Leadership and the Art of Surfing

Move Your Team Out of the Box and Into the Wave

(Teaching The Power of Open Systems and Random Relationships)

by Rick Hansen

Leadership and The Art of Surfing
Move Your Team Out of the Box and Into the Wave
by Rick Hansen

Printed in the United States of America

ISBN 9781619049369

www.xulonpress.com

"Chaos often breeds life, when order breeds habit."
-Henry Brooks Adams, American Writer and Historian

"We have a crisis of leadership in America because our overwhelming power and wealth, earned under earlier generations of leaders, made us complacent, and for too long we have been training leaders who only know how to keep routine going. Who can answer questions, but don't know how to ask them. Who can fulfill goals, but don't know how to set them. Who think about how to get things done, but not whether they're worth doing in the first place. What we have now are the greatest technocrats the world has ever seen, people who have been trained to be incredibly good at one specific thing, but who have no interest in anything beyond their area of expertise. What we don't have are leaders."
(http:www//theamericanscholar.org/solitude-and-leadership/)

"Every generation wrestles with the questions about its purpose. In the 1950's and 1960's, to be an able manager was to do four things well: plan, organize, direct, and control. Leading business thinkers conceived of managers as rational actors who could solve complex problems through the power of clear analysis. That view shaped the developing profession, but many questions were left unanswered. Planning and directing were essential, yes, but toward what ends? Organizing and controlling of course, but in whose interest?

By the 1980's and 1990's, one answer had come to dominate popular thinking: The purpose of management was to enrich a company's owners. Shareholder value creation had the advantage of being precisely and objectively measurable - and made CEO's like Robert Goizueta, Sandy Weill, and Jack Welch legends. Yet as a managerial mission, the pursuit of financial wealth has proved to be unsatisfactory. In the past decade as evidence that markets are far from efficient has mounted and much of the wealth created has been wiped out, basic questions about management have resurfaced. Today the focus has shifted to how management shout contribute to society, provide for environmental sustainability, and improve the lives of the people at the bottom of the pyramid... For those who have chosen management [or leadership] as their livelihood, these are not academic questions. They speak to the ultimate question that confronts us all: Has my life's work been important?"
(Harvard Business Review, December 2010, p. 87).

Table of Contents

Move Your Team Into the Wave

Hank parked his car along side the road, and with his surfboard firmly strapped to his racks, he eyed the surf while the tension of the day strained his vision. His car idled and merged its purr with the noise of the buzzing traffic. His scrambled thoughts swirled in his head and got tangled up with this newer shape of things. He was tired of trying to figure out ways to make sense of the rapid flow of flux and change along side the normal, daily stress of leading his organization. His Burberry tie dangled loosely around his slightly starched collar and he wiggled his toes stuffed in his Italian loafers while his sandals and beach towel sat listlessly in the trunk. He peered out at the surf hoping to make his day fade away. His ingrained "mechanical" mind-set stifled his spirit while the ocean breeze and salty air sifted through his nostrils and began to unwind knots in his mind. As he mentally sank into the sounds of the sea and unplugged from the outside world, the sea eased the strain. He thought to himself, "Why do these two worlds of my linear, mechanical precision of work life and the unpredictable, natural impulses of the sea have to hold such sharp contrast?"

The waves crashed in the distance as they ended their dance out at sea and rolled inland. He watched the uneven patterns of the water jostle together, clumsily merge, and form the shape of the wave. He longed to be on that wave and on that ride to ease the tension and feel the mist of the wave dust his face. He drifted in and out of the complications of the "office" as the sea flirted with him and lured him from his trance. The office would pull him back with the constant pressure to measure, calculate and manipulate while the newly globalized economy pressed on him with an intense competitive pressure. A wave would suddenly crash on the shore and jolt him out of his stress and back to the surf where he'd get lost in its natural calm. The outside system of the "office" seemed to drag him under with all of its layers and complications. Too many pulls on his psyche, on his family, on his employees, and on himself forced what seemed an unnatural way of living. He felt the disconnect between the attractive, chaotic surge and draw of the sea and the pressures of a system that manufactures premeditated outcomes.

He thought to himself as he took in the salty air that there must be a way to change. Another wave crashed and exploded with poetic force. He thought to himself how the system works in isolated and manipulated quadrants with sets of precise function and control. Then it hit him. What if the system began to work like a surfer does when he takes a wave. As a wave rolls in, he doesn't try to "change the wave," make it smaller, or alter its direction. He paddles to it, looks for the peak, folds into its cascading shape, and rides the wave as it peels overhead and falls forward. He doesn't fight the wave, or try to change where it forms, or manipulate its shape as it emerges. Instead he looks for a natural perch in the evolving face and rides its energy. He thought, I need to think like I do when I surf. I need to release my need to control and instead find out how I can make change the energy that drives me to create. I need to live the Art of Surfing.

He thought quietly, "What if there was a way to live and lead in a more natural way of thinking?" In other words what if he could learn to think like a surfer as he led his organization? He pondered the sea and its natural, random patterns as the waters and the currents endlessly intersected and connected. He thought about the more traditional thinking that is manipulated by control and precision. He stared out at the sea where the surfers dotted the horizon. He wanted to find a way to tap the natural, unfolding, and dynamic undulations of the ocean with all of its constant networks of change and apply it to how he lived his life and how he led his people. What if there was a more natural way to live and think? What if there is a different mindset that we are missing because we are stuck in a more linear, manipulative way of seeing life? What if we think more like a surfer that uncovers and then loosely converges on the natural power and energy of the wave? What if we learn to think like a surfer in and out of the water, "jump in" with board in tow, "get wet," and intermingle with the power and evolving shape of life? What if we try to understand its emergent nature and find a new connection to living and thinking like a surfer?

This thought began to stir something in his head. He slid from his car, changed into his wetsuit, grabbed his board and sauntered to the waters edge. The water slipped over his feet as the wave rolled up and eased back out. He sprang forward, threw his board and body out over the ebbing water, landed with a spraying splash as he slid across the water's surface, and headed out to the surf.

The waves were clean with perfectly stacked lines. The size looked perfect. The water was cold when it hit, but it snapped his soul into a calm. It jolted his mind from the office and the mechanical monotony required in organizational life. He dug his arms deep into the ocean, pulled himself forward in an alternating rhythm and paddled out to the lineup for his ride. His therapy began as each stroke of his arms moved him deeper out to sea and closer to the lineup. He reached the outside, pulled up and sat on the board with his legs dangling in the water and studied the horizon.

As the water lapped erratically over his board, he watched its uneven and mixed up percolating. The patterns were crisscrossing and behaving without a detectable rhythm. The water randomly bounced and danced. He kept watching and studying. Suddenly, he noticed something unique. There was a discernible yet erratic rhythm that was slightly chaotic. It wasn't distinct enough to predict but enough to feel an unusual harmony in random combinations. The water bounced and danced just enough to catch his attention differently than it ever had before. He thought, "What if we were to see life like the surf?" In other words, instead of disconnecting from his daily mindset at the "office" and shifting into the surfer mindset in the sea, we need to think like a surfer in and out of the water.

When a wave mounds on the outside and takes its shape, a surfer quickly paddles to the peak, positions himself in its evolving momentum, swings his board around, aligns with the peak, and thrusts himself into its cascading shape. A surfer knows that a wave is an evolving, dynamic, and interactive walk with change. He knows how to interconnect with the intimate probabilities of the ocean, not its precision.

Hank fought the cynicism in his head as he tried to formulate his clarity on surfing. He realized that the older, more traditional thinking lingered deep in his psyche. He pondered doubtfully out loud in the water, "How could this philosophy ever develop in a system that is riddled in controls? To someone who has never felt the spray of a wave hit his face, this will likely only sound like a personal, emotional whim. It's crazy to think that such a model of control would ever yield to the uncertainty of a surfer's spirit?" He pressed this idea against his forming wall of pessimism, but to his surprise it pushed back. Every time he got out of his car in the sandy parking lot of the beach after a hectic day at the office, he thought he was simply trying to shrug the "office" off his back. It turns out that the deeper he thought about it, he was wrestling with a mentality that rubbed against his natural lean. He was fighting a historic foot hold of a specific mindset. Just like a wave that held him under water long enough to make him slightly panic, he pressed through the doubt and nagging suspicion. This incessant need to be precise and predictable, to be in control, was from an older paradigm of an older era. Today in a world under a new and powerful shift of imprecision and random change, it doesn't work. Like a wave hitting him square on, he was jolted back to the probabilities of this new implication.

He saw his style of leadership and the structure of his organization was chained to his ankles, and they weighted him in the parking lot as he stared out at the surf. They were the need to control outcomes and put both people and outcomes into neat and tidy boxes. He shoved the surfer into a suit and a tie and shelved his surfboard in the rafters. He became a manipulator instead of a surfer that looked for the next wave to ride. He needed to inspire cutting edge creation in the system like he would look to create movements on the wave. He effectively quelled the potential and the probable by only looking for the certain.

He dangled his hands loosely in the cold water and instantly felt free and inspired as he connected with the system's movement. He sat back and undulated with the ebb and flow of the water and found the rhythm to calm his jaded meandering. As the water moved beneath and before him, he tapped again into its lucid energy and co-mingling entities to ease his mind and spirit to interact with the random and the unlikely.

To Tony who inspired me to write, my family who supported me while I did, and my wife who makes me a better man.

Leadership and the Art of Surfing
Move Your Team Out of the Box and Into the Wave
(Teaching the Power of Open Systems and Random Relationships)

10 Rules to The Art of Surfing
Rule 1: Innovate and Adapt
Rule 2: Recognize the Need to Change
Rule 3: Meaning Is Found in the Whole Thing
Rule 4: Find the Natural Principles of Living Systems
Rule 5: Recognize Light Disturbances to Highly Connected Systems
Could Have Tremendous Effect
Rule 6: Seek to Uncover the Deeper Order
Rule 7: Understand, Interconnectedness is the One Thing
Rule 8: Constantly Create the Crazy and Unusual
Rule 9: See a Relationship as not Limited to Meaning in Itself
Rule 10: See Dynamic Interconnectivity

Introduction

L eaders need to teach their teams to surf. Our thoughts about organizations are obsolete. In this time of rapid change, we need leaders and organizations that are able to quickly respond to an ever-changing environment.

The time has come where we can no longer control and isolate things to tiny and tidy boxes. Our current mentality runs short in this time where the current shift calls for leaders and organizations who are willing to adapt and navigate through a more undefined space. We have to be comfortable with uncertainty. We don't have to be whimsical and frolic in pandemonium and whim. However, we have to wrap our heads around the reality of evolving forward without a blueprint and leave behind this more anachronistic model of "top down" thinking. Whether you are an executive leader, middle manager, pastor, team leader, or teacher trying to navigate a new era with your team, we are in a monumental shift in a new global landscape that interconnects like the the waves of the ocean. As leaders, we need to be like the surfer that connects his team with this raw, indiscernible power of shift.

And yet we are stalled in a mind-set rooted in the Industrial Revolution while the world has become flat and interconnected. We tend to frame reality with an image of the assembly lines on factory floors with specific job functions. This older paradigm leaves us stranded. We need to connect to a more lucid set of bendable, malleable rules where communication channels are open and rules adapt to needs as they shift. Think of places like the ocean, the internet, the markets, and our emerging global landscape. Think about a surfer.

The surfer is deeply connected to the randomness of the ocean. He responds to unsuspecting movements of the sea, finds its hidden momentum, and surfs. He finds the peak of the wave as it emerges and rides its evolving shape. He is at home in this randomness and thrives on the edge. Only on that edge of the wave can he create. Only on the edge of the wave can he live. As leaders, we need to move our teams out of the "box" and into the wave.

Chapter 1

Rule 1: Adapt and Innovate
The Art of Surfing

"Today's organization design must ... meet the expanding need for learning and rapid response capabilities" (Twomey, 2006, p. 18).

"In scientific terms, it was akin to rolling a steel ball down an inclined plane to measure its velocity - only to watch the ball float into the air instead. It suggested that our understanding of the gravitational pulls on our behavior was inadequate - that what we thought were fixed laws had plenty of loopholes" (Daniel Pink, opening page, Introduction, Ch. 1).

"But in the first ten years of this century - a period of truly staggering under-achievement in business, technology, and social progress - we've discovered that this sturdy, old operating system doesn't work nearly as well. It crashes - often and unpredictably. If forces people to devise workarounds to bypass its flaws. Most of all, it is proving incompatible with many aspects of contemporary business" (Daniel Pink, opening page, Introduction, Ch. 2).

Leaders need to move their team out of their box and into the wave because the world is not just flat but intimately connected. Like the internet, our new world is now millions and millions of overlapping random networking cables, sloppily intertwining across a diverse landscape that interconnects everything and everyone. Because of this, it brings diverse and complex change that swirls in pulses and surges. As leaders, our landscape has become boundaryless. Our world today is interdependent with ideas and people constantly intersecting. We live in a time where we must accentuate adaptability and move to change like a surfer casually, but decidedly paddles into an emerging wave. As leaders, we must learn to be like that surfer on that wave, CO-evolving as he cascades down an "emerald wall."

Today, conflict and cooperation exist in a dynamic tension. Unlikely but mutual dependencies are as confusing as they are common and as vital as they are complex. The world today with its highly connected networks quickly bring random change, but we live under a mindset that prefers control, precision, and predictability. We like to put things under our thumb. Although this is not natural, it has become second nature. However, in this new landscape, we must turn to a natural order that is more random and evolving, less controlling. As leaders, we must use uncertainty to be innovative. To be successful and thrive as individuals, as leaders, or even as entire organizations, we must learn the art of surfing by leading our teams out of a confining box and teach our teams how to surf in an open ocean.

The Surfer

The surfer is tuned to the unfolding shapes and energies of the ocean. He converts the confusion of the water into energy to understand both the ocean and the wave. He finds the natural rhythm and connects. He's not confused or bothered by the chaos of the sea but rather he fuses himself into its lineup. He uses the random order of its chaos and becomes a part of it. He listlessly bounces in the churning waters but is tuned to the ocean's cauldron. He paddles into unsuspecting movements, finds its deep, hidden momentum, and interacts with its converging power. He surfs. He has no presets other than to surf the "line" and connect to the sea. He finds the peak of the wall as it rises from its 1000s of miles of travel, paddles towards it, positions himself in its emerging pitch, and rides its evolving shape. He is at home in the randomness and thrives on the edge of the uncertain, and only on that edge of the wave can he create. Only on the edge of the wave can he live. This "edge" is where we as leaders need to be, not as a location but a state of being.

Tumbleweeds?

Surfers are generally thought to be tumbleweeds that roll and bounce across the road at whim under no specific direction but the winds choosing. We are seen as flimsy and tossed around by a random breeze looking always and only for the next wave. Our attitude is thought to be, "Whatever dude" and "Dude, gnarly." The perception of the surfer - flighty, undisciplined, temporary - is actually quite different from the truth. Surfers, although a bit more relaxed and "sandy" tend to be acutely aware of the "alternative," the kind that doesn't look like there is much there, the kind that seem unlikely. However, a surfer sees those things as opportunity. We see a storm or the churning of the sea and know that from that comes the wave. We see the randomness of awkward patterns as potential discoveries and new frontiers instead of just unfamiliar and unchartered landscapes. In the more awkward and unruly, we become more flexible. We tend to be in tune with the nuance and whim of nature and the unspoken currents of change.

This ocean is a system of constant change, and we love this because this unpredictability creates our wave. It's the system that constantly interconnects with different swells, currents, and the wind that create evolving shapes. It makes every wave and ride different. Every session is new. We depend on this unpredictability. We live in this unpredictability. We happen to like that it's crazy, frenzied, and imprecise because that allows us to create and improvise. In that we find the intoxicating beauty of the wave and the powerful draw to the sea.

Listen to the professional surfer Chris Malloy, one of the well known Malloy brothers, as he artistically describes this connection to the unchartered rhythm of the water like an artist describes a portrait, "...[We] sat in perfect six-foot Santa Barbara point surf...He caught a long, tapering wall and then paddled back out... He paused for a moment as the orange twilight on the horizon was being replaced by an emerald green wall of water marching in thousands of miles from its birthplace in the Aleutician Islands" (Chris Malloy, Santa Barbara Magazine, p. 121, April/May 2010). The time has come where leaders can no longer control and isolate things to tiny and tidy boxes. We have to realize the unparalleled power existing in a newer global network layered with free-forming, random relationships and networks that evolve and connect. We need to be able to put ourselves in this framework of thinking. We need to be like a surfer that connects with the raw, indiscernible power in the open ocean. We need to find that emerald green wall of water and immerse ourselves in its unfolding. We need to find our own, more natural way intrinsic to our design and open up to systems highly connected.

Traditional Thinking Falls Short

Our traditional thinking falls very short in this paradigm shift that is calling for leaders who are willing to move toward a more evolutionary stance. It's something more fluid and adaptive. We have to be comfortable with unpredictability and details that may appear chaotic. We have to wrap our heads around the reality of evolving forward instead of articulating movements from a blueprint. The old guard of precision, control, and manipulation must yield to a high interconnectivity and interdependence. In other words, we have to be okay with the more messy, evolving order shaping the future.

More with More

I have a friend and mentor who was a previous professor in my post graduate studies. Currently he is an Executive Coach. His background is a founding partner of a very successful national health care organization where he served a number of years as Senior VP, and later moved on to become CEO in premier organizations. Recently, he came to speak for me as a guest lecturer in one of my classes at a University where I am an adjunct professor of Organizational Development and Theory in the MBA program. He made a comment about this change in the "landscape" and its affect on his clientele of "C" level executives. Referring to this idea that we are entering a new mindset where we are shifting from this hierarchical thinking, he said from his view point as senior leader, practitioner and now executive coach, that he has noted 4 specific changes while working with many prominent CEO's: 1) To succeed today, the work required by both the CEO and his organization require 110% effort with twice as many people versus the 75% effort that it used to take with half the people to achieve the same level of success. 2) He said another client who is a prominent Chairman of a large organization realizes he can no longer just expect execution alone from his CEO. Today he requires his CEO to both execute and build people and relationships beneath him to develop innovations and proper succession in his bench strength. Not only is the external community connected, but the need to build a internal, connected community to address accelerating global speed is vital for survival. 3) Another transition he sees is the shift in how organizations are structured. Typically, the organization is hierarchical and top down with the traditional structure of CEO at the top and the normal organizational "boxes" that fall beneath, like a pyramid. Communications are vertical. However, what has become commonplace is a matrix organizational structure. It's design and dynamic chains of horizontal and transparent communication systems are intimately connected. This model has moved from a distant theory only once discussed in a management classrooms to literal, commonplace structures in domestic and international organizations across the globe. 4) Finally, what is ultimately stunning is all of this has all happened in the last 6-8 years where the traditional structure has taken 150 years to become entrenched. The shift in global competition and an interconnected community has pushed everything forward faster and requires greater resources. We are in a shift.

A Surfer is Flexible, Quickly Adaptable, and Evolving

Both leadership and their teams need to be immediately flexible, quickly adaptable, and always evolving. Like a surfer on a wave, we must be all these things always. For example, if you watch the physiological phases of a surfer on a wave, you'd see bouts of "bursts" next to the calm of evolving, fluid adaptation as both the surfer and the wave seamlessly blend from an explosive state of change into one lucid state of emergence. Leadership needs to itself be nimble enough to implement this combination of speed and agility alongside fluid adaptability into its teams.

There are three distinct phases for a surfer when he rides a wave. 1) The explosion of pulling and paddling into the face of the wave and snapping up to a stance like a race horse bursting from the gates, 2) the smooth drop and rolling down the shoulder of the wave like a warm sip of scotch, and finally 3) riding and creating on the edge of wave in an innovative state of natural emergence like an artist sculpting a piece of art or the quiet splendor of a silent snowfall.

First, when a wave begins to build on the horizon, a surfer drops to his chest on his board and decisively *paddles to* the wave. When he reaches its crest or face of the wave, he quickly pops up, swings his body and board around 180 degrees in one motion, puts the wave behind him, and then paddles, pulls and thrusts himself forward into the rolling pitch. As it rolls beneath him, he sinks into the momentum of the face of the wave and connects to its form as it lifts him, pushes him forward into the emerging shape, and in one fluid motion he immediately pops his body into a standing position to career down the face of the wave. When he is in this stance and can find the invisible rhythm of the wave, he then begins to converge on its shoulder and methodically and creatively "carves" up and down the face of the wave like a sculptor driven with purpose and vision.

Two Mindsets

"The organization of the future will be based on the principles of adaptability rather than predictability. It will be an open organization that considers process more important than structure and human interaction more effective than impersonal chain of command hierarchy." (Dr. Brabara Mink) There are two types of mindsets that stand out more these days as we become increasingly intertwined with this flux. They are very separate and distinct. The *surfer* is adaptive and flexible and innovates when flushed with disturbances and complexity, and *the controller* force-fits things into prescriptive functions with strict marching orders. There is a clear line between the *surfer* and the *controller* mindset. They act and think very differently. If we put it on a chart in relationship to the symbol of the surfer, it might look like this.

<u>What a Surfer does</u>:

The Surfer	The Controller
Paddles to the wave	Measures the Wave
Interacts with the surf	Observes from a Perch
Creates on the wave	Predicts the next wave

<u>How a surfer thinks:</u>

The Surfer	The Controller
Dynamically Innovative	Perfectly Planned
Randomly Interconnected	Hierarchically topdown
Unpredictably Evolving	Manipulate and Control

23

Density of Data

We are headlong into an era where the density and velocity of data is redefining how we think and how we find and redesign success as a person, leader, or organization. We need to decide if we are going to lead with a nimble and adaptive response like the surfer or a reactionary and manipulative movement like the more traditional mindset. We have to decide how we are going to interact with this reality. As this information naturally presses, it is pushing us out and forcing our hand to do more. Instead, under an older way we are becoming frazzled in what Phyllis Tickle has coined the *"Great Emergence."*

When we become agitated - and agitate each other - about how we are drowning in information overload, in correspondence, and in the stress of unending "To-Do" lists, we are talking about the Great Emergence, or at least about one small part of its presence as a new time in human history. When, for example, we discover we can no longer do so simple a thing as running sums in our heads, but instead have to turn to our calculators, we are recognizing that we are storing more and more of our "selves" outside of ourselves and thereby creating a dependency that is, at the very least, unsettling (Tickle, p. 15).

We need to find interconnectivity within a system that is multiplying rapidly. We need to watch what the surfer does, and to some degree emulate his movements. I don't mean literally, although that perhaps might make things a bit more relaxing in flip flops and board shorts. What I do mean is that it will help us deal with the information overload like a surfer handles the surging and mixing of the mighty and great expanse of the ocean; he takes it in stride and looks to the horizon for the wave. Because of the depth and width of an era riddled with the constant of flux, we need to alter our mindsets and unwind our tight grip or it will be our peril.

The typically rigid, controlling mindset that rules through strict measurements, calculated forecasts, and fear needs to redefine itself. The system has changed, and our world has changed. Yet we have not. It's true like Phyllis Tickle says that we do operate increasingly outside of our selves and especially outside of how we used to think.

We are headlong into a new paradigm. Our older mindset however is holding us back because it corals us into prescribed boxes of high specialization where everything is determined and fixed instead of loosing us out into the open sea to surf. Both people and systems need to change. If we are to successfully lead in this climate and new culture, we need to learn the art of surfing so we can transform our teams.

Listen to Phyllis Tickle in her latest book as she poignantly describes how this cultural shift affects everything. Her primary focus in her book dwells on how this dramatic undercurrent of complexity and rising tide of change is altering the entire platform of how church and faith will be done in the future, but in this following bit she shows how everything else, along with the church is now immediately affected. In this excerpt, she talks about what she is calling the Great Emergence. Whether its music, religious institutions, the sharing of information, formal worship, personal connectivity, the discussion of science versus faith, pastoral care, artificial intelligence, computer science, or the hierarchical arrangement of the church, everything has been touched, affected, altered, or even birthed as a result of this new order.

We must recognize that the coming of individually programmed technologies like the iPod or the programmable cellphone made superb music not only accessible...but also highly participatory...

We cannot ignore the fact that computer science has unleashed upon us nanotechnology and artificial intelligence and concepts like the Singularity with all their concomitant legal, moral, and religious questions. The problem inherent in all of them is that we are public whose extant religious institutions have to date shown themselves to be ill-prepared both theologically and intellectually to wrestle with the practical implications involved in such intellectual and technological developments.

We must acknowledge as well that the world has indeed gone flat again, the Reformation's nation-state having given way to the Emergence's globalization. Cash, which replaced blood as the basis for power over to sheer information in the Emergence. And to some greater or lesser extent, every social or political unit is in thrall to those who know the most about how to destroy the most or expedite the most, whether such threatening agents be next door or three continents away.

We cannot ignore the passing of much religious experience, instruction, and formal worship from sacred space to secular space and, perhaps even more significantly, into electronic space. The progression from the radio preacher of the first half of the twentieth century to the television "sermons" or visits of Bishop Fulton Sheen in the midcentury to the televangelists of the later half of the century to the churches and worship sites of the Internet is an uninterrupted movement to a more and more interiorized or imaged religious praxis. Millions of Americans now receive their entire pastoral care and have their whole religious instruction and engagement on the Internet through websites ranging from the sociability of worship in Second Life to the prayerful quiet of gratefulness.org to the informational and formative offerings of sites like beliefnet.com.

Nor can we, in speaking of the computer and cyberspace, forget that both have connected each of us to all the rest of us. The hierarchical arrangement or structure of most extant Churches and denominations is based on the hierarchical arrangement of the Reformation's evolving nation-states. It is, however, quite alien and suspect, if not outright abhorrent, to second-generation citizens of cyberspace where networking and open-or crowd-sourcing are more logical and considerably more comfortable. In our connectedness, of course, we also experience with immediacy the pain and agony, incongruities and horrors, of life as it is lived globally, forcing the question of theodicy to take on a kind total humanity angst or urgency that has not accrued since the Black Death leveled the earth five and six centuries ago (Tickle, p. 106-107).

We need this more nimble way for three reasons. First, as you can see, we live in a world of accelerating and complex change. We live in a global, flat, and interconnected landscape that is ushering flux faster than any leader, leadership committee, board of directors or organization can handle. This isn't to say that these communities aren't smart enough or capable enough, rather it's that a leadership mindset of control is no longer effective. Under the older way we manipulate outcomes and calculate variables from more determinate patterns, but now increasingly is unpredictable "to second-generation citizens of cyberspace where networking and open-or crowd-sourcing are more logical and considerably more comfortable" (Tickle). Second, this sheer mass and speed of change is creating complexity that we can't understand and make sense of fast enough. It cannot be approached and methodically unraveled like things used to be. Finally, because it is all interconnected through networks that continually multiply randomly over and over, unless we learn to think differently, see differently, and adapt to the randomness, we will become disconnected from this shift. We will become entangled in these networks instead of fluidly moving with and through them. Several things will happen from this:

> First, a new, more vital form of [thinking] does indeed emerge. Second, the organized expression of [the older mid-set] which up until then had been the dominant one is reconstituted into a more pure and less ossified expression of its former self...The third result is of equal, if not greater, significance though. That is, every time the incrustations of an overly established [way] have been broken open, the [thinking] has spread - and been spread - dramatically into new geographic and democratic areas, thereby increasing exponentially the range and depth of [its] reach as a result of its time of unease and distress (Tickle, p. 17).

Obviously, painting such broad strokes may seem just that - broad - but it's necessary when realizing the pervasive nature of the current way of how we think. I know every leader and organization is distinct and requires unique attention, and perhaps re-socializing might shake the footing of those entrenched in the past. However, it's safe to say this current framework where we manage by control and predictable outcomes are rooted in the Industrial Revolution that created assembly lines on the factory floors and management became a science. Instead, the leader for today needs to learn to how to surf and teach his/her teams to immerse themselves in the ocean and ride the "waves" of adaptability and flexibility.

What a Surfer Looks Like

We need to symbolically "look" and "feel" like a surfer: a bit sandy, the skin a tad sun drenched, and streaks of dried salt water lining across the body. It helps paints a symbol of a slightly fresh attitude and it poises us for a unique view of the horizon. A surfer's ultimate concern is the next wave, the green emerald wall, and how he's gonna catch it. He is aware that every wave emerges and takes on it's own shape. He doesn't seek to control and manipulate the outcome, but he intends to engage and interact as it unfolds. He wants to intersect and alter its shape and form by the influence of his own moves on the wave.

I am not proposing we need to say "gnarly dude" and "totally tubular." Maybe a "dude" here and there placed strategically in meetings might loosen up the rigidity of a corporate assembly, nonetheless, the point I am trying to make is that we need to become more flexible in our thinking, nimble in our behavior, and innovative in the momentum we infuse into our leadership and the organization(s) we lead.

Not only in our thinking as leaders but the teams that we lead need to go through their own shift. We need to be able and willing to connect in unusual ways to unfamiliar relationships. A surfer is never held to one spot or one "break" when he paddles out because the system allows him to paddle to where the wave emerges. He paddles to the energy. He flexes and adapts versus paddling to a "spot" and waiting for something to break in that precise point of entry. He makes decisions on the "fly" as the information comes available. For example, businesses must interact more with vendors, data, employees, to learn adaptability and communicate in transparency. Bill Gates in his latest book encourages businesses to set up "central nervous systems" so data and information can be transparent, interactive, and pushed to high points of interests quickly throughout the organization.

All types of organizational leaders need to administer a system that puts their people in direct contact with the vitals so information is real, timely and hopefully interactive. Even a church might need its pastor to let go of the reigns of control in how he/she typically organizes, delivers, and teaches his/her sermons by creating a forum where the members interact more with its shape. Maybe he/she needs to loosen the reigns of the organization and how the staff is structured and even how the church service is set up, or even what the Sunday message will be.

If we continue to stay entrenched in reports locked up in towers of strict order that determine our next step, hunch over excel spread sheets laden with determinate patterns, or the hold fast to the hard line of predictability and control in hierarchical organizations, we will undoubtedly stay stuck in the quagmire of the past.

Look for the Story and Not Just Data

Because everything is increasingly connected, knowing what to measure, what's important to measure, and how to interpret it is becoming more difficult and more important. All of this information swirling around the internet, throughout this flat world, and in our heads changes the game and alters how we play in the game. We need to look at measurements, data, and the sheer mass of information differently. We don't per se need to ignore the data or reconfigure it. We need to instead find where more things connect, how they interconnect, and what then is the impact and emerging trend of the moment and its potential future connections. We need to see the ripples affecting other ripples and those ripples affecting again other ripples to realize that at some point this is all a result of a myriad of connections through multiplying narratives.

We need to *find the story* and then become a part of it. We need to realize the vital role we play in this is not to manipulate the cogs, but create a place where organizational life can thrive. When we do this, the whole system can interconnect with multiplying, random unfolding relationships, but if we prescribe only to numbers and isolated events, we miss the narrative and the wonderful subtleties of development. We miss the learning and the power of the "central nervous system" as it uncovers the dynamic interconnectedness.

Learn to Measure What Matters

This new era of data demands that we learn to measure what matters, measure qualitatively and quantitatively, and be open to measurements that we used to think unimportant or arbitrary. For example, instead of looking into and measuring an event in isolation, we need to understand its connection to the whole story. It's not that measurements or events are unnecessary and whimsically random. They are the results ultimately from other influencers that need to be considered. Ripples affect more ripples and therefore create more and different but connected ripples. Measurements are important and quantitative movement is essential, but today information is diverse and more robust. This information, instead of static snippets, is kinetic and moves through the agents or players of the system. We must flatten the system so that organizational life becomes part of the story's unfolding. This way, instead of telling what story to write and manipulating its outcome, we become a part of its development as the ripples are free to interact and intersect.

An organization that is historically an icon for the traditional command and control structure is learning that they must restructure their entire understanding of leadership and communicating internally and externally in world where the landscape of historic warfare has been completely changed. The "leaderless" terrorist cells of Al Qaida that have forced the mighty US Military to shift its entire tactical strategies of leadership and communications, and specifically negotiations. For example in a recent Harvard Business Review (November 2010) there is an article called "Leadership Lessons from the Military" :

It's often not easy to 'get to yes,' particularly given the pace of business and the structure of organizations today. CEO's and other senior executives are under extreme time pressure, managing complex, high-stakes conversations across functional areas and divisions, with alliance partners and critical suppliers, and with customers and regulators. Many report feeling that they are constantly in negotiation mode - trying to gain approval for deals in which hundreds of millions (and sometimes billions) of dollars are at stake, in the shortest possible time frames, from people who may hold the company's (and even the leader's) own future in their hands. To these executives, negotiation isn't just about transactions anymore; it's about adapting to rapidly changing information and circumstances.

...But the perception of danger prompts business and military leaders to resort to the same kind of behavior. Both commonly feel pressure to make rapid progress, project strength and control (especially when they have neither), rely on coercion rather than collaboration, trade resources for cooperation rather than get to genuine buy-in, and offer unilateral concessions to mitigate possible threats.

...U.S military officers serving in Afghanistan have found themselves trying to hold these pressures at bay while engaging in, often daily, in dangerous negotiations. Over the past six years or so, we've studied how they resolve conflict and influence others in situations where the levels of risk and uncertainty are off the charts. We find that the most skilled among them rely on five highly effective strategies: 1)understand the big picture, 2)uncover hidden agendas and collaborate with the other side, 3) get genuine buy-in, 4) build relationships that are based on trust rather than fear, and 5) pay attention to process as well as desired outcomes.

...Avoid assuming you have all the facts, "Look, it's obvious that..." Avoid assuming the other side is biased and you're not. Avoid assuming the other side's motivations and intentions are obvious - and probably nefarious. Instead, be curious, "Help me understand how you see the situation." Be humble, "What do I have wrong?" Be open minded, "Is there another way to explain this?" (Harvard Business Review, Nov 2010, p. 68).

The older way tells us *how to write the story and what its going to be about*, but today we are being called to write the story together by opening and connecting our relationships and systems. We don't know how it unfolds until it does. We must learn to listen to the conversation and help give it shape in tandem with the other voices instead of trying to control the conversation. We need to get to information efficiently, learn about its potential contributions, and then disseminate it out. The article in HBR continues,

Avoid threats, "You better or else." Avoid arbitrariness, "I want it because I want it." Avoid close-mindedness, "Under no circumstances will I agree to - or even consider - that proposal." Instead, appeal to fairness, "What should we do?" Appeal to logic and legitimacy, "I think this makes sense, because..." Consider constituent perspectives, "How can each of us explain this agreement to colleagues?" (Harvard Business Reveiw, Nov 2010, p. 68).

In a flatter, open system, like the ocean, there are no designated, specifically assigned players with limiting, defined roles. Everyone participates and plays together under defined values.

> [An open system is] very amorphous and fluid. Because power and knowledge and are distributed, individual units quickly respond to a multi- tude of internal and external forces - they are constantly spreading, growing, shrinking, mutating, dying off, and reemerging. This quality makes them very flexible. Think of the Internet: each day thousands of new Web sites emerge and countless others fade away (Brafman and Beskstrom, P. 50-51).

Today, everything is an infinite influence on something else that then becomes an infinite influence on another something else. When people are encouraged and allowed to move where they are inspired under commonly shared values and where they can contribute the most benefit, innovation becomes natural. When a surfer finds the wave, he is free to paddle to it and surf.

The Bible?

This might be a slight aside, but it has critical merit to our idea of *the story*. Scott McKnight wrote a book called the *Blue Parakeet, Rethinking how we read the Bible*. In it he talks about how we must read the Bible as a story instead of picking and choosing specific passages that fit our argument or individual verses we want to contest. Reading the Bible in bits breaks apart the truth into shades of gray. It doesn't tell the story because it is only a gives snapshots or vignettes. The transparency is lost. Most anyone can take any verse and bend it to their angle and then build a platform, or even a cult. But McKnight challenges people to read the Bible as a story from cover to cover so that one can master the plot and understand what is being said considering its diversification.

He argues that if you read the Bible thoroughly, individual verses that might on their own elude, or confuse might be clarified and even enriched when exam- ined and explored against the whole. The full story summons the truth according to McKnight and exposes the gray or the "hard to read" when considering the plot. Listen to his charge on interpreting and deciphering the complexity of the Scriptures if we take it in random bits and make those bits the whole. Instead, he contends that we can master the plot of Bible. "We do so not by charting our own path through the thicket but by mastering the plot and the *story (italics mine)* of the Bible so that the path we take is the natural [one] ... that will guide us to the waters in our world in our own way" (McKnight, p. 162).

We must master the plot of the story and not jump in and out of chapters at our own convenience to be selective with the facts that benefit our viewpoint. Leaders and organizations do this well. We generally fail to read the story for its whole plot. We tend to take on event mentality. In other words, we take snapshots to tell the stories. The more traditional approach is to pour over reports and numbers and create stories that tend to be skewed by someone else's end game that provide only portions of the systemic truth.

Central Nervous Systems (Bill Gates)

Two things need to happen, 1) real, live information must be connected to everyone all the time, and 2) it must be spread out and dispersed constantly for quick evaluation, interaction and action. In this book, Bill Gates applies this idea of connecting information to his "central nervous system" for companies in order to attain TRANSPARENCY and VISIBILITY. His focus is in business, but for our purpose we can easily apply it to the idea of an open system and leadership. In other words, leaders need to create a central nervous system mentality in their leadership paradigm and in the company's shared information systems that distributes transparency and visibility to the community. "Very few companies are using digital technology for new processes that radically improve how they function [and think], that give them the full benefit of all their employees capabilities, and that give them the speed of response they will need to compete in the emerging high-speed business world" (Gates, p. xiv). He believes information dispersed like this provides a greater chance for the community to adapt.

Instead of compiling information in the ivory towers of senior management, if the information becomes both visible and transparent, the people and the organization can create a dynamic future by interacting with it in real time. This will help to create a flexible and adaptable organization. Therefore, we can take his idea of the central nervous system that creates universal visibility and apply it to how we must learn to interject ourselves, our team and our people into the story and interface with it where we see fit.

Going forward, we must ask ourselves these questions: 1) Is our mindset open to a paradigm shift? 2) Are we too susceptible to the comfort of precision and predictability or do we seek to dig into an undisclosed "rhythm" of the sea? 3) As leaders, do we push into our natural order of connectivity and relationship or live under an older system of controls, protectionism, isolation? 4) Do we let the swirl of information, conversations, and varying plots stir together and connect? 5) Do we practice the ancient principle and natural rhythm of Kaizen - constant information and feedback loops that provide a continuum of learning?

Measurements Need to Coincide with the Plot

What we measure needs to connect to the plot. Often, there is so much more going on behind the "measurements" than the limited story they appear to tell, and yet we constantly gage movement on those numbers alone and their immediate and alleged impact. The question isn't do you or don't you analyze performance and analyze metrics whether you are an organization, a leader, or an individual. Analytics are vital. A surfer always needs a surfboard, surf wax, an understanding of swell dynamics, and insight into currents and their influence on the wave and the water.

As a leader in a company, I understand it is very critical to know where your organization is and to weigh its productivity. Let's face it, increasing the efficacy of the organization and then measuring its performance is a primary way to log quantitative movement. However, the question goes from *what* are we measuring to *why* are we measuring and *what* is its relationship and significance to past, current and future movement? Certain questions need to be asked: Does it inspire and innovate or does it manipulate and suppress? What is the story behind the measurement and what does it tell about our past, what story might it help create for our future, and what specifically does it say that we have not even considered? What is the connection?

For example, a surfer with access to the internet can check the surf any time and figure out its size and then go to his local break for a "session." However, if he doesn't know the direction or the size of the swell, he might show up at his local break only to be disappointed by "ankle slappers" lapping gingerly on the shore like a lake. In this case the information is extremely pertinent because the size of the swell conversely determines the size of the wave and its direction determines which facing beaches will take the surge. From that, the surfer needs to then consider the tide and the local topography of his favorite break and how that then influences the surf. Real, transparent, and more timely information allows for better decisions.

Open and Accessible

Just because a leader has access to critical data and alone can understand its alleged and interpreted connection does not mean he has access to the whole story nor the total ability to determine an effective response. Simply because there is a preacher behind a pulpit doesn't mean he/she has it all together or that they have all the answers. The real problem is that we have been conditioned to believe that only special few people have access to key vital signs of an organization, whether it is a company, a church, a school, or even a nonprofit. There is a current that underlies our behavior that says only a few, only the "special" few get to know and get to decide.

It is this sense of the "proprietary," this false sense of control that permeates our mindsets. Whether a worker, middle manager, senior executive, teacher, or senior pastor the mentality is that only the "top" really knows how to act and make proper decisions. For some reason we believe that is how it should be. But I believe we are starving for a new type of transparency and interconnectivity. We search for a place where we can go and see things for they what they are, believe in what we see and hear, and then act on it. We are tired of being told what to determine and how to determine it. We long to participate and feel a part of something other than ourselves, a fresh perspective with significance with a core of intrinsic value and truth. In this new complexity, we have for the first time in a long time an opportunity to change the flow of things.

It'll take the re-sculpting of our organizations and corporate culture, the incubation of new art forms, new languages and expressions, new symbols, flexible ways of being organized and led, and even a fuller explanation of what we know...We're looking for something that fits what we know to be intrinsically true. We're hungry for it. We sense the urgency of it (Gibbons, p. 36).

Bill Gates talks again about this digital nervous system. He says information needs to be more transparent, accessible, and open to the whole system and not just senior leadership so that it can be shared, responded to, and acted on in real time. On the corporate front, he believes in this era that for companies and organizations to succeed, this digital nervous system of transparency is essential. In leadership and organizational life, we need something akin to the digital nervous system where we can incorporate a more nimble way that creatively and adaptively processes information and change. Organizations crave this transparency because it can add value and incredible flexibility. Leaders need to believe that people are valuable and should help shape this discussion. This then will help us to move intelligently and in real time with critical information.

Under this connected landscape, several things are affected. 1) Transparency becomes paramount, 2) communities become empowered and connected, 3) and they also get irritated when things are aren't transparent and they can't interact with the information. People of the organization, the company, the church, the school, are being taught to crave transparency (Twitter and Facebook) and the power to connect to this information of the system where people can interact and move without restraints. Mr. Gates talks about how we need to do away with this mentality that I mentioned above where only a few select can access vitals. It is ineffective and dare I say "old school."

Two things happen when leadership conceals information: it limits innovation and the system remains inflexible. If our mentality is trained to simply take numbers and reports "blindly" and implement assumptions and correlations without input from the bottom up, we will miss significant opportunities to develop living systems.

Gates proposes that the digital nervous system provides actionable data in real time throughout the organization or community so that the whole system can innovate intelligently in real time. Most important is that this information will be spread and bring flexibility and innovation to the community. Like the internet and the digital era has flattened the landscape, it has also flattened the mindsets of the masses. We too must have a "digital nervous system" of sorts or at least a mentality where our system intimately interacts and adapts as it gathers and views information on the quick.

When I sit down with developers to review product specification, or with Microsoft's product divisions to review their three-year business plans, or with our sales groups to review their financial performance, we work thorough the difficult issues. We discuss feature trade-offs vs. time to market, marketing spend vs. revenue, head count vs. return, and so on. Through human intelligence and collaboration, we transform static sales, customer, and demographic data into the design of a product or a program. *Information work is thinking work.* When thinking and collaboration are significantly assisted by computer technology, you have a digital nervous system. It consists of the advanced digital processes that knowledge workers use to make better decisions. To think, to act, react, and adapt...To do information work, people in the company have to have ready access to information. Until recently, though, we've been conditioned to believe that "the numbers" should be reserved for the most senior executive.

On today's computer networks you can retrieve and present data easily and inexpensively. You can dive into the data to the lowest level of detail and pivot it to see it in different dimensions. You can exchange information and ideas with other people. You can integrate the ideas and work of multiple people or teams to produce a well-thought-out and coordinated result. We need to break out of the mind-set that getting information and moving information around is difficult and expensive. It's just basic, common sense to make all of your company's data - everything from the latest sales numbers to details of the 401-k plan - just a few clicks away for everyone who can use it (Gates, p. 15-16).

Share the Information With Everyone

Anyone can look at a surf report and loosely learn about the surf that day. I can look at the swell direction, the size, and tides and figure out where to surf from the data, but unless I understand how to surf, the specific break, the unspoken subtleties of the wave and the beach, the unwritten code of the surfer, and the peculiarities of the sport, it's all just data. We live in a time burgeoning with data that we must learn to transcribe and then adapt to its complexity. By exploring the Art of Surfing, we can learn to unconventionally connect to a new era of emerging change, open wide random relationships of discovery, set up nonlinear thinking, and lead through the power of innovation. If we don't learn to surf, we will end up corralling information into silos that hoard it instead of share it. It will become useless like the "U.S. steel company [that] discovered that the information provided by the new tool led senior executives to ask more questions of their subordinates, who didn't have the information to answer them" (Gates, p. 17).

I Hate Putting on My Tie

I hate putting my tie on every morning for work. I like looking sharp, but I hate ties because, like a good metaphor in a poem, it represents my displacement in the workforce. (I am more of an open collared, untucked shirt kind of guy) I am intrinsically bound through the slacks, the long sleeved collared shirts that are stiff and scratchy with starch, and the dress shoes that bind my feet like combat boots-Italian leather or not. I try to accentuate a little style with a spiked, disheveled haircut, but the noose around my neck casts a pale shadow over my reality.

Even though I am a business leader, I always feel ensnared by an organizational model and industrial machine that feels like a manufactured structure of "place and order." I feel the tug of history on my actions where things were very hierarchical with monarchs, sovereigns, nobles, and kingdoms. Like the factory assembly line of the Industrial Revolution, everyone and everything has their place and responsibility.

The Tie - A Symbol of "Place and Order"

Shakespeare was such an organizational conservative who held strictly to a fixed place, a fixed function, and a fixed order. He, like many others then and now, believe that order and function are essential components of productivity. He felt it mirrored a hierarchical order in nature and that *place and order* are essential. He firmly believed, like many do still, that we all belong to a "line of order," and if we stray from it mutiny will follow. He says in *Troilus and Cressida* in a speech by Ulysses, "But when the planets / In evil mixture to disorder wander, / What plagues and what portents, what mutiny!" Later in *Henry V* he writes about the hierarchically ordered universe and under that we are all assigned specializations, social ranks, and formal obligations. We are all to fall under our "place and order."

Therefore doth heaven divide
The state of man in divers functions,
Setting endeavor in continual motion;
To which is fixed, as an aim or butt,
Obedience; for so work the honey-bees,
Creatures that by a rule in nature teach
The act of order to a peopled kingdom.
They have a king, and officers of sorts,
Where some, like magistrates, correct at home;
Other, like merchants, venture trade abroad;
Others, like soldiers, armed in their stings,
Make boot upon the summer's velvet buds,
Which pillage they with merry march bring home
To the tent-royal of their emperor.

However, as one who earned my BA in English Literature, I love Shakespeare. It's rich and wonderful literature with language that drips with the good stuff of verse, and yet I still say that this mindset of "place and order," even when worded eloquently by Shakespeare, today is less likely to work. It's a tough sell in this global landscape, and its implementation is as difficult. It might have feigned allegiance during a time where stringent commands of "place and order" forced the hand of people to pay homage to Kings and Queens. It may have done well on the factory floor in moving productivity in the Industrial Revolution and even later when management became a science, but in a world where connectivity replaces mere function and transparency has become common, the older way must give way to the surfer.

Place and Order were Cold Place Holders

Place and order never created believers and passionate followers of the system. It did however create cogs and efficiencies. Homage was paid but out of duty not inspiration. Instead of it enabling a stealthy performance from employees where there is a meaningful exchange for both the employee and employer, it tyrannically and dispassionately measured predetermined outcomes. The very design of this *place and order* restricted the organic make-up of our innate design and the natural order of the living system. Intentionally, it had no central nervous system.

My Tie

Similarly, like this practice that causes me to dictatorially coordinate behavior, the tie that I slip around my neck symbolizes such control and precision. The only thing snug around my neck that I am okay with is my wetsuit. It's not that ties are bad or that this current form should be instantly and totally disbanded, but the tie around my neck and this practice of "place and order" is merely a traditional platform of operational thinking.

What if there is a totally different and unique way that looks and acts contrary to this older way? What if dress codes are only manifestations of control and leadership is not meant to manipulate but inspire and loose unrealized potential? What if we were meant to surf and roll around in the world of the dynamic and not get stuck in the streets of unimaginative ruts of routine? What if the unknown and the uncertain was the engine behind real change and not something to be feared? What if we are not to have a predetermined "place and order" but random evolving networks.

Deterministic Behavior

What gets me is that both the model and my perfectly perforated tie aren't natural. Neither of them are natural styles per se; rather they are both adorned in a deterministic behavior. Instead of innovation, a picture plays in my head of a cog on a wheel rolling down an arduous trail that aimlessly drones forward and ultimately rolls nowhere. As I have questioned this tie around my neck every day for years and this way of leading, I finally realized that this anachronistic model that parallels a common way of thinking ultimately has very little power to alter true and deep change. It creates a machine of movement and does little to create and then sustain development. It's a mindset that is deterministic and calculated, predetermined if you will to the expectations of an arbitrary calculation. The people and the untold individual narratives of the network are ignored. Like the tie around my neck that doesn't really change anything about me, except an image of control, our current thinking also pegs a false image of what we can really accomplish.

Every morning, the routine was generally the same. I synched a stylistic tie into my desired knot, matched it strategically with a crisp shirt and slacks, slipped on my less than comfortable dress shoes, gave my family the standard "see you tonight" salutation, and waddled like a predictable penguin out the door to work. As I backed down the driveway and watched the garage door slowly grate down its metal rails, I'd painfully watch my quiver of surfboards hanging distantly in the foreground as they silently remind me of my disconnect. As I drove to the office, constantly shifting my psyche as I wrestled with my tie, I realized I was a part of the herds streaming down the freeway pressing forward to the mechanism. As I siphoned my frustrated spirit into the cauldron of my workday and sipped my Starbuck's, my body would begin its typical writhing as I felt my tie choking out my soul.

Fit?

I, along with the majority of Corporate America, realize that I don't necessarily identify with a J.O.B. Not because I have worked for bad companies but because the human soul has been stuffed into a mechanized world that answers older mantras. I'm a surfer by spirit and trade yet a cog by practice. I am stuck in a line of thinking that inhibits me and limits my potential and ultimately the teams that I lead. There is something in my role, my position and function that grind against the slate of my natural intuitions, and its the spirit of calculated outcomes and precision.

As a senior leader and president and owner of my own start-up, I feel pressed to perform, calculate, and manipulate outcomes to seemingly canned forecasts. It is not where I work, the company that I own, or the jobs that I've had that is the culprit. It is however the system of corporate organizational life that finds its roots deep in the practices and science of traditional management that stretches back 150 years to Newtonian mindsets. It's this cloak that hangs heavy over organizational life that is the antithesis of image of the natural, powerful rhythmic dance of the sea.

I realize that I have a significant responsibility and unique opportunity on several levels concerning organizational life. I follow dutifully the traditional learned model and plan around predetermined projections and strategic targets set by corporate and market. However, always in the back of my mind questions rage from a traditional leadership perspective: Who defines and quantifies forecasts? Who determines the formulas to predictions? Why do we do things the way its been done for 100's of years in a time that is ultimately different? Where is the human spirit of innovation and why is it so routinely suppressed? Why is the system so disconnected from itself? Why do we determine five year plans when we don't know what the market is going to yield at the close of business that day? Where is the power of the individual or organization to author true change? Where is our power to create and where is our ability to inspire? How does the natural inclination of the divine human spirit play out in a mechanized world of management?

Even as a leader, I punch a clock, fulfill a role, worry that all my people are on post, calculate overtime, micro manage numbers, panic and sweat when results seem anemic, only to re-strategize under the same rules, and press to meet or exceed our next target. Then I turn around and do it all again. Even though I don't like to generally lead under this sense of control and manipulation, I've grown warily accustomed to the model that says this is how it's supposed to work – precise, controlled, calculated, predictable, determinate, disciplined, and manipulated.

I am told this system, this way of leaderships is tested. It's the hand of precision like a finely tuned clock droning out its "tick-tock, tick-tock, tick-tock" which gets the results. It's the manipulation of systems and people that reach toward the predisposed target, but compared to the wonder of the human spirit and its creative potential, the result I see is meager. Its like listening to the water in your bathtub or shower shoot from the faucet versus the waves in the ocean randomly colliding and exploding with symphonic roars. To me it feels so unnatural to lead like this because I know I only can really get lackluster results from a workforce that is potentially and intrinsically filled with rich and unusually dynamic solu- tions. Clearly, under this cloak of leadership the true capability of the person, the leader, and the organization hibernates in a deep slumber far away from its true potential.

We Work to Live?

I try to find my place after I am home from the office and the gym. I love being father and husband, but the majority of time that I spend living involves a dispassionate outlook because as the cliché aptly pens, "We work to live." In other words, like the majority of Corporate America we are disconnected from a meaningful venture and bound to something that merely provides a means. Work in general is not a place where meaning is exchanged for meaning or a place where creativity flourishes or is inspired; it is a place of compartmentalized functionality. I am structured under the hierarchical mindset. Still, I understand, I have an important job as a leader, I provide a valuable service, I help shape a company's future, provide jobs for my employees, and provide for my family, but the overall exchange is arid and mechanistic.

The Mentality of the Tie

As a people, we are wandering the desert floors parched and beaten by the sun. Under this current, more tyrannical model of thinking and acting, the exchange on both a micro and a macro scale is disconcerting for both the people and the organization. Until change becomes innovative through natural and random interconnectivity connected to central values, we will stay stuck in the mire of an industrial mindset where hierarchical control suffocates true, sustainable learning and vital innovation. While the world is quickly spinning webs of flux and change, our general mind-set is static and linear. Symbolically speaking, we are all a bit cinched by the ties around our necks. Like the Reformation called to question the hierarchical liturgy and control of the Catholic Church, we too are at the cusp of dramatic change, a monumental shift. In a way, the current flux of change in a global landscape has nailed its own "95 Theses" to the church doors and claimed the "Priesthood of all Believers."

A revolutionary leader in the field of business and a stalwart evangelist of a democratic workplace spins this traditional model of control and manipulation upside down and challenges this notion of pure calculation and precision. He challenges this "mentality of the tie." He advocates the human potential through transparency and accountability. I know this sounds like an oxymoron but listen to how it might look. His name is Ricardo Semler and he is the CEO and President of a company named Semco located in Brazil. His leadership style is highly controversial but measurably effective. His philosophy and practice is to release his people to perform under their "natural inclinations" through a system where the behavior is dictated by community conversations and group accountability and natural outpourings. He strongly believes in a thoroughly democratic workplace where the people influence and the people direct virtually every move and venture of the company in real time. Not an Executive Board or "C Suite" leaders, but the people decide the direction and the movement.

In his organization, there is a revolving circle of leadership that direct and hold the course, but conceptually and practically the power is spread across the floor of the company and every member shares in its force communally. The people and the company seems to thrive off of doing what feels and seems natural while being held accountable by the unforgiving, stringent arm of free market enterprise and simple peer pressure. Later we will hear more about him, but listen to a vignette from an interview from CNN.com by Nick Easen:

He breaks down his philosophy in his typically candid, layperson's terms in an interview with Nick Easen on CNN.com:

"Q. It is part of a reoccurring theme in your book to treat people at Semco as adults, not as children. Do you believe that companies often treat employees like children?

A: Yes, I see a lot of what happens in companies. It is similar to the situation in boarding school – where pupils and teacher both know that things need to get done. The teachers know that they cannot trust the pupils to decide everything on their own. That is why they always check on arrival times? Are pupils sitting in class, what are they saying to other pupils?

Here at Semco we are doing something else – we are saying everyone is a responsible adult. Currently, staff already makes decisions about their kids. The elect governors and mayors. They know what they what to buy and what they do not. It is absolutely crazy, the idea that people are still concerned about how things are done. The bosses here do not say – you are five minutes late or how come this worker in the plant is going to the bathroom?

In life we do not give employees enough leeway. If you look around at Semco's office there are plenty of empty desks. The question is – where are these people? I do not have the slightest idea, but I am not interested.

I am not interested in saying I want to make sure that my staff are here and that you are giving the company so many hours a day. Who needs so many hours a day? We need people who will deliver a final result. I need to make the bank happy. With four hours, eight hours, 12 hours in the office – showing up o Sunday and not showing up on Monday, it is totally irrelevant to me.

Today we have a lot of problems with customers, because the customer has certain mentality and they like to see everybody in suits. And I do wear a suit but very rarely.

The point is that if we do not let people do things the way they want to do them, we will never know what they are really capable of and they will just follow our boarding school rules" (http://edition.cnn.com/2004/BUSINESS/05/19/go.semler.transcript/index.html).

I realize this is a tall order and that what I am about to present may not be for every person, leader or organization, but we all should at least sincerely ponder its ramifications on the core of our communities and specifically on the core of our person.

If we are to succeed in today's landscape, we must at least pay attention to it and eventually and hopefully shift our behavior through a new structure of thinking. From a philosophical slant it bears significant merit, and from a business perspective, Semler's ideology is persuasive. His employee growth, 1-2%

turnover, and profitability surge is unarguable. He has grown from several hundred employees when he took over to over five thousand at last measure and he has surged from several million dollars in revenue to billions under his managing without managers' philosophy. His democratic work society where the employees hire and fire their managers, decide their own work schedules, and come and go at leisure sounds like letting a dragon loose on a castle to have its way with the villagers; it's sheer madness. He has no dress codes, voluntary meetings, and mandatory vacation times.

I know making blanket statements and overreaching generalizations dulls the potency of a unique idea because one thing cannot apply to all things and meet the parameters of critical details in every corner, but conversely what I propose carries the potential to alter true and significant change to people, leaders, and organizational life across multiple boarders – families, churches, businesses, companies, governments, industries, non-profits, education, boards of directors, etc. It does challenge the very model of hierarchical thinking, but this type of change needs to happen more often and in more lives. And if we ignore all the facts around us throughout the world and in our local communities, we will miss a critical piece of our design which is not only to develop ourselves but those we come across. The pace of change that we are facing won't allow us to continue the same way we are going now.

I realize this magnitude of change is a direct affront to traditional structures that reach back centuries that mandate control from top down. And yet, it is very unlikely this very traditional type of leadership can reach forward to the future effectively and command the attentive hand of flexible, adaptive networks. It manipulates change instead of inspiring it. There is no room for elaboration, collaboration, and innovation from random communities or from the bottom up. Typically, it is all stayed and in the form of template. Sure it has historically moved the needle and performed measurable effects, but can it continue to do so in this environment of probabilities and velocity? The old way restricts the very amazing and probable results that we could produce if unfettered through a more democratic and participative structure.

Lifeless

Most of us have compartmentalized ingenuity right out of reach and cemented ourselves into a mentality of lifeless production and depersonalized systems. We fiddle with widgets, but our innate design and intuitive gifting scream out for more. Our imaginations crave attention.

Under the current models of leadership, organizational structure, church elder boards, and hierarchical mentalities, true creativity that emerges from spontaneous needs from random people are considered "unstructured" and too messy because of this strict assembly of top down. It's been this way for far too long. No real event on the horizon or in our present has brought much to challenge this way of "doing." However, things have changed, are changing, and only will continue to change fast and faster. And under this diverse climate, this older way is becoming more like the insecure kid in the corner of the room that bellows his false vibrato like the schoolyard bully. It cannot sustain its rule in this day or this age because change today is slippery and evolving and entirely more emergent. It demands a more nimble mindset.

Going back to the metaphor of my tie. I finally realized that it isn't really the tie that was suffocating my psyche and crimping my soul, it's not the scratchy and stiff dress shirts pinching my brain, or the slacks and dress shoes that restrict my gait, or the job that I have, but it is the imposed, manufactured precision and discipline rooted deep in the bedrock of our mindsets that churned against my natural state. I am caught in the machine. I have become a cog in the wheel of mechanistic thinking only to forget the rush I get as I drop down the face of the wave. I forgot the power of salt water as it sprays on my face that draws me into focus and puts me into center. I have forgotten the power and the art of surfing and how it releases the soul.

The Inflection Point and Moore's Law

There is nothing more difficult to carry out, nor more doubtful of success or dangerous to handle, than to initiate a new order of things (Booz, Allen, Hamilton, p. 1)

Exponential change is the global currency, and we are at an inflection point, a tipping point (Gladwell). There is a video on Youtube that has become a small phenomenon demonstrating this transformation called "did you know?" It talks directly to the amount and speed of change and how it causes dramatic shifts. According to Youtube search and credits it's called "*did you know 3.0.* - A Newly Revised Edition Created by Karl Fisch, and modified by Scott McLeod; Globalization & The Information Age. It was adapted by Sony BMG at an executive meeting they held in Rome. Credits are also given to Scott McLeod and Jeff Brenman" (http://www.youtube.com/watch?v=LUtxEsc10B&feature=related). If you can, watch it and let the visual embolden the message and imbed its thought provoking observations into your psyche. What I have here is the text and the message. It is much more dynamic with music and the visuals of course, but the text still conveys this idea that shift happens more now than ever as we live in exponential times:

Did you Know?
If you're 1 in a million in China there are 1300 people just like you.
China will soon be the number 1 English speaking country in the world.

The 25% of India's population with the highest IQ's

is greater than the total population of the United States.

Translation: India has more honors kids than America has kids.

Did you know?

The top 10 in-demand jobs in 2010 did not exist in 2004

We are currently preparing students for jobs that don't yet exist...

using technologies that haven't been invented

in order to solve problems we don't even know are problems yet.

The U.S. Department of Labor estimates todays learner will have

10-14 jobs by the age of 38.

1 in 4 workers has been with their current employer for less than 1 year

1 in 2 has been there less than 5 years.

Did you know?

1 out of 8 couples married in the U.S. last year met online.

There are over 200 million registered user on MySpace If MySpace were a country, it would be the 5th largest in the world (between Indonesia and Brazil).

The #1 ranked country in Broadband Internet Penetration is Bermuda, #19 is the United States, #22 Japan.

Did you know?

We are living in Exponential times.

There are 31 Billion searchers on Google every month

In 2006, this # was 2.7 billion.

To whom were these questions addressed B.G. (before google)

The first commercial text message was sent in December of 1992

Today, the number of text messages sent and received everyday, excels the total population of the planet.

Years it took to reach a market audience of 50 million

Radio - 38 years TV - 13 years Internet - 4 years iPod - 3 years Facebook - 2 years

The number of internet devices in 1984 was 1,000 in 1992 was 1,000,000

in 2008 was 1,000,000,000

There are about 540,000 words in the English language

About 5x as many during Shakespeare's time.

It is estimated that a week's worth of New York Times contains more information than a person was likely to come across in a lifetime in the 18th century.

It is estimated that 4 exabytes (4.0 x 10 ^ 19) of unique information will be generated this year.

That is more than the previous 5 thousand years.

The amount of new technical information is doubling every 2 years

For students starting a 4 year technical degree this means that half of what they learn in their first year of study will be outdated by their 3rd year of study.

NTT Japan has successfully tested a fiber optic cable

that pushes 14 trillion bits per second down a single strand of fiber

That is 2,660 CD's or 210 million phone calls every second.

It is currently tripling ever six months and is expected to do so for the next 20 years.

By 2013 a supercomputer will be built that exceeds the computational abilities of the human brain.

Predictions are that by 2049, a $1000 computer will exceed the computational capabilities of the entire human species.

Did you know?

During the course of the presentation

67 babies were born in America

274 babies were born in China

395 babies were born in India

And 694,000 songs were down loaded illegally. So what does it all mean?

Shift is happening as information becomes significantly available and more complex through a flat and flatter world. Its influence on everything will force our hand. Who would have thought just a few years ago it would be understood whether in pop culture, everyday language, business meetings, or current technological conferences to "just Google it." Things are changing at significant speeds and the complex is becoming the normal. Take for example an article that talks about this change and its affect on church parishioners and laypeople from the Los Angeles Times called "Event Explores Religion in Web era" (LA Times, Mitchell Landsberg, AA4, March 15,2010). "Church 1.0 is all about creeds and doctrines, whereas Church 2.0 is kind of like wiki-theology."

"That was, in fact, one of the terms used last week during a three-day conference about the future of American Christianity at the Claremont School of Theology. Pagitt was among about 150 ministers, laypeople and academics who gathered to discuss "Theology After Google." The consensus: It's a whole new world out there. Churches will ignore it at their peril. "I think things like denomination and ordination are part of the old system of control and domination that has to go," Pagitt, 42, said as he relaxed after the conference's first day at the Theo-pub set up for participants. Around him, beer flowed and conversation leaped from Twitter to evangelism for church formation...The premise of the conference had been laid out earlier in the evening by Philip Clayton, a professor at Claremont who talked about the role of gunther's printing press in the 15th century. By making the Bible available more widely available, he said, it democratized religion and led directly to the Protestant Reformation.

"Ladies and Gentlemen," Clayton said, "we are talking today about a transition equally as great..." Jon Irvine, a 30-year old Web designer who works with the "emerging church" movement, said the church of the future will have to be less hierarchical and more free-wheeling and ecumenical: "Church 1.0...was always about a big council of big brains getting together and telling you, 'Here, we've gone into a room and we've decreed that you need to believe.' Church 2.0 is more bottom-up. Every man is capable of learning and providing feedback. Church 1.0 is about creeds and doctrines, whereas Church 2.0 is kind of like a wiki-theology."

At least half the audience multi-tasked on laptops, iPhones and Blackberry's while listening to speakers. And many contributed comments in the form of Twitter 'Tweets' that were scrolling up a screen behind the podium. In addition to those in attendance in Claremont, organizers said about 1,300 people watched a streaming video feed of the conference from around the world (LA Times, Mitchell Landsberg, AA4, March 15,2010)

This robust complexity is hitting the business world, organizations, leadership, church, religion, and individuals. It doesn't show favoritism to institution, creed, or belief. It is all around.

The boundaries are disappearing and borders are blurred and the complexities of the information era are mounting. The way we did things is not the way we can do them in the future. It's all so much and coming so fast that it can disrupt total systems if our thinking is disconnected. It will be our peril. If a system or person cannot disseminate the information fast enough or connect and process its evolving content within an interconnected network, it will be overrun by the sheer amount and more specifically its complexity. Like ants rushing a dollop of sweet bar-b-que sauce on a picnic plate in the park, so is information pervading our homes, our families, our businesses, our churches, our schools, and our organizations. It doesn't matter what you do as a leader, your role in an organization, or even your responsibility as an individual because the amount of information swarming like a bee hive is challenging how we think at every level.

And because of this, we are in a quandary. Whether we realize it or not, we don't quite know what to make of this new shift. We are usually under unique pressure to increase performance and fix all the problems hindering progress anyway. Now, we are in a more difficult place. The information is more complex and difficult to unpack, and there is more of it. So we react in a typical fashion. Like a hunter we shoot; we react. We try to make room for brain space and try to peck the problems off one at a time like shooting cans off a fence. It's the hierarchical mindset. It's that control that wants to take over and manipulate the outcome.

I will use myself as an example. As a leader in a company, I feel this pressure but mainly because I think too top down and not enough bottom up. I get stuck in the menacing limitations of the hierarchy. For example, I get hit with a slew of problems and feel like they all rest on my desk alone because I am plagued by a pyramid mindset. I think I have to fix all the problems. I am not talking about mere delegation. I am talking about a mentality that needs to learn to let go. The world is becoming a network of networks, hierarchical thinking with a singular point of control is becoming archaic but more important it is ineffective. These times are about collaboration that randomly happens when an emergent problem creates an unlikely need.

Two things happen here that I am trying to show. First, we cannot go it alone because we need the resources of the network and emerging networks. There are too many complex issues at once to solve for any one person. I need to flatten my hierarchical power grid and open up the capacity of an emergent community to respond on the fly like a surfer does to a wave. A surfer see's the wave emerge on the horizon and takes to it. I must therefore contribute to the needed solutions as they arise by instilling in my mind-set the authority of the community to implement innovations that bring real change in real time. The information and the ability to act must be as close to on the spot as possible.

The second thing that happens on the macro scale if we restructure how we think, is that we will learn to innovate through this unrecognizable mass of change. In this newer format where a flatter landscape brings more flux and change, it is easier to confront this evolution and unpredictability if we are meeting it with nimble structures. We meet natural evolution with natural innovation using the connectivity of an open system. We can break out of our confined space, interact, and respond with our natural core instead of the static mindset that we adapted off the assembly line.

Islands and Bridges

These traditional mentalities, like islands dotting an ocean, are too isolated and disconnected. Picture a myriad of disconnected little islands peppered all over the ocean. Each island represents a person, leader, or organization and a static, traditional perch. Each island is fragmented and disconnected, separated by boundaries and distance. The island, like the person, the mindset, is used to things in their place and function instead of interconnectivity and networks. He/she cannot make sense of a whole system held together by random networks, like the ocean where everything is an influence on everything. They are limited to the shoreline. Our mentality is like the islands; it is rigid, linear and used to restrictions. We are familiar with limits.

However, what if overnight, unknowingly a maze of bridges appears and connects all the islands in the entire sea, and those bridges not only connect the islands but they instantly connect all the information and diverse content of the islands to other islands.

The islands in a sense become intimately connected, accessible by all the others. At once, information becomes rampant and instantly accessible to almost any one island who is curious of another. The islands edge cease to limit or strictly define their reach. At once all the islands make up a new and highly elaborate connection of knowledge centers. Boarders cease to exist and the sea becomes an interconnected network of information. Instead of one island "wondering" about the other island or being confined by their own natural restraint, they simply tap the power of the "bridge" and access any of the other islands at whim.

Instantly, the myriad of isolated islands become a giant network. They are interconnected, and the bridges become superhighways of information. Networks are everywhere. The islands reality is no longer their shores but their limitless, dynamic interconnectedness.

These bridges also allow for random and instantaneous movement of data. Information becomes transparent and accessible, and the individual islands overnight become a part of a conglomerate of connected knowledge centers. Instantly, they have to deal with a new and dynamic change. Not only do they have learn how to function within an interconnected landscape, they quickly must learn how to handle a *different world* burdened with rapidly changing and ever increasing amounts of data and velocity.

This is obviously a simple example and so much more could be unpacked, but the point I am highlighting is that the world is fast and flat. And its not just data but data that is mixed and tossed together by the random power of free forming connectivity. *These swarms of information bits united by "bridges" exponentially expand and converge and create a new way of life.*

It's not that this then necessarily makes people smarter because they have more information or that more information is scary. It simply means that almost anyone has access to almost any type and amount of information any time they want. We have new rules. It is a core component of these exponential times. "Each of these applications of digital information is approaching an inflection point - the moment at which change in consumer use becomes sudden and massive. Together they will radically transform our lifestyles and the world of business (Gates, p. xvi).

Like the bridges represent the internet and its expansive world of interconnections bringing together the global landscape, it also represents the exponential growth of both the speed of connectivity and the amount of information now accessible. We can see it in "the wild pace and large scale of the exchange of ideas, information, and insight that is taking place 24/7 across the 1.5 million miles of fiber-optic cable now connecting every continent on earth" (Gibbons, p. 90). It specifically affects how we live, how we think, and how we can tap into the power of a randomly evolving momentum.

In short it's like Wikipedia says of Moore's law: the measurement of the capabilities of the world of digital electronics grows at roughly exponential rates. Specifically, Gordon Moore, the cofounder of Intel observed that the number of transistors per square inch-data density - that can fit on integrated circuits has doubled roughly every 18 months since 1965, and it will continue to do so for years to come.

The world landscape will continue to indulge in tremendous technological change which will bring obvious and accelerated advancements across how we live, think and connect. This will spearhead social ramifications and increase random communities that will cross pollinate and CO-create new realities because of their ability to connect. This advance will continue to change our life as we know it, permeate our future, and change the way we think. The overall "density of data" will be increasingly compressed and fit into smaller and smaller spaces-technically, socially, and organizationally. This translates to more data that we will need to process in the work place, in the organization, in the church, in the school, in our homes, and in our world.

In the digital age, "connectivity" takes on a broader meaning than simply putting two or more people in touch. The Internet creates a new universal space for information sharing, collaboration, and commerce. It provides a new medium that takes the immediacy and spontaneity of technologies such as the TV and the phone and combines them with the depth and breadth inherent in paper communications. In addition, the ability to find information and match people with common interests is completely new (Gates, p. xvi).

The "bridges" are changing the worlds technology, social dynamics, organizational DNA, the pace and rate of exchange, and our way of thinking. We can't sit down and bureaucratically saunter through a maze of disconnected parts and pieces to figure it out. Unless we evolve and learn to make sense of an "open ocean" for example, the rate and complexity of the bridges (Moore's law) will leave us dizzy.

Web 3.0

At the D7 or "All Things Digital Conference" held in Carlsbad, California, the Wall Street Journal officially declared Web 2.0 was over and that Web 3.0 had begun. Web 2.0 refers to the second generation of web development and web design. Wikipedia says that 2.0 "...is characterized as facilitating communication, information sharing, interoperability, and collaboration on the World Wide Web. It has led to the development and evolution of web-based communities, hosted services, and web applications [like] social-networking, video sharing sites, wikis, and blogs..." Like the 20th century marked the end of an era and the 21st century now marks a new frontier, so too does the end of Web 2.0 and the beginning of Web 3.0 mark a mile stone of change for communities all around the globe. It is the latest innovation in computing that has paved the way for seamless and simple applications that unwind real-time complexities. The Wall Street Journal said,

"So what's the seminal development that is ushering in the era of Web 3.0? It's the real arrival, after years of false predictions, of the thin client, running clean, simple software, against cloud-based data and services. The Apple iPhone and iPod touch are the tip of the spear. It's more than just those two products, of course, but it's what they represent: the complete integration of computing into every part of our lives in a way that is seamless, ubiquitous and, ideally, dead simple. From using easy gestures to grab any piece of information from the Web to having powerful computers in the palm of your hand to being able to quickly dip into complex social networks to getting real-time information from across the globe as it happens, this is an era when computing could become as integrated and invisible as electricity and just as important...While we could make a lot of lofty predictions, in truth, no one knows where it will all lead. More important, few can predict the impact it will have on all kinds of businesses...Because whatever name you want to slap onto what's happening, the pace of change does not wait to be defined" (Wall Street Journal, Tues. June 2, 2009, R1, Technology).

A pastor, CEO, COO, teacher, Chairperson, Director, parent, or any organizational leader is under pressure to disseminate and make sense of this undefined influx for their team members. As the article said, the structure has now become to exist as "the complete integration of computing into every part of our lives in a way that is *seamless, ubiquitous and, ideally, dead simple.*" (italics mine)

Seamless, ubiquitous, and dead simple, that is the future we are headed toward, and this is what we have to get our heads around as we unravel it all. And this diverse and seamless stream makes our current structures unable to move with the flexibility that we need. We are too stiff and too tightly organized. This current structure, when put up against what is coming, is like a loosely sitting wall of sand trying to hold back a surge of water. Because the traditional structure is too top heavy and too big to move quickly, it can't comprehend or create new realities.

With this unconventional movement, it requires our minds and our attitude really to be nimble and flexible. Dynamic change is everywhere and because of the interconnectivity (like the islands) on a global scale, we are meeting with change that will not wait to be defined. Because of this global network of connections, just about anyone can access almost anything. Therefore, at some point and in some way we are nearly all connected. Conversations are different and more "intercontinental" with a greater reach. Language is even changing and narratives are being amended, and if we are not attentive to the shift, we will lose our footing.

Who would have thought just a short time ago that words like wiki, blog, online communities, social-networking sites, virtual worlds, and even twittering would become every day vocabulary whether you are talking with your friend or at a formal business meeting or in a church service. "Oxford University Press recently announced it will be dropping words like 'dwarf,' 'elf,' and 'devil' from its children dictionary to make room for words like 'blog,' 'Euro,' and 'biodegradable'" (Wall Street Journal, Friday, December 19, 2008, W11).

Take for example the ramifications these recent events have etched and their velocity of travel: 1) The tragedy of 9-11 that forever reshaped our view of the world, 2) a pervasive and deep global credit crisis that demoralized and imploded both lives and institutions, 3) a catastrophic fall out for the automotive industry that changed American Icons and total industry, 4) and manifestations of deep, intrinsic change with the first ever African American President. And because of a global e-connectivity and flatter landscape, these changes in a matter of days altered total mindsets. Listen to a paragraph from an article called "The Permanent Tea Party" in the Wall Street Journal clarifying the new type of change:

> *This isn't just another turn in the business cycle.* (Italics mine) On September 15, 2008, the economic structure of the U.S. imploded. Lehman Brothers, a synonym for the American financial bedrock, filed for bankruptcy. On June 1, 2009, General Motors, once a symposium for American economic primacy, filed for bankruptcy and was effectively nationalized. In the nine months between these two iconic events, the American people were riveted to news of economic distress" (Wall Street Journal, November 5, 2009, Opinion, A17).

This rate of its travel is akin to Bill Gates title of his book, "At the Speed of Thought." The Great Recession ripped chasms throughout the global community and leveled industries and institutions, and the credit crisis spread a thick blanket of trepidation over the windows of hope. And this all happened virtually over weeks instead of years or decades. The "closeness" of the global community has sped up change to move more like a Formula One Race Car versus the cathartic river boats that used to leisurely paddle their way through the Mississippi. "True, this global halt is the dark side of the information technologies and globalization that have created so much wealth and generated so much activity in the past 20 years. The frictionless, instantaneous flow of capital is possible only because of the Internet and the electronic exchanges" (Wall Street Journal, Friday, December 26, 2008, A13). Because of the startling "commonness" of this current rate of travel, change is changed by more change and it will not be defined by time.

It is this speed and mass of change that has become the uncanny connection across industries and the global community. Listen to a recent event from Wall Street that demonstrates the uncanny speed and connectedness of a particular segment.

> "Soon after the Black Monday crash of 1987, exchanges and regulators scrambled to enact new rules to prevent a repeat of the biggest stock market shock in 50 years. Even then, they worried they hadn't done enough... After two decades of rule changing and technological advancements, those comments seem haunting, especially as investigators of May 6's "flash

crash" stumble upon echoes of the Black Monday meltdown. Technological advancement has been widely touted as having made the market efficient, and more resilient. Instead, the May 6 drop - while much smaller than the 1987 crash - showed that technology mainly served to speed up trading and mag- nify the market moves.

On May 6, "The velocity of volatility was stunning, beyond anything I had ever seen, with the exception of October of 1987, when I was on the trading floor," said Ted Weisberg, president of Seaport Securities in New York...On Oct. 19, 1987, the Dow Jones Industrial Average tumbled more than 20%, and the swoon extended into the following day, before a rebound. Floor traders, working by telephone, dominated the action and computer-generated trading was still in its infancy. Dark pools and high-frequency trading were stuff of science fiction. Trading reached 600 million shares, according to the SEC.

Fast forward to May 6, 2010: The worst part of the lightning descent lasted roughly 10 minutes and the decline hit 9.8% at its worst. Trades, many executed in milliseconds, reached 19 billion shares (Wall Street Journal, Tuesday, May 18, 2010, Money and Investing, C1).

Similarly, we must think systemically. We must learn how to readily adapt, respond, and maintain flexibility. We are under a drastic movement of change whether we admit it and embrace it and innovate with it or whether we ignore it, miss it, and then become changed by its force. It's all around and we need to tap into a new vein of flexibility and innovation. Mark McDonald, a group VP at the technology consulting firm Gartner, Inc. said, "The world we're working in – and we're all trying to be successful in, and have our teams be successful in – is changing so dramatically and so fast. People have a natural desire to look for some kind of framework or a way of explaining what's going on" (Wall Street Journal, Monday, May 5, 2008, B6).

Too Top Heavy

However, we are likely incapable of making such leaps because we are top heavy and deterministic. In our current framework, we are about as effective as a sailboat tied and anchored to a dock trying to catch the wind and skim through the waters or like a little ski boat trying to pull a freighter through the open seas. We may be disciplined and highly specialized, but we are untrusting, suspicious and controlling. Unless we learn to nimbly respond collectively with transparency and accountability, we will stutter and stall. This older idea of authority must be dispersed and flattened instead of isolated in a perch. We need to let go and not hold so tight.

When we are confronted with this complexity, we must be able to see it for what it is, quickly disseminate its value as a disturbance, and flex enough to use that disturbance to innovate. To handle this velocity and volume, we need to undo years of hierarchical habits and put them through an overhaul, like when a boat is dry-docked so the barnacles can be scrapped and the bottom repainted and repaired. Like the world has become flat and interconnected, we too must flatten our perception of power, the meaning of power, and the pyramid flow of its directives.

We still need to collect input and data to more effectively steer the ship and make decisions. A leader still needs to help hold or change direction and continually shape and re-carve the vision. However, we no longer can afford to use input and data to suppress and manipulate. It must become a central nervous system that helps build valuable conversations and corporate wide visibility, but the data and input in itself is not the value alone. The conversation becomes the critical piece that really begins to foster qualitative movement. The older overarching arm of control that manipulates the effects of data discourages creativity, quells accountability, and infringes on sustainable learning. In other words, whether you are a leader of any type or simply a person trying to forge ahead in this time of velocity, if rigidity is paramount to your structure, you will be unable to rally and flex with emergence and self organizing. Like Semler said of Semco in its earlier days,

> "Semco appeared highly organized and well disciplined, and we still could not get our people to perform as we wanted, or be happy with their jobs," he wrote later in Maverick. "If only I could break the structure apart a bit, I thought to myself, I might see what was alienating so many of our people. I couldn't help thinking that Semco could be run differently, without counting everything, without regulating everyone, without keeping track of whether people were late, without all those numbers and all those rules. What if we could strip away all the artificial nonsense, all the managerial mumbo jumbo? What if we could run the business in a simpler way, a more natural way?" (http://www.strategy-business.com/press/16635507)

In the past, organizing anything into a tight and snug system seemed efficient, but in todays climate we will run ourselves or the organization short if we are ruled by it. We will fall short because the system can't experiment with full, unbridled potential and random creativity. Everything is too corralled. This type of highly organized and disciplined culture of old acts more like a group of levees that restrict and control the natural flow of moving water to corral it into designated aqueducts, reservoirs, and channels.

Instead, our new mentality needs to act more like a network of free-forming rivers that naturally move their way across the valley floors and through unrefined landscape until they find their own, natural way to the end. We need this because this emergent and massive *flow of information* is uplifting familiar landscape and creating new, unrecognizable masses, new roads, new passes, new bridges. Not only do things look different but they move differently. It all used to be manageable and understandable because we could think in bits and therefore control informational flow. We used to be able to eat the elephant one bite at a time. Now it seems there is a relentless herd of elephants stampeding forward every day all day long.

This reality is three pronged: First, the information now is coming from knowledge centers around the world that are all connected and the proprietary has now become common. Second, this new reality is evolutionary with unfamiliar and random behavior. Finally, and most crucial is that we need to think more like Semler and find a more "natural way."

No More Secrets

Globalization, the landscape of *.com*, and Google have made our world boundaryless. Hard lines that used to hinder the sharing of information are gone. There are no more secrets. The reality is that information is flowing like a swollen river etching and carving its own path. The books have been opened, and the islands have been connected. Bill Gates says,

> Business [and life] is going to change more in the next ten years than it has in the last fifty. As I was preparing my speech for our first CEO summit in the spring of 1997, I was pondering how the digital age will fundamentally alter business [and our lives]. If the 1980's were about quality and the 1990's were about reengineering, then the 2000's will be about velocity. About how quickly the nature of business will change. About how quickly business itself will be transacted. About how information access will alter the lifestyle of consumers and their expectations of business [and life]...These changes will occur because of a disarmingly simple idea: the flow of digital information (Gates, p. xiii).

Developments like Napster, Limewire, and iTunes opens the masses to shared music files from Boston to Bangladesh. Collaborative software and open source software like Wikipedia are developed by way of open networks of trust and accountability from Indiana to India. Companies employ designers for projects from California to China. Electronic and networked gaming makes it possible for a kid in New Jersey to play "war games" with a kid in New Delhi in real time. It's more common for randomly developed global communities with a common purpose to develop open source software like Wikipedia thorough spontaneous and emergent participants as opposed to the highly structured process for selecting a corporate committee tasked to handle a new project within its own walls. The internet has become the great equalizer, made geography virtually useless, and has leveled the playing field.

> But Globalization 3.0 differs from the previous eras not only in how it is shrinking and flattening the world and in how it is empowering individuals. It is also different in that Globalization 1.0 and 2.0 were driven primarily by

European and American individuals and businesses. Even though China actually had the biggest economy in the world in the eighteenth century, it was Western countries, companies, and explorers who were doing most of the globalizing and shaping of the system. But going forward, this will be less and less true. Because it is flattening and shrinking the world, globalization 3.0 is going to be more and more driven not only by individuals but also by a much more diverse-non-Western, non -white - group of individuals. Individuals from every corner of the flat world are being empowered" (Friedman, p. 11).

Whether you want to live in a virtual world, designate an international work team, or learn about topography in some remote location, just "Google it." It isn't necessarily how do you retrieve information but how much, in what format, and from where in the world do you want it to come? It's because of this that it is near impossible for the traditional framework to handle the conundrum that gets funneled to our doors. If we act and think alone with a focus on centrality and pretend to be the all powerful "Oz" behind the curtain, we will miss the vitality of evolving relationships necessary to move forward and forget that its all just a clamoring noise.

The Great Emergence (Phyllis Tickle)

Phyllis Tickle, again in her book called the Great Emergence writes about this new type of change and how it alters the rules of the game.

> Like every "new season," this one we recognize as the Great Emergence affects every part of our lives. In its totality, it interfaces with, and is the context for, everything we do socially, culturally, intellectually, politically, economically. When, for instance, a book on global economics can become a mega-seller, what we are really acknowledging to ourselves at a popular level is something we had already sensed but had not wanted to acknowledge, namely that the world really has gone flat again. Among other things, we are admitting at last that classic economics do not apply nearly so well to a service-based economy as they once did to our production based economy ones. We are acknowledging as well that national borders and national loyalties no longer hold as they once did. We are accepting as well the absolute fact that now even a small nation can hold a large one hostage, because technology and the knowledge of how to use it have leveled the playing field. No one is privileged anymore, or at least not in the old ways of physical wealth and sheer manpower (Tickle, p. 14-15).

Every part of our lives is affected. We sense it but now we have to acknowledge it as we are forced to examine a new world stage. Namely, we have to reassess how we handle information, how we process it and then how we maximize it within our community. Now as this information becomes more complex and dense, our older style is restrictive to the leader, the person, and the organization. The flow of new data requires fresh perspectives and a cacophony of viewpoints and contributing voices so that it can flow out. It's simply too much and too tangled to make sense of it alone.

For example, I have this huge crate of legos at home that is filled with thousands of pieces from when I was young. If I sat my 2 year old daughter down today in front of that box and told her to create as many probabilities as she could, she might put together a block or two or put a helmet on one of the little space men and say, "Dally, wook." However, if I put her together with my 5 year old daughter, my wife, myself, the grandparents, and my sister and brother-in-law, I bet we could take that huge box of colors and shapes and come up with cities, landscapes, transportation systems, space stations, neighborhoods, and perhaps even a light rail transit.

"Of course" you say, diverse teams brings together more people, which create more possibilities, which drive more options. This isn't new. And yet my example extends way beyond the idea of diverse teams coming together to break down and reassemble things. Diverse teams work for certain things, but for what we need today they are too prescribed and maybe even too canned for what we are trying to tackle. Sure, if you put all of my family together with my daughter the result is far greater and perhaps impressive, but what is coming at us today needs more than more people. It needs more than just a diverse team. If a diverse team is intentionally put together to handle this new flow, who is to know if that particular team is going to work to solve those new problems or be able to address one's that we have yet to see. Or how do we know that the person(s) who assembled the team understands what is needed. Maybe their biases skewed the team and it won't be effective for what is needed. If the team is purposely assembled, we are back to the same problem. It's all still static and linear and controlled. The team didn't assemble randomly or emerge to address a problem with mutual interest. They were brought in with someone else's predetermined thinking of what and who was needed to solve the problem. This is not to say to then let the groups or teams form like weeds at total random and wherever they want. There is a system, there is a way that smartly teaches networks, instead of teams, how to emerge and address the issue. If we develop networks that connect and seek each other out instead of having a senior leader selecting his/her favorites for a diverse team, there is a greater chance that the network will address the issue through a more organic, natural, and ultimately more effective way with mutuality. Autonomy can create effectiveness.

The networks need to come together and connect as the emerging problems formulate. This looser parameter will encourage the network or system to be flexible enough to come and go as the solution works itself out through the combining players. We need to unhinge our stiff and mechanized patterns that we normally use to find our way and begin a new way of "doing," a more interactive way that is connected to our intricate, complicated and wonderful design.

To extend the example, unlike the static box of legos that my family and I were using, this conundrum is a bit more messy and potentially overbearing if we hold to our older ways. Remember in this *Great Emergence* we are dealing with a whole new quilt of change. Phyllis Tickle above said it "affects every part of our lives. In its totality, it interfaces with, and is the context for, everything we do socially, culturally, intellectually, politically, economically."

Instead of a static problem that require a static approach with categorical responses, here's a symbol of what it might look like instead. Take that same box of legos in my garage, set them up to creatively assemble whatever your pleasure, and then add multiple conveyor belts from all angles of the garage that endlessly pour more legos into that crate and around the floor. All the while from above and from the sides, different cranes swoop in from all angles and intermittently take out structures you built, pieces you may need, or even topple structures that you are in the middle of building. These cranes along with the conveyor belts effectively dismantle and make useless the need for blueprints. Legos are constantly coming and going with no discernible pattern. You have to improvise on the fly. It makes planning nearly impossible, or at least the planning we were used to doing.

In other words, the conveyor belts constantly pour out endless inventory and change and the cranes constantly come in and take what you have, what you may need, or what you think you want to use. Through the mass and the ever changing content, blueprints and plans become arbitrary. Your "lego" project must now be nimble, mobile, and perhaps even obsolete. You might need an endless stream of people flowing in and out of the garage nonstop to forever deal with the open stream of lego pieces pouring in as well as the constant change and flux of the that inventory by the cranes moving out.

In other words, the current digital age of flux and random change is about connectivity, like the bridges joining the islands, but what that does on a hyper level is dump and move mass information all over the place as well as remove and shift information at whim to different places. In the meantime, we are still thinking in isolation with our egocentric behavior trying to make cities of legos from piles that always change and continually compound at unpredictable intervals. We are faced with virtual conveyor belts constantly dumping new and random information into organization, churches, cities, government, families with big virtual cranes altering and changing that information at whim.

I'm not trying to spread panic or be a conspiracy theorists to say that we better change or else. I believe conversely that this is one of the most exciting and revolutionary times to be alive, "...globalism truly is what historians call a disruptive force, because it's making for a very different, new world: culturally, economically, socially, technologically, commercially, and politically" (Gibons, p. 35).

The opportunity to learn new ways of thinking and living is incredible. If a system or an individual can come together and act on what is called *whole system thinking or a living system*, the person, organization, or leader can converge on complicated networks of data, collaborate through communal wisdom, and share real authority to act with transparent information, amazing things can shake our more stayed mentalities. We will be surprised and we can personally, socially, intellectually, and spiritually evolve. People never before able to connect and network can now at whim and at random find new meaning and purpose with shared values. This flattened landscape could be the catalyst to intimately unite entire segments and cause unusual evolutions. Listen to what David Gibbons in his new book about what he is calling the Third Culture titled the *Monkey and the Fish* says about this new change. It's lengthy, but listen in:

Around the world, things are changing fast these days, and in ways that seemed unthinkable only a few years ago...People who are students of culture couldn't help but notice that new topics and questions are looming large in the most important conversations talking place today. There are conversations about how China is upending the world economy and culture, and about how China is eclipsing the United States in so many ways. There are conversations about grassroots social change around the globe - which is being fueled by the internet's vast potential for helping people leap barriers of time, distance and culture - is far outstripping institutional approaches to crises and problem-solving, whether the institution is political or religious or otherwise.

There are conversations about how the world demands that business not only be good for profits but also be good for the planet and good for people. In business, it used to be that one bottom line - profit - separated the good from the bad. Now there are at least two bottom lines to attend: profit and cause. This new reality, this new way of doing things, has huge ramifications for the thinking, methods, and game plans of for-profit organizations and business entities of all kinds. Many in the corporate and non-profit domains are pretty sleep-deprived these days trying to figure out this new world we live in and what it means to be cause-oriented and socially conscious with their gains. This is in large part because they recognize the profitability of cause marketing.

What does all of this have to do with those of us in the church? Well, just as the spheres of commerce and government are being fundamentally reshaped by globalism, so is the domain of the church. Again, it's not new but a wake-up call to return to our roots, our calling as lovers of the marginalized.

Globalism applies to the many colossal shifts occurring in the world today because of an intense interdependence that countries, culture, and people are experiencing with one another. The world is shrinking. By the day, it seems. Distances that once took months to cover now take hours. People and cultures unknown to us, let alone ever personally encountered by us, are an integral part of the fabric of our lives. For example, experts have said that if you take out the undocumented worker in places like California, that will wreak havoc on our economy. People in politics and business, in education and the arts, people throughout all our institutions, are finding it difficult to keep up with the new way the world is changing, to understand what's happening and why, and to adapt (Gibbons, p. 35).

Take for example an organization started by a young woman with a very keen passion to connect to the poor people in third world countries. Through a very dynamic website, she helps to build relationships that multiply freely and create strings of emerging networks that evolve over and over. She established and helped to create kiva.org - loans that changes lives. It's a portal that allows someone simple like me to connect to a real person with real needs countries away from me through the internet. What kiva does is it lists profiles of entrepreneurs in poorer regions of the world that need a small business loan like $25 (yes I said only $25) for example to start a small business so he/she can feed their family, pay for their kids to go to school, put a roof over their hut, or keep their lights on.

Their site (www.kiva.org) answers "what is kiva?" Their mission is "to connect people, through lending, for the sake of alleviating poverty. Kiva empowers individuals to lend to an entrepreneur across the globe. By combining microfinance with the internet, Kiva is creating a global community of people connected through lending." Some of their core beliefs are that they deeply believe that all people by nature are generous given the right impetus, the poor are highly motivated, and by connecting people they can create relationships beyond financial transactions, and build a global community. They don't believe that it will just happen, however. The platform has to have a loose structure that allows participants to build on itself, and their core has to have specific qualities and characteristics that bring out generosity, motivation, and relationships. They have three key pillars: dignity, accountability, and transparency.

Today as I am typing they have a repayment rate as high as 98.57%, 742 gift certificates purchased, $1,503,425 lent, 4,265 entrepreneurs funded, 20,677 lenders made a loan, 3,206 new lenders joined, with 1 loan every 13 seconds.

I can peruse the site, study profiles of people or small groups, and pick one person or twenty-one people or small groups that I can connect with in some fashion and help fund their venture. Maybe its Jonalyn Laggui's Group with 10 entrepreneurs from the Phillipines who need $315 per entrepreneur. Maybe it's Abdulato Nazarov from Tajikistan who need $1,200 for his spare parts store. Or maybe it's Samrith Pov from Cambodia who needs $1000 for her little grocery store. The point is through this flat landscape, I can pick anyone like these or 100s of others and connect with a part of their lives, and in so doing I build a random relationship. I become a part of their story.

But for an effective community to grow and for the network to continually connect and expand, there has to be accountability and transparency. How they do this for example is that the site doesn't simply give a hand out without obligation. It validates their venture, underscores it against the need, and weighs the probability that it might work. The evolving community thrives because the interconnectivity multiplies through an exchange of value for value. After the loan is processed and the profits are calculated, the money is paid back. When they do that, I can take my repayment money and become a part of another community, and do it again. I pick another person(s) to loan that $25 to again. Through the internet and the transparency of kiva's network, I can create interconnectivity within a wildly evolving network, establish a connection through mutual causality or a common limit, become a part of a community with like interests, and build random relationships that evolve again.

Years ago, to touch someone in the third world like this involved huge organizations that kept you at arms length, or contributions to favorite charities, or dropping money into the offering plate at church. At no point was their dynamic interaction to the extent of kiva. You may have felt good if you gave to the Red Cross for example, but you were not literally dynamically connected. Your power of working together directly with the other side was extremely limited. Now, I can go to the internet, type in Kiva.org, connect to someone I want to directly because I like their story, affect them through being a part of their need, contribute an offering, and build a relationship with that person through micro-finance and a flattened power grid.

I immediately affect change and intermingle with change because the flattening of the system and the amazing sensitivity of highly connected networks. Simultaneously, I establish relationships within the community of kiva by connecting to people trying to contribute like I am. Instantly, through multiple emerging, evolving, and random kiva networks, I can affect change, move with change, and be an author within random relationships that connect and reconnect. Because of this high connectivity of the network, tiny movements like a contribution of $5, or a click through of the site, or the very story I am telling you now, and the whole system at once expands, evolves, and grows. The community multiplies relationships through dignity, accountability, and transparency. It's complexity brought on by the power of the bridges between the islands and the complexity of the conveyor belts and swooping cranes that ultimately bring this new opportunity where I can help build a bit of Samrith Pov' life in Cambodia.

I never would have been able to connect with these people before if not for this flattened landscape, and I never would have been able to participate or be aware of their needs before our previous life of borders and fences. Nor would have someone had the idea or notion to birth kiva with its inherent simplicity. Our mentalities and the splintered, physical constructs of our world wouldn't allow it. The hierarchical mindsets couldn't disconnect from linearity long enough to envision such a touchable community that can be immediately impacted. I wouldn't have known how to participate, and I would have been acutely disconnected from the need. However, now I can connect to the heart and passion of a young woman desirous to effect real change through micro-finance, interconnect to an evolving and unique network, author change with her, and bring life to her dream of using loans to change lives.

Her organization is very much akin to the idea of "circles" in a decentralized organization.

"The Apaches, for example, lived in many nonhierachical groups spread across the Southwest. Though they shared a common heritage and tradition, each group maintained its own particular habits and norms. Each Apache group resembled a circle: independent and autonomous...That's the thing about circles: once you join your an equal. It's then up to you to contribute to the best of your ability.

In the days of the Apaches, communication between different communities was difficult, and sharing information took days or weeks. But the advent of telephones and cheap transportation has made communication virtually instantaneous. Until the Internet Age, circles were confined to physical location. People could join an AA circle, but in order to take part, they had to show up at a meeting. The internet has allowed circles to become virtual: members join from their computers without ever leaving their home.

The barrier to forming and joining virtual circles has become dramatically lower. Joining circles is so easy and seamless, in fact, that most of us, whether we realize it or not, are members of a decentralized circle of one kind or another. Take Craigslist, for example. If you browse the ads, post one yourself, or contact a seller, you've just become a part of a virtual craigslist circle. It's not a close-knit group of people, but the sense of community and support is still there. The site has many circles, each based in metropolitan community: there's San Francisco craigslist, a New York craigslist, and so on" (Brafman and Beckstrom, P. 88-89).

Going back to the legos, I am not saying by their example that that we all have the capacity of a two year old if we try to do something on our own. What I am saying is that things have radically changed. If we stay stuck in the bureaucratic "goo" of our past, we will be overwhelmed and unable to affect the change confronting us. What is important is to acquire an ability to integrate multiple angles of change by connecting and building communities to the information creating that change. Then we can possibly meet the speed of change with the flexibility of a system of leadership that moves with the nimble reactions. Like a surfer, we must immerse ourselves into what seems like a brewing cauldron and find how to connect to its force instead of being taken and undone by its complexity. We need those circles.

Unlike Apache circles [that were exclusive], anyone can contribute to organizations like Wikipedia. As they've become virtual, circles have also become more amorphous and difficult to identify. There are't groups of Wikipedia users meeting together in rooms somewhere. Instead, a Wikipedia circle is made up of individuals contributing to a particular entry. Some members write the article, others edit it, still others beautify it. Membership becomes heavily fluid...Though virtual circles have become more anonymous, they're still based on trust. Contributors to Wikipedia trust one another to edit their articles. Craiglists users feel that the site is a community and tend to put more faith in a fellow craigslist user than they would in a person off the street. Members assume the best of each other, and generally that's what they get in return" (Brafman and Beckstrom, P. 89-91).

Find Connections to Randomness

When a surfer is out at sea waiting for the next ride, the ocean can be overwhelming. As kiva.org breaks down the overwhelming size of world poverty to individual people and actual lives, it makes real and dynamic change believable and something worth engaging. Making tiny connections within the system brings it all closer. Every time I plunge my arm in the water to paddle, the ocean becomes smaller as I connect to it with my immediate movements. It makes change exciting and immediately tangible. Kiva makes the immensity seem small. The surfer learns to do the same thing in the ocean. He enters the water and becomes a force of its rhythm instead of being swallowed into the vastness as it stretches and blurs itself into the horizon. As we learn to surf and systems become flat, we to will become enthralled by the moving and developing rhythm instead of overwhelmed by the mounting complexity. The art of surfing helps make the global landscape small enough to navigate as we travel throughout the interdependence of the system.

Like the slew of conveyor belts dumping legos out to the garage floor and cranes from all angles swooping in to randomly pick them out, the ocean like our new world, is filled with interactive communities that are alive and moving and combining and changing. Like the internet and like our new reality, the ocean and the world we now live in is a constant body of interconnecting change.

In the ocean, the sea life, steady currents, spontaneous rip tides, rogue waves, wind chop, storm swells, ocean topography, the sway of the water, etc., can make you think more about the apparent chaos and mess instead of the next wave. If you stay disconnected, you will miss the chance to interact with the ocean's "otherness." If we get confused by this new reality, we will lose focus, the vision, and the wit to combine and connect to the "mess."

Don't be Spooked by Vastness

My brother-in-law was snorkeling off one of the local beaches here in Southern California in the kelp beds just about 100 yards off the shore. He said something interesting that applies to this discussion. He said, "When you're surfing and sitting above the water, you know there is all kinds of stuff under you and around you, but we tend to block it out of our minds cause it's a bit freaky, a tad overwhelming. You don't realize how much there really is under and around you until you swim out, put your face under the water and look around." He took a breath and chuckled nervously about his experience. "At one point I was in about 20 feet or so of water and about 20 yards in front of me I saw the buoy that marked the drop off point. It went a mile straight down." He continued, "The kelp was swirling, my body was swaying with the currents, the water a bit murky, fish were all around, and the water was alive with so many things. But when you stared off toward the mile marker of that buoy and stared off into the deep, deep vast expanse of the world beneath the surface, then you realized how much is really out there. It's spooky. Really spooky."

Trying to process all the possibilities at once messes with your head, like trying to fix world poverty or change a leadership paradigm. To try to tackle all of this new reality at once and alone is pointless. We must instead begin to grasp the idea of connectivity and non-linearity, move with its "currents" and feel its rush so that we can connect with it in bits.

The Beautiful Flurry

I remember when I was a lifeguard, the ocean's brought together all kinds of things. It was alive with seagulls flying, seals swimming, the water churning, the wind blowing, the waves crashing, the tides moving, the fish intermingling, the crabs crawling, and the surfers surfing. It was constant movement. In its own way, it was uniquely intertwined and a highly connected network. To be sure I couldn't control it all, but I had to at least be aware of the beautiful flurry. I was responsible for my "water" and what happened, but not all the activity. I could only control what I could control. The wisdom came in letting the system exist as it was and monitoring its activity to gauge the level of influence I needed to exert to engage the balance of powers and ultimately keep people from drowning.

For example, a few hundred yards off that beach was a canyon ledge that dropped straight down about one to two miles deep. The same one my brother-in-law just described. This shelf as a structure increases the possibilities I spoke of earlier. It acts like the internet in its ability to create random relationships. This shelf causes the surf on a big swell to surge to sometimes dangerous levels; it keeps the water extremely cold, the rip tides are frequent, and it draws a variety of sea life. It brings and creates connections. For example, it wasn't uncommon to see massive whales gently floating on the waters surface and gingerly mixing with the currents, seals basking in the sun rolling in the water like lions lounging in the desert, dolphins playfully dancing with the waves and chasing each other like kids in a playground, tides and currents moving and shaping the waters like liquid clay, and even an occasional shark swirling its fin out in the distance. My point is that the ocean and my surroundings were teeming with activity and what seemed like fascinating distractions. I was a small piece but nonetheless, I was oddly a component of the system's activity. I was in a community of random relationships.

We often don't get this part. Namely, like a lifeguard as leaders we sit in the tower for power or perspective, we ultimately are separated from this flurry because of our static view from the perch. Actually, we are detached. Instead of engaging the system and interacting with percolating networks, we keep what seems to be the pounding of distractions at a distance. We'd rather feign a sense of control.

I'm not saying a leader or an organization needs to do more as they come out of their "perch." We don't need to for example, jump in the waves and swim with the dolphins and whales. That might be a bit overwhelming and even dangerous. Rather, we must learn to let go of this need to control and manipulate and stay strategically disconnected but utterly engaged in the activity.

The key in this newer surge of complexity is to merge with the unrealized and unfettered power of the system. Interact with it. Move with it. Create within it. Work with legos as they come and/or go, find the emerging wave, and don't be so committed to a blueprint or the structure that you spent hours building. We must be nimble and flexible. This is not to say that it looks and feels messy and chaotic, but that a natural, undulating rhythm is allowed to swirl like the oceans waters. The disturbances, or the consistency of flux and change for the leader, the organization, or the person can actually create greater opportunity instead of bringing what may look like and feel like chaos.

The system before us whether it is a country, an organization, a small business, a church, or a family is alive and brewing like the ocean and the internet, whether we interact with it or view it from our perch. It takes on its own form and its own shape. It will do this with our without us, but if we integrate our minds into this game we get to be dynamic participants that intermingle with change instead of being undone by it.

Held Captive by Wonder

Our new reality thrusts a new and robust surge that is unparalleled. However, what happens when we get off our perch and intermingle with a system that is very alive, the power to understand and move with greater intelligence exponentially multiplies. The system beckons us to share its life and tap into an undisclosed reservoir. It won't drag you in by force, but it will beckon you forward like a minstrel in the cool, dark night. However, to maximize this potential, we must enter into an almost mystical and confusing darkness. A surfer shares this type of wild but intimate connection to the sea.

The wonder of being able to tap into this surge is to touch an aspect of the Unseen. If we open up to this wild momentum and multiplying variables, we will be held captive by the wonder of discovery like a surfer cascading up and down the shoulder of a wave where the edge unlocks a system and transforms change into innovation. Like when I was a teacher, the greatest experience was when I was able to lift back the veil of a student's fear and lead them through the wonder of learning and into discovery. If we interact with this emergent system of networks, it will do for us what the ocean does for the surfer and what teaching did for me.

Paddle Out

When I was in that life guard tower, because the water was so cold and the currents erratic like I mentioned, the other lifeguards and I would take turns on the rescue board and paddle a mile or so out in the water to stay familiar with the cold and the currents. From far out, the beach and my tower looked small, the water was mind altering cold, and my sense of vulnerability was pricked as my feet dangled like bait on top of the water's edge. I was quickly small and insignificant, but I became a part of the system. What happened next was the most important. Out there in the water, I experienced a "place," an otherness. By paddling out, I converged with the system and became a part of it.

Whether I was life guarding or surfing, the ocean wrapped itself around and through me if I engaged it. If I let it, its largeness and unstated power mesmerized me. I could have easily gotten swallowed, but I learned to take it like kiva does poverty so that it becomes exciting, almost personal. However, when I entered the system I had to harness the apparent confusion and transpose it into order so it could play like a wonderfully complex symphony lucidly composing.

There are four points we need to understand as leaders why it is important to engage and interact with this new confusion. If we do this, we can experience the freeing and beautiful power of connectivity and its direct link to innovation. 1) If we stay in our perch, we stay disconnected. Our viewpoint from our lofty perch is comfortable and familiar, but it keeps us from the symphony. 2) We need to let go of our need to control. We must engage our environment and immediate elements to grapple with the realities of change and connect with networks and emerging communities. We must plunge into the water and taste its salt, its current, its chill, and its vastness. 3) Finally, we must interact with our system to connect to its vitality. When I surf and enter the water, I am instantly aware of its pulsating movement. It has an undefinable, chaotic, and mysterious surge that taps my psyche and strangely releases me to an unfettered paradise of calm. However, if someone is new to the sea, new to the board, new to this surge, and new to surfing, he/she could be undone and overwhelmed and panic if plunged directly out to sea.

Surfing is about direct interaction - the drop, the rush, the pulsating, rhythmic sea. Yet we fear its mass and power. We miss the wave and stay locked in sameness. Surfing for a leader or an organization is about connecting to what is natural, and then tapping into networks to become a part of its unpredictable and indeterminate creative reality.

Our Meddling Intellect

I know what you are thinking. By jumping in the water *with* the confusion there is instantly more complexity. Understandably, that is the first glance. "Surfing" you might think will breed fear and confusion because you are *in* the ocean instead of watching from *a safe perch*.

I realize that "headspace" is important to all of us. However, getting wet and tasting the salt of the sea and even getting racked by a wave doesn't take away our "space." It actually creates space as it shakes you from sameness. It opens the mind and soul. Sure, at first it might feel like things all of a sudden get crazy. I remember the first time in the water when a wave tumbled and tossed me around, I freaked out and my board got washed to shore. When I composed myself, I realized the power of the ocean and eventually learned how to move with the wave. I quickly learned how to duck dive under the base of the wave with body and board. You come out the other side a little shaken, but unscathed and ready for the next wave.

The ocean, for example, like an open system does not grow the burden, rather it increases probabilities and possibilities and lessens tasks and busyness when you release control. When you actually release yourself to the wave and surf, the connection to the "otherness" is revitalizing.

There are two feelings that stand side by side as I drop down the face of the wave. 1) I have this immediate sensation of reckless freedom as my mind's eye is caught in a flurry of release, and 2) it pushes me to metaphysically saunter over my human restraints. It is at that moment where the chaotic and a sense of purpose intersect and converge into a moment of divine ascension. It is in the very moment that I surf. I know this sounds a little zen, but this is where sustainable learning happens; it's the kind of learning that goes deep into the soul, the mind, and stretches out ultimately into the network of the global landscape. This is where mentalities are changed. It's where the transformation reshapes the individual narrative.

To experience this, we need to flatten and decentralize authority and information and push for communities to emerge, participate in the scramble for understanding, and then press the discovery. We must learn to build systems of natural components instead of cogs.

However, we are historically set up to be disconnected from the process and each other. We are funneled into parts and pieces that fulfill functions. The older system figures it's best to set up a rigid structure to maximize the control of systems by separating parts and pieces into a place and order to increase human performance and therefore increase efficiency. Instead, this puts our divine creation to sleep. Perhaps it's akin to Wordsworth's warning in his "The Tables Turned" (1798). "Our meddling intellect/ Misshapes the beauteous forms of things." We can choose though to challenge this way and re-pollinate a new vision. We can use transparency, accountability, and community to awake our inner purpose and natural bend and spread the conversation through the power of the network.

How does this work? Each leader and organization will have to figure out what best works for their culture, their needs, their industry, their segment, or their vision. Just as each surfer defines his own style by surfing, so to the leader will have to determine what works in the world that they lead. But several things do need to happen to start the process. First, we must learn to listen and interact with the system so that we can open and connect the system to itself. Second, the people and the system, if the power and the information is disseminated, begin to learn how to decide for itself what works and what doesn't by exploring the content and its relevance. Third, the structure must form itself in the image of the "webbing" of the internet - unrestrictive, multiplying, random connections under common value - so that it can move to discovery and then respond, like open source software. In reality it needs to follow the model and principles of kiva.org or Facebook where highly connected, emergent, transparent, diverse, and simple systems connect and convert activity to measurable, effective outcomes.

In practice, we need to follow Wikipedia's model of transparent and accountable editors and contributors, or Facebook where connections intertwine and expand random communities. Information needs to be funneled in and then quickly shared and edited and recreated by all players or agents. This speed, if there is connectivity and transparency, will bring functionality and multiplication, and through unpredictable surges it can translate that information into movement, adaptability and innovation.

Scary Concept

The concept scares us to some degree. We think it's like a pirate on the open seas. However, power is not removed and given to anyone at anytime for any purpose. It's not anarchy. Instead, the power is shared and distributed and corralled under purpose, vision, and core values. With more participants and more connectivity, there is far greater accountability and productivity. More people have actual voice in the decision and approval process and therefore hold each other and the system accountable to its course. This will generate a more productive, efficient, and versatile people. Listen again to Semler's pragmatic argument for change:

> If successful business depends on innovation, why are automobiles made essentially the same way today as they were in Ford's first assembly line 100 years ago? Parallel parking is one of the 'stupidest things we do,' says Semler.
> 'If we had a day, could we not by tomorrow afternoon figure out a way to make a car' that handles better in this common situation – or, on a grander scale, escape from the 'silly concept' of oil dependent transportation altogether? The problem, Semler figures, is that there's something fundamental about organizations and...leadership that makes it almost impossible for people inside a business to change their own industry.' Industries are based on 'formats that are basically legacies of military hierarchies,' says Semler, which neglect or deny the power of human intuition and democratic participation. In Semler's own firm, there are no five year business plans (which he views as wishful thinking), but rather a 'rolling rationale about numbers.' A project takes off only if a critical mass of employees decides to get involved. Staff determine when they need a leader, and then choose their own bosses in a process akin to courtship, says Semler, resulting in a corporate turnover rate of 2% over 25 years. 'We'll send our sons anywhere in the world to die

for democracy,' says Semler, but don't seem to apply the concept to the workplace. This is a tragic error, because 'people on their own developing their own solutions will develop something different' (http://www.strategy- business.com/press/16635507)

Social Networking - Dignity, Transparency, Accountability

Despite the glaring rise of the social networking phenomenon, we continue to disconnect. We're afraid of things not controlled or put in proper place. We erect fences and boundaries. We fail to see that a free-forming community rich in random relationships guided by immediacy, transparency, and accountability will produce greater results. There is a sense of significance and value, and a community filled with common and random connections will share some sort of mutuality.

There is a fairly common saying usually held by upper management which runs contrary to this idea of connectivity and rich, random relationships. It's the mantra of hierarchical leadership and it's about control: "It's *only* in what you inspect (control) and not what you expect (trust)." I believe this works to a degree, especially if the structure and mind-set is hierarchical. We need to make sure things are running and working. We need to investigate and make sure the ship is floating and on course, but this message given the usual sentiment of top down is all about control not innovation.

Remember back just a bit when we talked about kiva's principles? Their core beliefs said they believe *all people by nature are generous given the right impetus, the poor are highly motivated, and by connecting people they can create relationships beyond financial transactions, and build a global community.* They build this on those three key pillars: dignity, accountability, and transparency. This sounds idealistic, but kiva has made it pragmatic and real. In essence, they believe we are generally good, we can become better and help others if information is transparent, we are treated with dignity, and we are held accountable. The management mantra of the older way can't buy into this in its entirety. It's just too scary, too trusting, too cooperative, too collaborative, too open. Notice though how kiva says that people by nature are generous under the proper circumstances and motivation. It has to make sense and appeal to a higher good, something that beckons our belief system, something with intrinsic truth.

So I am not saying just to spread out authority and hand out all information and let the natives have the rule of the land. There has to be a qualifying appeal, transparent conversations, and the contributions and results must be held to some kind of accountability under specific mission, vision, and core value. We are good if the purpose and ultimate end game taps into our core belief, a core component of our design, and is directed forward from the same foundation.

People aren't always honest. That's naive. But we can be taught to practice honesty. People don't just naturally work hard out of the goodness of their heart when no one's watching. That too is just foolish. However, given the right arena,

I believe the older mentality might be surprised by the level of work performed within transparency inside of a collaborative community. What will happen is the pillars of dignity, transparency, and accountability become central to our mindset, the results will surpass those of the "inspect what you expect."

Like the model and structure of Facebook and Twitter, the propensity to develop up and out is very likely. However, if the system is put into constraints through control and fear, the results will be meager. Adaptability will remain marginalized.

As people, we are meant to light up the sky with our creativity and potential. If our soul is unfettered and certain pillars are in place (like kiva) we can dazzle, but more often under the older way we look like the flicker of a candle. Additionally, when we connect with others who also feel this same stirring, we become charged and inspired. Our soul awakens from slumber.

Here is a fiscal example of the value and influence the market sees in the architecture of these social networking communities. The young 20 something owner of Facebook - a commodity of massive networking - turned down a mulit billion dollar offer from a major corporation for his college "project." And Youtube was purchased by Google for a whopping $1.65 billion back in 2006 while MySpace was purchased for $580 million by news magnate Robert Murdoch. Major corporations are seeing the power of people in evolving communities and what their connectivity can bring to the bottom line. This interdependent power of collectivity is translating to fat profits. They may not actually believe it works, but clearly by the check they write, they believe in the results created by the movement that is a transparent, evolving conversation.

Sure the companies see these vibrant, evolving sites for advertising venues as profit centers. None-the-less, they believe something about it works. They are trying to create a network, a community. They understand the power of connectivity simply because of its massive appeal and the value these numbers can then translate to the bottom line. Whether they wholly believe in it or not, they cannot ignore the number of random subscribers to these emerging communities and its power to wage influence. They are setting up Twitter, Facebook, MySpace, and Youtube pages with links to their corporate sites because they are seeing the power generation X and generation Y and especially the millennial has placed on the might of social networking and open, unrestricted forums of conversations.

The premise of these sites is sharing information, promoting opinions and preferences, and encouraging discussions. If you start a conversations that is attractive, clever, and relevant, your conversation might go viral and you will get approved by the amount of followers you have. You could become a person of influence.

The May 10, 2010 issue of Time Magazine titled its focus "The 100 Most Influential People in the World." Not to surprisingly, one of the benchmarks they used to measure these people of influence were stats derived from the pages of Twitter and Facebook - President Obama, Ashton Kuthcer, Oprah Winfrey, Glen Beck, etc. They used what they called a social-networking index grid to rank the person's influence. This is the formula they used to quantify the leads and they called it the Formula for networking index: (Twitter followers) x 2 + (Facebook Connections) / 2.

If we lived in some kind of Orwellian dystopia, we could hook a nanobot to everyone's brain and scientifically measure just how much influence each human being has on every other. Whom do we trust? Whom do we fear? Whose ideas shape our view of the world - whether or not we even realize it?Fortunately, that's pure science fiction. But it is becoming easier to quantify certain kinds of influence. Social-networking sites such as Facebook and Twitter, for instance, can provide some basic information about the breadth of a person's brand. The measures are far from perfect: they tend toward to reward the young rather than the old, artists and entertainers rather than scientists and thinkers. Lady Gaga has nearly as many Twitter followers as Barack Obama does; is she really as influential? Probably not. But in other cases, the comparisons are apples to apples. On our index, Sarah Palin's social-networking score is about 45 times that of Nancy Pelosi. Conan O'Brien may have lost the Tonight Show wars, but he emerged with almost 20 times as many Twitter followers as Jay Leno (who was one of the TIME 100 in 2009). Pelosi and Leno might hold more prestigious positions, but there's little doubt about who has more ability to change the course of our conversations at a moment's notice - and in an interconnected world, that's what influence is all about (TIME, May 10, 2010).

There is obvious influence and power in these open, "conversationally based" networking communities. They are the places where people meet online, talk, tweet, post, communicate, splinter off to subgroups, build value, and collaborate seamlessly with a certain level of transparency. The success is in its architecture, and this same thing can happen in an organization, a business, or a church if communities are allowed to form freely in an open system.

Take the model and intended purpose of these sites like Facebook and Youtube and their intended, emergent qualities and build them into your organizational structure. You will begin to surf. Watch and be intoxicated by the power of the ocean working new currents in your company, church, or school as creativity, spontaneity, and innovation pushes you dynamically forward.

Listen to this example of a random connection. I had a customer in my store in Southern California that was, shall we say, rather hot under the collar. He wanted and eventually demanded something we could not nor would we do. It was impossible to meet his demands in any shape or form. He was visibly upset, very argumentative and unwilling to listen to reason or explanation. The only way he would have been happy was if I allowed my managers to make a very bad business decision without merit, mutual exchange, or economic value. Needless to say, we apologized for his frustration and turned him away. This confrontation with a customer is not abnormal unfortunately nor is it my point, but what happened next is a small glance into the reach and power of a system that opens itself to random connectivity.

That very next morning I got a voice mail from one of my very best friends who lives in Princeton, New Jersey (the other side of the country) telling me about a friend he knew that was upset with my store. (This is where I get invigorated because of what this very small example demonstrates.) As it turns out, his friend was that same angry, unruly customer from the day before that made me hot under the collar. Now mind you he didn't call my buddy and tell him about this experience because he knew him to be a friend of mine. He didn't even know I was the VP. I simply overheard his rant. He simply voiced his opinion at whim to his evolving community on Facebook. He posted his perceived value of the experience at my store on a thread on Facebook which then began a conversation with everyone in his immediate network who then shot it over and into those connected to other networks via his network and on and on and on. (Sadly we got a lot of bad press in that one shot)

The simplicity of the evolution was intoxicating. A thread on his Facebook "wall" stated he was "disappointed with our store" in LA. My buddy in New Jersey, on the complete other side of the country, was in his network of friends and his community which therefore allowed him to read his posting which is only visible by those on his "friends list." So my friend, not knowing the details of the situation or that I knew what happened called and asked me to help. So as I listened to the voice mail from my buddy about his friend and our client that he learned about through Facebook, I instantly realized how this "closeness" interconnected and flattened the world. My store was connected to a community with members virtually and intimately intertwined in both LA and Princeton via Facebook's networking, evolving communities and conversations.

What's important to note is that this wasn't a phone call that this customer asked my friend to make to me. The customer and I have no known connection that would prompt this reach out by my friend. This "connection" instead was utterly random. What this demonstrates specifically is the power of unpredictable, random, spontaneous solutions that happen at whim via open interconnectivity. This customer's post was a quick and random 30 second thread to a community of networked subgroups that interacted and caused a reverberation back to my store from the other side of the country. The thread began in LA, meandered its way through a complicated and close network of connections to the East Coast, and then shot back through another complicated and close but utterly different network of connections to LA via transparent conversation and open structure. The world became ultimately small and deeply interconnected by a brief quip that formed random connections and ultimately caused movement. This is the power in the art of surfing.

Post it for Free

There is a video series on YouTube called the trunk monkey where an auto group developed this character of a "trunk monkey" (literally a monkey in the trunk of a car in various scenes) and made a series of vignettes on YouTube. They touched thousands of new communities because of the network and a "conversation" of perceived value. Because they were so clever, unconventional, and "non-car-dealerish," they went viral. The community loved the dynamic message. The people approved. The community approved. The network responded and branded the auto group slogan as non-traditional and innovative and spread the word via number of "views" and ratings.

Instead of expensive cable advertising, they created low budget ads and posted them for free and communicated a distinct message that encouraged random conversation for anyone interested in their message. A random network of connections helped to develop a brand. The network created a labyrinth of new networks that connected via a common conversation - the trunk monkey - and a community within communities was born. As an ad campaign, it was a resounding success, but more importantly it was a valued conversation that generated new unlikely relationships.

The question we all need to be asking is not *will the conversation take off* and can we use this unorthodox venue (transparent conversations), but *what is the question* and *how many questions* and *how often* do we need to ask *so that* the conversation begins, continues, and evolves? It has to start, be able to take on its own form of relevance, and then it has to emerge and branch out and up and over. If the conversation is relevant enough and if you connect with and tap into something that carries a valid message, the new value will power the conversation and the community. Bono, the lead singer from U2, recently said in a excerpt from

New York Times that the content of "the conversation" more and more is about *value* and not necessarily and only *values*.

Although the example of the trunk monkey was a simple campaign and my angry customer was a small connection, networks of connectivity in Twitter and You Tube demonstrate how simply and functionally one can design and inspire seemingly complex networks through open conversations through transparency and immediacy.

On Twitter, you can follow the moves (or Tweets) of people from President Obama, to Bono, a favorite business, or close friend. Whoever you choose to follow, you can listen in realtime as the person decides to post whatever it is they are doing. You can follow them if you approve of their content and value as it pertains to your interest or you can "block" them from your connections. This architecture and structure moves innovation forward, but the people generating the conversations are the ones that truly author this revolution.

Draw, Luck, and Iterate

Jack Dorsey, one of the cofounders of Twitter, was recently speaking at Behance also known as http://the99percent.com about the starting of Twitter and how its structure came about. He talked about three keys to Twitter's success. And these points affect our conversation here: 1) Draw- Get your ideas out there, 2) Luck - assess and measure the market readiness and timeliness and "place" of your idea's intro to market, 3) Iterate - Be a rigorous editor; listen to feedback; refine your idea continually. His three pillars are, interestingly, very similar to kiva's (Dignity, accountability, and transparency). Twitter's architecture was built around immediacy, transparency, and accountability. He says that through the community being the primary contributors of the changing shape of Twitter, Twitter's primary role became that of an editor. He says a really good editor is not one that just listens to the loudest voice and makes that change to appease that voice. A strong editor takes in all the inputs, all the information, all the develop- ments of the crowd and implements the change. Like the internet and its web, the ocean and the wave, and the people and our mind-sets, if we are to move up and out we too need to be diligent editors of this new content and listen to the populace.

For example, Twitter's original tag line was "what's your status?" Then it changed to "what are you doing?" And finally, as it reads today, "What's happening?" Jack Dorsey said what was important was the question wasn't generating a conversation that opened transparency and people weren't enticed enough to join. So, through the suggestions of the community and Twitter acting as an editor instead of a top-down machine, the question changed to what it is today.

His latest project is called "Square" and will be more visible in the coming months, but his impetus of its launch (Point #2) was the financial crisis of 2009. The older model blew up. Totally and completely blew up. No one anywhere really and truly understood the complexity of the global financial market. It was run with abstractions and secrets. When the Great Recession happened, the total system clashed and it became an implosion. It brought all of the hierarchical machines to their knees. They then scrambled how to figure it all out and quickly innovate and fix what colossally broke and tumbled down.

What Dorsey has seen work so well in this new era is in the underpinnings of Twitter. First, the older model wants things perfect and calculated, but Twitter sees things are more rough around the edges. Second, the older models wanted long and unmitigated speeches to emphasize their overarching control and manipulative hand of power, but Twitter sees the benefit of the constraint of 140 characters. It allows everyone to speak and contribute more often. Finally, the older models want seamless flow of executive orders from directives to implementation, but Twitter sees power in the rising influence of an interruptive nature. Twitter, instead wanted to expose all of the secrets of the older structure and break down all of the abstractions to simple bits understood by anyone. As Twitter took on this role of editor, they learned how to use the suggestions of the community, the total populace, the crowd and implement the change. Twitter became an engine that could draw something out, recognize it for what it is, and then share it to the whole system. This is where approachability, immediacy, and transparency became their capstones that allowed them to evolve through collective wisdom.

Take for example the institution of the church. The general structure of the church at large is the power of the pulpit and the power of the organization. It virtually has no interaction or live engagement. It's very hierarchical as compared to something like Twitter.

As Twitter has exposed the new era of this immediacy and approachability, the church at large must also deal with the change. Its not just that Twitter has created a venue where we can all Tweet. Although that is true. What is most revealing is that it exposes how an entire mentality, and older model is shifting to a brand new way of thinking. If systems are to be innovative, they have to learn to become the editors through approachability, immediacy, and transparency within a changing context and crowd.

A Tweeting Church

I know of a pastor who is looking to a younger pastors to Tweet his sermons on Twitter while he is preaching. In other words, while the message is being spoken live to the community on a given Sunday by the senior pastor, he wants my friend to tweet vignettes of the sermon's content and key insights from the sermon to their followers. That way, anyone in the circle who has elected be a part of the network (a follower) can interact with the sermon live and give real time, interactive, honest feedback as the sermon is happening. There is no delayed feedback. No extended waiting to figure out what is being taught. There is no need for anyone in the conversation who wants to be in the conversation to not be heard. No one is screened. As he speaks, you can integrate your thoughts, your Tweets to his words. There is this sense of approachability, immediacy, and transparency. It's all fast and faster.

Look at the movement now President Obama instigated on his campaign trail through social networking. Obviously his message of "Hope" and "Change" was a foundation, but it was also argued his ability to spread his conversation through a valued content gone viral through a flatter world with an emerging community that ultimately won him the White House.

People through these developing communities are connecting through this power like dry brush being met by a forest fire. The hunger for transparent information and approachability is unprecedented, the information flow is almost unlimited, and the possibilities of what it might look like is constantly moving. We drive this revolution. It's in our DNA. Our natural hunger to connect and meet with meaning is pushing the power of social networking and its more powerful effects outward, and this force is only trumped by their power when they connect.

In these groups and forums, diverse and unlikely communities and relationships are emerging, disappearing, reinventing themselves and then reappearing somewhere else as something else. These social networking sites -Twitter, You Tube, Facebook, Myspace, etc. - allow nearly anyone to create a profile, identify their preferences, and then connect with others who have contented their identities with similar information. Whether they are in London or LA, if their birthdays, for example, are the same they can connect and join a community in India that likes flying fishing (random I know) with people that share their birthdays. There is an entire generation coming on the scene that brings a newer mindset to a com- munity across a global and flatter landscape. Globalization is now a phenomenon of community and conversation and not just a political discussion concerning the WTO for example. There is a newer mentality. The thinking is non-linear and the applications take on a different form and translate into new shapes all the time at random intervals. The only dependable notion, like the ocean for the surfer, is the constant change.

And yet, life in its current form of man made functions and plastic destinies disassociates our meaning and our purpose from our core design. We miss the inherent power of life to translate our dormant creativity into dynamic solutions. Instead, we act more like we hold a place in the factory lines while the world is ablaze with a Facebook and Twitter mentality.

When we learn to connect a newer mentality to how we lead, these evolving relationships become far more interdependent. "The organizations that will truly excel in the future will be the organizations that discover how to tap people's commitment and capacity to learn at all levels in an organization" (Senge, p. 4).

Because this global interconnectivity is real, indeterminate outcomes have become more constant. The only steady in this flux of unpredictability is its unpredictability. We must learn to open up and connect so the system can become interdependent. We need a perpetual and sustainable state of deep learning. A fundamental key then in this radical shift is to learn to unhinge our organization's creative ability from an older model that corralled us in.

We need to learn how to unleash relentless vitality through dignity, transparency, approachability, immediacy, and accountability. It's imperative that companies, organizations, schools, churches, Wall Street, and Main Street encourage hybrid relationships and total interconnectedness to randomly occur over and over again. Executive committees and employees. Church elder and church layperson. School administration and teachers. Executive managers and frontline employees. Companies need to be adaptive and "jiggy" enough to "dodge, bob, and weave" like an NFL running back slipping tackles and innovating a run pattern on the fly to come out of a pile and head for the end zone. If we stay stuck in staunch hierarchical stance, we will likely be derailed. If we dictate behavior in lieu of transparent communication, nimble innovation, *creative behavior*, and indeterminate patterns, failure is more probable than success.

Micro Communities

Organizations do not need to simply and only outsource with vendors to increase efficiency, market major price reductions, outmaneuver the competitor with cheap labor in India, or move manufacturing to a warehouse in China to maximize production. Although some of these strategies might need to accompany all this, we need an interconnecting network of micro communities of 6-12 members that spring up like popcorn in a microwave that innovate within the interdependencies of the system through a conversation under the pillars of kiva and Twitter. Then those teams need to be able to interconnect within the world of other micro communities, that then connect again with the community of the whole organization, that then usher in real change by acting on real information.

It is imperative that transparent conversations happen instead of supervisors monitoring an employee's clock time and then scold them for being 5 minutes late. The question becomes, "How do you encourage innovation while minimizing fear and panic that is entrenched deep within the structure?" The premise for the solu- tion, although very layered in its unfolding, is to open transparent, participative, hierarchically flat conversations so that the information becomes shared and com- munal in order to find dynamic answers to evolving realities.

We must learn to look within our organizational walls whether it is a church, a school, or a company and tap the sleeping spirit of innovation deep within our core. We need to find unfound answers in unlikely relationships by letting go of the nuance of power. This notion of manipulation produces an unreal sense of productivity, and it may look good on excel spread sheets to shareholders and executives and church members. Where in actuality, these excel spread sheets animate and contort results like hand puppets. The key is in the people, but it isn't necessarily just asking one employee at a time what the answer might be. Instead, it's about collective wisdom from a whole bunch of random employees interacting freely together that also have the authority and autonomy to interpret, think, respond, and act.

I am not advocating the need to do away with tough choices within any firm – downsizing, layoffs, mergers – nor am I saying the employees should have the run of the show under a leaderless society. What I am saying is that like Ricardo Semler believes, we need to learn to manage without managers. We miss the mark when the dominant framework is ruled through a perception of power.

Historically, we have been herded like sheep, shuffled around like chess pawns and sacrificed for a "checkmate." In many companies or organizations, when things are difficult or "tough" decisions have to be made, the categorical response has been to cut pay or cut people. As a businessman I understand the logic to a point, and I clearly understand cutting expenses when revenue is superseded by heavy expenses. I have hired, fired, and cut expenses when it is necessary. I have lived through a downsize and forged ahead in a downturn. Excess is generally just bad business and running a lean and tight organization is a fundamental and a key discipline. However, the answers for the future days are not just that cut and dry. You can't just open the butcher drawer when things get tough and dice away thinking everything that doesn't contribute perceived revenue is fat. It's true that lean is crucial but for actual betterment and sustainable innovation, dynamic and unlikely relationships are a primary component.

The people in this incredibly evolving landscape of change, the new workforce of the Facebook and Twitter mentality, will no longer tolerate such blatant disregard of their potential and of their person. The companies can no longer afford to misstep the handling of their greatest asset in this exploding change - the people. If we are to survive, we need to recognize that typical models can no longer innovate at the level that is required to excel. We must turn our mindset into the highly evolving internet or the rapidly expanding pages of communities on Facebook.

The global landscape of organizational effectiveness is forcing entire companies, churches, businesses, and schools to leverage their resources and become and boost bottom line – philosophically and economically – is to tap the people's unfound talent and the connectivity of the system. I am not advocating the concept of *using* your people to simply benefit the executives and company bottom line. I am talking about providing evolving solutions with the ability of an organization to sustain that change over time *thorough and with* their people.

Nor am I ignoring the essential ingredients for certain organizations to continue, like profitability for business or income for churches and non-profits, but I am saying that learning to recognize emergent patterns and the concept of evolution in an open system as a primary characteristic trait is fundamental to our survival. Organizations and people need to become transparent, let information become fluid across divides, and promote conversations through the convening of random and unlikely communities and individual relationships.

"There has to be a King..."

However, the older model in spite of this reality continues to compartmentalize. It prescribes caned solutions, stifles operations, inhibits fresh approaches to problem solving, limits innovation, and then files us into labeled file drawers that are outdated and rusty? We are too splintered in the structure of the system and in the space of our minds to really be flexible and uniquely creative.

Dave recalls that their questions were 'based on the concept of it has to be centralized, there has to be a king, or there has to be an emperor, of there has to be a - something.' These key investors - 'probably thirty people in a room in one of the five-star hotels,' Dave recalls - were a 'very intelligent group of people,' but they didn't get it. Dave tried another approach: the sand networks, and they all share the burden of communication.' And they said, 'But who decides?' And we said, 'No one decides. It's a standard that people subscribe to. No one decides.' And they kept coming back, saying, 'You don't understand the question, it must be lost in translation, who is the president of the Internet?' And honestly, I, I-I tried to be very up front in describing [it] the best way [I could], but I was deeply unable to.' (Baufman and Beckstrom, P. 33).

This problem looms across the board. The way we led and thought in the past cannot be the way we will lead and think in the future. The problem exists in our roots. The way it used to be done as compared to how it needs to be done have collided, and the results on either side of the pendulum will be nothing short of tremendous. We think there has to be a king. There has to be someone in charge to rule and decide.

The goal, then, is to build organizations [and people] that are capable of continual, trauma-free renewal...Automatic. Spontaneous. Reflexive. These are words we typically use to describe deep change in large organizations. And therein lays the challenge: to make deep change more of an automatic process – to build organizations [and people] that are capable of continuous self-renewal in the absence of a crisis (Hamel, p. 43).

Surfers Innovate and Adapt

- Learn how to adapt like a surfer instead of walking in a rutted path of calculation and precision.
- Substitute a machine like mentality with nimble flexibility.
- Learn to use this "density of data" to overcome and innovate in a time of shift and exponential change.
- Spread authority and information out so it's open and accessible instead of keeping it isolated

- Mimic the structure of the internet and the ocean as open systems that seamlessly connect through a web of networks and random relationships.
- In a highly connected system, use disturbances and disruptions as positive events to inspire innovation.
- Develop communities and mind-sets rich in uncommon, interdependent relationships that push creativity and provide solutions.
- Tap collective wisdom through open conversations with the pillars of immediacy, transparency, and accountability.
- Unwind and unlearn the older way because its filled with abstractions that inhibit and create borders and walls.
- Embrace edges and co-evolution as an infrastructure that create unlikely solutions.
- Use interdependence to draw things out, instantly recognize them for what they are, and share them in transparent conversations.
- Become an active editor that tries to understand the whole plot and not just listen to the the loudest voice or be the loudest voice.

Chapter 2

Recognize the Need to Change

"The factory of the future will have only two employees, a man and a dog. The man will be there to feed the dog. The dog will be there to keep the man from touching the equipment."

-Warren G. Bennis, Universtiy of Southern California Professor of Business Administration; advisor to Ronald Reagan and John F. Kennedy

"A company is stronger if it is bound by love rather than by fear...If the employees come first, then they're happy." -Herb Keller, cofounder of Southwest Airlines

"The significant problems we face cannot be solved at the same level of thinking we were at when we created them." -Einstein

Complexity is the New Norm

Think of this, I could be writing this while flying Virgin Air somewhere streaming music on my iPhone, watching You Tube videos via Virgin's Air inflight WiFi on my iPad 2 while checking my email. Things aren't what they used to be. Everything around us has changed except the way we think and the way we lead. "The reasonable man adapts himself to the world; the unreasonable one persists in trying to adapt the world to himself. Therefore all progress depends on the unreasonable man." (George Bernard Shaw, Maxims for Revolutionists).

As leaders, we have to look at things from an entirely new paradigm. What we are grappling with and looking at is different. From a surfer's viewpoint, this newer type of flux is like a strange wave, an anomaly building on the ocean's glimmering edge.

A Strange Wave

Imagine, you are a surfer sitting in the water on your board waiting for a wave in between sets, and out on the horizon the water begins to surge and roll as a large mass churns and forms under the water's surface. Your head perks up and scans the horizon. You see the wave. Your heart starts to pound with a familiar rush of an almost spiritual sensation as you anticipate the feeling of surfing the wave. It begins to flutter in your soul. You drop down to your chest on your board and paddle your arms deep into the blue liquid pulling your body forward. Then you stop paddling and your arms fall limp in the water as you scan the wave again. Something's not right. Something is not familiar. It seems like a wave but it doesn't move like a wave. It rolls along lifting the water like a rolling pin beneath the surface, but it doesn't behave "normal." You see it and acknowledge it, but because the wave looks unruly, disheveled, indeterminate, and just plain feels different, you paddle out to it, over its mass, and slip by its strangeness. You hope the next wave is like a "normal" wave.

You're puzzled. It didn't form like you're used to seeing, and it didn't roll like it was scratching the belly of the water's surface. It didn't look like the wave would peak up and pitch out like you knew. So you paddled over the wave. As you paddled down the backside of the wave, you look back over your shoulder only to watch it undulate and wobble with an enticing strangeness and then crash into shore with an unearthly, unsuspecting force. You turn back to scan the horizon hoping for a better a wave that your are more familiar surfing, but to your surprise you only see another wave just like the first – odd, erratic, meandering, lumpy, unrecognizable, and completely unfamiliar. You can't notice a pattern, a shape, or a form. You hoped the first wave was unusual, a freak randomness, but as you looked out there was yet another strange mass building with the same odd complexity. Right behind that one you saw another and another and another. As each wave lifts you up, you see the horizon is filled with lines of these strange masses lining up endlessly. You're confused and baffled for in the same spot you'd surfed for years, with the same ocean topography, climate, currents on waves that you "knew," it at once became complex, unruly, indeterminate, and unrecognizable.

This new global landscape is similar to the image mentioned above where the "weird" surf was once recognizable and its behavior understandable, but now this new unrecognizable mass is moving toward us with wave after wave of indeterminate influence and an evolving nature. Until we learn to recognize the new characteristics instead of predictable, determinate patterns, we can't adapt, innovate, or truly create. We will continue to paddle up and over the wave, only to miss it. Only to paddle on by.

The Changing Surf

There comes a point...when a great truth dawns on those involved: The inevitability and wisdom of the ongoing change is finally understood, and the new reality accepted. And what typically evokes this realization? Not hard data, nor a new process, nor an edict from above. What best crystallizes and reinforces change is powerful imagery that appeals to the primal emotions within human nature (Booz, Allen, Hamilton, p. 1).

This stuff coming our way is difficult to sort through its randomness. We need to have a surfer's spirit to handle the flux. We have to learn to innovate and anticipate change randomly and quickly adapt like a surfer studying the shifts in the water's surge and pull. It's a an image we have to grapple with in order to get our minds around a new era, a new time and a new way of leading. If we visualize what is coming and use this image of a surfer as he listlessly hangs in the water ready to pounce on emergence as it forms, then we might be able to let go of this older way that says we must control and manipulate. If we learn to see that we can't afford to paddle over this "strange new wave," then we will begin the process of transitioning to a place that is messy, unorganized, and evolving but utterly dynamic. Although that may sound erratic and thoughtless, it is a result of the place and time we are now living, and even though this mind set isn't familiar, we must become students of our more diverse and emerging future. We need to become a part of the conversation already unfolding and learn to take the wave that feels unruly and unfamiliar. Ultimately, like a surfer, if we paddle into it, we will experience a spiritual sensation as we preen down its emerald face that will far surpass manipulated outcomes.

Like I mentioned, I am a surfer by nature and by mentality. We tend to have a slightly different bend from the crowd and we tend to ebb and flow like the rise and fall of the tide. We track the phase of the moon to see if the tide is spring or neap. We wait for swells and live for the rush of the "drop," the stoke, the calm, spiritual experience of connecting with the sea.

The surf is always changing, but we anticipates this. We wait for it and watch it, and we know every time we check, it will be different. We are aware of the highly connected ocean that has enormous power along with unique subtleties. The surf can change in an instant under multiple influences like the tide, the wind, an odd current, underwater topography, sea anomalies, a storm. We watch and anticipate it so we can maximize the "ride" by learning where it *might* break and hold the best shape. There are websites complete with tide charts, swell direction, surf cams to view live breaks, wave models, surf forecasts, etc. Even surfing has become more connected, more public, more accessible, more open, more communal, and more inclusive, through electronic models and trending of data. The conversation has expanded through transparency, immediacy, and openness. For example, I can log onto my favorite surf site on my iPhone and check the surf via web cam and tide charts in Ventura, CA and then with a click bounce almost instantly internationally over to a live web cam in Kuta, Bali to check the local break. There are two points here: 1) Although I can *check* the websites and "be informed" in real time of the surf, 2) the world, like surfing, because of expanding interdependencies that create volatility, can erupt and change in a flash.

Like I mentioned earlier, the change we are under is different. It's like the strange wave and the legos with the swooping cranes and conveyor belts. We have to learn to surf and understand how to always adapt and flex. We can't afford to reach back and use what used to work.

Whether the executive, the church leader, the school teacher, the senior manager, or the entire organization, we are all facing this extreme environment. Leadership is used to dealing with change from the interpretive lens of older models, but today those models are incapable of innovating fast enough and creatively enough to find dynamic solutions. Rapid advances are being made on entire organizations and communities, and we are fraught with anxiety scrambling for new solutions.

For example, General Motors represents an American icon, and yet they are now blended with the government society. Who would have thought a short time ago they'd be dancing with disaster as they pleaded to Congress for help, filed for bankruptcy, and then restructured by severing the heads of several of their key brands? Their demise and timeline highlight the speed of change, and their linear mindset helped accelerate their fall. They weren't nimble enough to see what was coming or flexible enough to adapt.

This particular pace and speed of change that currently manifests not only in the melt down of Detroit, but in the housing market, the credit crisis, the banking turmoil, Greece, Germany, and the EU typifies the pace and severity of global change we can come to expect.

Overnight, not only companies collapse, but entire industries implode. I don't want to delve into the arena of markets, industries, and economics because I am by no means an expert or even deeply knowledgeable. I am simply amazed by the speed of the unraveling.

We must change. Our mind-sets must change, and how we deal with change must become non-linear. We must tap into something deep within ourselves and our design to figure a way to undulate creatively with the velocity of the swing. We have never had the global connectivity that we do in this age, and because of this global and local interconnectedness and the emerging markets developing every day, change is a unique blur. We don't just need corrective lenses to realign our ability to see. We need new eyes.

We must learn to recognize and then encourage evolving relationships, inde-terminate change, and unrecognizable patterns as positive things. We need con-nectivity and its power to innovate. If we learn to roll with the wayward waters and tumultuous tides like a surfer does after a wave's pounding crash, we may come up a little shaken, but it is probable they will come up ready and more importantly, anticipating the next wave.

The Pounding of a Set Wave

Like our times and like a "set" wave, we have to lead with the awareness of the surfer. We have to 1) recognize the surge and pull of the water as the set approaches, 2) either duck dive the wave and pop out the backside ready for the next waves, 3) or paddle to it and position yourself for the drop.

1. Recognize the Surge and Pull:
Knowledgeable surfers recognize what are called set waves that emerge way off in the horizon. They usually roll in about every 7-12 waves, are much larger than the rest, and they come in sets of 2-3 waves, e.g. set waves. As a surfer, these are the best rides because they are potentially the biggest and most erratic waves with the greatest power and form. It is important that you are ready for them, and in order to be ready for them you have to recognize their approaching. This set wave produces a strange lull in the ocean, a "pulling" out of the sea, and then a distinct surge in the water. You must immediately respond and then paddle into their peak, hopefully beat the crowd rushing the set, flip your board around and drop in on the shoulder of the wave as it peels forward.

2. The "Duck Dive:"
When a surfer is avoiding the pounding of a wave whether in the impact zone or just out at sea, he/she will do what is called a "duck dive" where he/she pushes the nose of the board down and under the water at the base of the wave. This way the wave, given it is not the size of a "tow in" wave like Jaws in Maui Hawaii (50-70 feet), will tumble and tussle them a bit, but they will ultimately push through the bottom of the wave, under its power, and away from it force so that when they pop up on the back side, they are angled and prepared for the next wave. However, if a surfer tries to just hold their breath and hit the face of the wave or the crashing white wash head on, he will get pounded. If he gets stuck on the inside of a big enough set, you get caught in a tossing, tumbling cycle like being inside a washing machine. This is a bad place to get caught.

3. Paddle to It and Ride:
You can either ride the wave or "duck dive" beneath its base. However, if you anticipate the set by *recognizing* its dawning and catch the drop, the ride catapults your soul into a rhythm. The rush is transcendent and almost surreal. It can bring a sense of freedom to the mind and a unique awareness to the soul.

Like the surfer, leaders must recognize the conditions of the change and be willing to get tossed around a bit while maintaining perspective on the horizon. After we duck dive beneath the base of the wave, we will come up a bit disoriented, salt water burning our eyes, and a bit out of breath, but we will be ready anticipating the next wave cresting on the outside line-up.

You hope to take the set wave, but if you miss it you must duck dive and hope you can position yourself for the next one, or at least be prepared to maintain perspective on the horizon. We have to be willing to get messy, disoriented, feel unpredictability, push through and under, and then move ahead of what is coming. We have to adapt quickly.

What we have to come to terms with is that there are greater things at work here than just multiplying networks and random relationships. There is something deeper and natural. What's most fascinating to me in the discussion on our new global reality is that it has underlying principles. Although I use words like *complicated, chaos, randomness, emergence, messy, unpredictability, and evolving,* there is a deeply ordered structure that we are only recently discovering. It's not one big mess. It just may feel like one because we are used to words like *control, manipulation, patterns, predictability, discipline, command and control, and order.*

As leaders, our goal should be not only how we deal with these newer words in our new reality, but what is really the power moving this whole thing. How does it work? There are principles that contain a deeply structured order with natural laws and we need to uncover them. We need to recognize that this this flux is from an interconnectivity that has an order deep in its layers. It is called *a living system.* (I will break this down in later chapters).

Two Major Problems

We don't know how to create because we don't possess the capacity to think differently. We accept the conformity of traditional expectations and limitations because we allow ourselves to be shifted off course through entrenched bureaucratic thinking. Scott Belsky in an article from his website called www. the99percent.com about Steve Jobs' ability to hold vision explained his discipline to see beyond those demons, "These are our demons - the self doubt, the fear of failure and the impulses to meet others' short term expectations and the expense of long-term possibilities" (http://the99percent.com/articles/7074/ Vision-Without-Obstruction-What-We-Learn-From-Steve-Jobs).

That said, therein lies two of the major problems. First, the problem isn't how to find the answers, but how we are *not prepared* to create and then process the connectivity in order to find those answers. We are too linear to unravel it, and yet the world's interconnectivity is so dense and webbed that we need the collective wisdom of crowds to unravel it. Second, our mind-sets or the *factory mentality of top-down thinking,* doesn't allow us to connect through randomness. It's too fractured into too many pieces and so is our thinking. If we see the rule of the law still ascending from the top down, then we will never be able to access transparency, immediacy, and accountability. Discipline and control will still be the imperial guard.

If we stay in this frame of mind, we are not instinctively ready to innovate and author continual change without receiving orders from the top. Our older mindset has disconnected systemic reactions, and as organizational leaders, we have a real difficult time finding effective ways to deal with it under the paradigm we are used to using. If we stay in this current form, we will become incapacitated like an army tank tipped on its side in the desert sand.

Historically, leadership is reactive. We are used to just pulling our proverbial pistols and firing shots at problems that are too deep to "just" fix. We don't understand interdependence, adaptability, and flexibility, and we certainly don't know how to utilize and harness *collaborative and horizontal communication channels that evolve freely.* Most certainly in our current state, we would never view it as a living breathing system.

It's not Complicated just Complex

Its critical we find better answers, but in this awkward and furious pace, our more traditional discipline keeps us stuck. We can find better answers if we open the system up to the power of connectivity and flatten out our grid. We can find the answers through inserting an adaptive, flexible, and nimble structure into how we lead and we can do this under a context of random transparent relationships that have the freedom to emerge and evolve.

The global landscape and the way communities and individuals interact now is different; we are all connected. And consequently, we are also then interdependent. It's all about relationships, or as Desmond Tutu says it's *ubuntu.*

> Ubuntu is a concept that we have in our Bantu languages at home. Ubuntu is the essence of being a person. It means that we are people through other people. We cannot be fully human alone. We are made for interdependence, we are made for family. When you have ubuntu, you embrace others...

-Desmond Tutu, God Has a Dream (Gibbons, p. 69)

I am proposing that as leaders we are charged to examine the power of *becoming fully human through other people - through relationships in the system and with each other.* And because we are talking about natural organisms, it applies to people and organizations that live and breathe and move with natural impulses.

Connected and Interdependent

Like the traffic on the freeway or in a mall or a train station, the world is highly connective and interactive. It's a developing, evolving, constantly changing organism making immediate decisions from active, live information that then affects everyone around, in front of, and behind.

For example, in traffic if I tap on my brakes all the cars behind me are immediately affected whether those right behind me or others miles back. In a crowded train station I might abruptly stop, move right or dart left and the people immediately around me are impacted by my movement as well as those behind them.

Or if I'm snowboarding down a crowded run in Mammoth, CA for example, my movements affect the riders all around me. They may have already picked a line, but my movements might force them to immediately change. It's like dropping pebbles in a pond. Its ripples upon ripples affecting more and more ripples. The surface observation is my actions affect the movements of others. My movements creates ripples. What I do interacts with how they move and then influences their move through our immediate connection, whether the people in a train station, me snowboarding on the mountain, or the cars on the freeway.

However, the deeper level is that it's not only my movements that authored a chain of reactions around me, but my movements are a result of someone else's influence on me from somewhere else and they were responding to other movements from someone else and so on and so and so on. The deeper law is the millions of points of connectivity interacting with millions of other points of connectivity all the time. It's an endless myriad of activity that goes back to the beginning. Sure my actions did effect change around me, but I was playing a role in an already faster moving ring of activity undulating within the millions of multiplying connections. I became a ripple affected by previous ripples interacting among other ripples that then go forward to create other ripples.

The older discipline or event mentality would view my movements mentioned above as the center of the event where the other actions spun outward from me. My action was the catalyst that started the ripples moving because I am the center and everything spins outward form me. But in an open system and in the world that we now live, my movements are merely ripples rolling along in a pond already filled with ripples interacting and intersecting with other ripples and _together_ we perpetuate the actions of a living system. Here is the key, our interactions co-mingling add to the system's emergence and evolution. The ripples alone aren't moving the water's surface, but together they become dynamic turbulence bouncing and rolling and colliding.

In traffic or in the mall, there is a high degree of this unnoticed, but sophisticated connectivity. In our new reality, the world is similarly connected. It's in this connectivity that then creates this interdependence that allows for random relationships. It creates dynamic instead of static connectivity. Today, we live in a world that is a traffic jam, a crowded train station, a busy mall, and we have to realize that every movement is a result of a myriad of other previous movements from millions of connections that spin this labyrinth of global and local interdependencies. Our movements continue the chain as a cacophony of interacting ripples. Because the world is flat and interconnected, the interdependence will only continually expand outward at exponential rates.

Therefore, to become effective and be a leader that can perpetuate the development within our own lives and the people we lead and the organizations we shape, we must transition from an "opaqueness" that comes with the older tradition to a more transparent lens that comes with the emergent generation. Our thinking has to change. Notice that this isn't change for the sake of change. This isn't a call to "rise to the challenge" or a half time pep talk to a team that is down by two goals. The world is ripe with a new reality; we are under a great shift. Therefore, the way we think has to change and so must our behavior.

Like I mentioned before, "It's a time in history when technology and global culture have made neighbors of all of us" (Gibbons, p. 83). We have become about relationships, nuances, stories, questions, learning, evolving, and connectivity. Of course its not just simple relationships, but when you boil it down to its raw essence, relationships and their unfolding, intersecting stories are inherent to its core.

The older way is about the individual, the silo, parts and pieces, and event mentality. This new way is about relationships and the story they tell from their diverse and limitless connectivity.

"...there is no guarantee that what has worked in the past will work today in a new generation and in a new world of information and superhighways linking nations, cultures, and people like never before...We must be about something that is fundamentally meaningful to others...Each generation must create a new language that connects with the soul and life of their community in their era. It must also create new forms not only to help carry the message, the truth, the content into a new generation but also to create a greater hunger for that message" (Gibbons, p. 90).

This thing is not overly difficult or heavily complex, but what might be difficult is unlearning this entrenched older way so that we can then relearn. We must step away from the human animal and move closer to the human spirit. We must study the nuances and highly meandering subtleties - the ripples - of what is called a living system.

It's Been Put to Sleep

Using words like a living system may sound thick and "complicated," but actually, what is presented next and continued in later chapters should begin to resonate within your soul and flirt with your mind. It's not hard to figure out, but it's hard to change. Whether it's in a dark corner of your soul, off to one side, or smack dab in the center, you will resonate with it at some point because it connects to a universal, intrinsic truth - the power of the relationship and its power to use change to make things better.

In brief, the complexity sciences propose that this world of highly connected, multiplying networks and emergence are not only signs of different times, but they are natural operating principles deep within the DNA of natural organisms like people and organizations. Although the concept may sound new and different, its core is like an old treasure covered with the vines and dust of ancient time. It goes back to the beginning. And that is why this pace of change is so rampant because it is so natural. Its buzz is already in us. It has just been put to sleep.

Captivating not Obscure

This concept of flux and living systems captivate the attention of leaders world wide from economists, scientists, sociologists, engineers, business people, and church ministers. It's core principles are in the introductions of mainline books, newspaper articles, and magazine articles. Its connection to our everyday life is becoming more evident. It isn't found only in the obscure yet prominent Santa Fe Institute that performs deep dives into complexity theory, rather its reaching out from these labs to the ways we live out life, the way we do business, the way markets are connected, the way countries operate, and the way we interact with one another. It studies relationships and their tie to significance and value. In it are models that can help us interpret and understand the world in which we live. My goal here is to break it down to practical applications and understandable theories that can help us lead with greater efficiency and develop systemic responses in our organizations, teams and communities. These are some of the common concepts:

- tipping points - moments when unique phenomena become common.
- collective (crowd) wisdom- crowds can make better decisions and move more effectively than individuals.
- six degrees of separation - the idea that it is usually no more than six steps before you can find a connection between two random people.
- emergence - new properties and processes emerge unexpectedly and randomly from what is called complex systems.

The complexity sciences are concerned with what is called *complex systems or living systems* and their unique process of adaptation and innovation. People, relationships, organizations, ant colonies, traffic, crowded malls, crowed ski runs, a crowed wave, for example are all complex systems. As we unpack this model, we will begin to understand how to unwind our current times.

Let's define it. A complex system or a living system is more than just being "complicated." *It's a group of diverse agents (people, ants, economies) that are all somehow relationally connected through actions and behaviors that are interdependent and show adaptation.* In other words, a living system can be an organization of people because they are consequently connected, gather real-time information, converge on the data together, analyze it, propose collective insight, and then make decisions. It can be a colony of ants that notice a leaf that fell in their line of travel, act on its intrusion, determine a solution, and then the "first responders" act in chorus for the rest of the colony and move the leaf and then communicate back to the group its movements. It can be the cars behind me in traffic that respond immediately to me tapping on my brakes and hit their brakes or speed up and veer right and then those cars behind them that then move from their actions. Therefore, a complex system is a collection of interdependent actions and decisions made from immediate information from a community versus relying solely on a slow moving, top down decision model.

Here, in a living system, the people closest to the situation with the most insight provide the communities with the best solutions which then pushes timely decisions. They gather real information as it happens, circle around the issue, participate in transparent conversation about its influence and consequence, innovate around it, and adapt to the change. It uses mutuality and interacts with mutable or bendable laws, and this permits them to flex and adapt as they see fit. It's like the interactive, changing, evolving, editing, webbing of the internet. Leaders need to encourage organic, dynamic movement in the church, in the com- pany, in the government, in the community, and in the global landscape.

A Plotted Course

As a leader, we need to see our evolution and that of our companies as expanding and adapting to change instead of staying stuck in familiarity. Understanding this concept of living systems will help us grow our organizations and the people we lead. If we allow our souls and our minds to network with dis- turbances, we will become intimately flexible with an era of flux. We will develop with far greater latitude and longitude than the the top-down world ever thought possible.

We need to learn to open our traditional ways that have been influenced by command and control thinking and instead see dynamic potential through flattening the power grid. We need to break out of the mantra shouted by genera- tions that have plotted a course of disconnectedness and determinate outcomes. If we don't become intimately connected to both the ripples in our organization and intimate communications, we will be forever static and planned. If however, we let them act as a catalyst to stir up our system, then we can grow, connect, and evolve.

Firing Neurons

What's key about this field is not only its possibility to organizations, but what it implies to the leadership and the teams they lead. Our consciousness is an ultimate example of complexity as billions of neurons in our brain perpetually converge on each other and communicate the mystery of our awareness. Our meaning is found in the random relationships of the neurons forming at whim in our brain that determines what we are thinking right now about the bewildering reality of our own presence. If you think about it, those random relationships help us become more human. The complexity of their random intersections make us more alive, more diverse, and ultimately more passionate about our existence.

We can see these things manifesting in living systems like cities, churches, police stations, countries, governments, weather patterns, financial markets; they all organize themselves into a varied flurry of random evolving rhythms and patterns through their own connections and preferences that are rallied around their specific values. Each one is unique to itself but their ripples communication create relationships that can use disturbances which bring emergence. Some common

characteristics: unpredictable, deeply connected, and capable to withstand disturbance and variation.

To really grapple with how a living system works, we need to understand and
explore what are the *operating principles of these natural organisms*. If we can
understand it on a macro scale and grasp these underlying principles that are the
bedrock of our own existence, we can participate in understanding their application to our own organizations and teams.

The complexity sciences and therefore the complex adaptive systems like an
organization, like our new global landscape, like you, and like me consequently
share some "fundamental properties – specifically non linear processes" that are
intrinsically innate to our nature. (We will break into the details in later chapters.)
However, for our discussion, the idea of a living system contains these properties:

1) It's appearance is chaotic, almost disorganized but this connectivity allows
it to be robust enough to withstand hard hits. 2) Because of this connectivity, small
disturbances either have no effect or a great effect. 3) Continuing random relationships power its emergence.

With our new reality and the random influx of these "thrusts and bursts" from
a flat world, our current leadership structures can't handle this type of unintel-
ligible flow. Our own minds can't handle the change unless we learn to undulate
with the flux that we encounter and realize the fundamental properties mentioned
above. Until we take out our linear lenses and put in our non-linear ones, it will
all just appear blurry.

For centuries, we have been taught to ignore our natural rumblings about how
things should and could work better. We have been told by the CEO's, executive
teams, the pulpit, and the teacher, that things are the way they are. Where in reality
our souls and our minds have been shackled. We have been disconnected, too top
heavy, and way too thick to nimbly move about.

We, as well as the complexity sciences, are trying uncover these principles
and learn about them so that we can apply them to the outside world of leadership,
governments, markets, teams and relationships. However, our natural ways are
suppressed and manipulated by our current thinking and the very structure sub-
dues adaptability. As leaders if we are to succeed, we must embrace the reality of
the traffic, the ants, and the crowded mall. We must learn to think with a "flatness
and adaptability" so that we can surf.

Machine like Precision

The traditional discipline of organizations and individuals use control and
manipulation with machinelike precision while we are quickly learning that *natural organisms with natural and intrinsic impulses, like these complex systems,*
cannot work under such prohibitive structures. You cannot throw machinelike
precision at organic structures and expect dynamic output. At some point, the
precision will be repelled by the strength and natural order of its design and only
produce to its "learned" capacity.

As we study these *natural organisms, we are beginning to see how they "work."* Consequently, as the global landscape is changed by this power of connectivity and interdependence, we are seeing those realities apply to our own natural order and the organizations and teams that we lead. First, what the world is penning as chaos or an awkward global flatness is actually the rumblings a living system. Like the ocean is a cauldron of energy because of its boundaryless structure, it creates a place where open, subtle, and violent interactions perpetuate its energy. The world is now its own cauldron of intensely evolving relationships and interdependencies. Second, the machine like sense of control is ineffective under these properties because it was meant for manufactured production and precision. Consequently, it gets lost in a natural, emergent order. Finally, this must dawn a new leader to bring us forward in a world utterly changed.

How it Works

How it works: Living systems in the natural world – churches, schools districts, companies, governments, classrooms, people, ant colonies, traffic, a crowed ski slope – all contain diverse agents that interact and interconnect and mutually affect one another (relationships). They then produce novel behavior. If a system is top-down, it can't be a living system that adapts. It's told what to do instead of interacting and learning what it needs to do on its own.

However, if the system is open or flat, these agents then interact with one another to form emergent behavior that can evolve and adapt and change in response to disturbance whether from internal or external influence. In other words, through mutually interacting with each other, we are capable of becoming nimble and adaptive to the radical conditions surrounding the system if we are allowed to interact and provide immediate solutions. By letting loose of typical hierarchical control, the relationships become the strength and intelligence of the system. It allows it or the person to withstand shocks because of its strength within its relationship.

Therefore, the science of complexity probes the actual intuitive nature of organisms by trying to understand how they become so flexible and nimble. For our new reality, this adaptability is our new currency. We must understand this so we can innovate under the duress of indeterminate change and unrecognizable patterns.

The business world is experiencing accelerating, revolutionary change, driven by rapid technological innovation, the globalization of business, and, not least, the arrival of the Internet and the new domain of Internet commerce. The change toward what might be called the connected economy rivals the onset of the Industrial Revolution in its impact on society and the way commerce is transacted. Managers are finding that many of their long-established business models are inadequate to help them understand what is going on, or how to deal with it. Where managers once operated with a machine model of their world, which was predicated on linear thinking, control, and predict- ability, they now find themselves struggling with something more organic and nonlinear, where limited control and a restricted ability to predict are the norm.

This of course, parallels the current revolution in science, with the rise of complexity studies and the recognition that much of the world is nonlinear and organic, characterized by uncertainty and unpredictability. The long established reductionist approach has produced a substantial understanding of the world, both in science and in business. But in the new economy, as in the new science of complexity, the limitations of the mechanistic model are becoming inescapable (Lewin, p. 197).

This global change has developing consequences. Therefore, I propose something with much higher stakes than simply adjusting strategies to compete against a new competitor, realigning the salesforce to meet new challenges, working harder to be a better employee, striving more to climb the corporate ladder, or restructuring boxes and personnel on an org chart. Winning alone is not the impetus. That's linear thinking.

I propose that we become leaders who are about innovating in order to surpass the static, disconnected mentality of the past. I propose we utterly change our thinking, our mind-set, our patterns of leadership and find what is naturally deep within our core - *connections, community, interdependence, transparency, emergence, messiness, evolution, immediacy, and relationship*. I propose we find a way to break free of presuppositions and find our natural, innate way inherent in our design that wants us to be the editors and creators of life that inspire change and people. To do this, we must undo our perception that control alone is effective and unleash the power of our natural order to find the way of the nimble, the way of the flexible, the way of the interdependent.

Today, systems thinking is needed more than ever because we are becoming overwhelmed by complexity. Perhaps for the first time in history, humankind has the capacity to create far more information than anyone can absorb, to foster far greater interdependency than anyone can manage, and to accelerate change far faster than anyone's ability to keep pace. Certainly, the scale of complexity is without precedent...Similarly, organizations break down, despite individual brilliance and innovative products, because they are unable to pull their diverse functions and talents into a productive whole (Senge, p. 69).

We must ask specific questions and arrange new approaches to this shift: How can we change? Why should we change? What do we now look like? How do we deal with fluctuations that challenge hierarchy? How can we develop fronts where change is embraced and solutions are created within that change through the relationships? How can our new level of innovation be the normal behavioral pattern that is adept at unwinding, reinventing, redesigning, and implementing and then doing it all over again and again under different conditions? How do we let go of control?

Understanding evolving, unlikely relationships and their interconnectedness is a key for the changing, blurry boundaries and the unconventional future. Change must become an impetus to inspire better answers. When change bumps up against us, it should rattle us enough to take notice, learn its story, share the story with others, see what they think, and then act.

Like Wikipedia, we must all become transparent editors of the system. Change is the only constant – unpredictable, evolving change. We cannot sit down and layout perfect plans anymore because it's difficult to forecast and plot with a future that is forever shifting and reinventing its course, description, and behavior. Consequently, there is great potential for us to innovate our own lives, our businesses, our government, our homes, our minds, our souls. It's all moving fast and faster and we must be ready to engage that speed with flexibility. Organizations, churches, companies, school districts, executive committees, shareholders all need to brace for a new wave, a different wave and learn how to tackle the more messy unfolding that is bound for our shore. For example in business, in an article in the Wall Street Journal titled, "*Thinking About Tomorrow*," Chaman Jain and Mark Covas talk about making forecasting more effective in this now global and complex economy.

> Forecasting has never been more important – or harder. Customers are less loyal, and global competition more fierce, making it more difficult to predict where sales are going. Adding to the problem: Products, sales and distribution channels all have proliferated, and the life spans of product have gotten shorter. As a result, some companies are being forced to adopt new ways to improve forecasting and planning. And a common theme links them all: collaboration (Wall Street Journal, Jain and Covas, R10, Monday, July 7, 2008).

We need to become the surfer in the water, meandering with intent as the waters roll and undulate and wait for the wave to emerge. We must be able to flip our boards around, paddle to its peak, and set up for the ride. Until we are able to look through our minds eye with a mentality of connectedness and the spirit of the surfer, the event mentality, pedestrian compartmentalization, the blame game, static snapshots, isolating silos, and rugged individualism, will unhinge and undermine the the potential of a world burgeoning with change and unforeseen potential.

Surfers Recognize the Need to Change:

- "The significant problems we face cannot be solved at the same level of thinking we were at when we created them." -Einstein
- Leaders must infuse teaching and perpetual learning into our organizations because traditional methods tend to disconnect this mutual exchange of value.
- In order to become a catalyst and understand its role, leadership has to become his/her own change before he/she implements a new organizational mindset.
- Leadership currently interprets change through models that are now incapable of innovating fast enough, and they are fraught with anxiety scrambling for new answers.
- If leadership can recognize significant change like a set wave and dive beneath the base, they will come up a bit disoriented, salt water burning their eyes, and a bit out of breath, but they will be anticipating the next wave cresting on the outside line-up.
- Leadership is not prepared to deal with new the velocity and complexity because the current structure itself is too linear.
- Traditional leadership cannot discern the flux forming on the horizon, so it must learn how to recognize the new face and movement of a new landscape.
- Flexibility and adaptability in a living system produce dynamic discovery because of its ability to produce nimble responses.

Chapter 3

Understand, Meaning is Found in the Whole Thing

"The ability to live in the question long enough for genius to emerge is a touch-stone of creative success. In fact, a 2008 study published in the Journal of Creative Behavior revealed tolerance for ambiguity to be 'significantly and positively related to success'" (http://the99percent.com/articles/7085/Uncertainty-Innovation-and-the-Alchemy-of-Fear).

Looking at one wave or even sets of waves at one break doesn't tell you enough about that swell to understand where its coming from or what were the probable conditions that caused that wave to break on that beach that way. You may have an idea, but the wave crashing on the shore is a result of numerous conditions and multiple variables way out at sea that you will never know first hand. There are vast and various interdependent actions that surge and collide because of an open system. It's a culmination of activities, a dynamic unfolding of iterations that have combined randomly together to move towards the shore, build into a swell, form a wave, and crash onto the beach.

A wave is never just a wave. It is a manifestation of all these multiple relationships that randomly intersect in the intimately connected open system. Each one is dependent on nearly a myriad of others before it, and if you remove one from the system, you could upset the entire chain of events. It is a result of unfathomable amounts of combining elements because the structure creates numerous random relationships that go out and create even more.

The wave that finally hits the shore has traveled usually hundred's if not thousands of miles and is influenced by disturbances that have made it *that* particular wave: the magnetism from the moon pulling on the earth moving the tides, the natural spin of the earth's axis directing swells, numerous storms that generated incredible energy, the force of the wind on the waters surface that pushes power deep into the sea, the ocean's floor riddled with complicated textures that rise and fall at whim like a random reef jutting up from the ground forcing a wave to crest, other waves from other storms intersecting with those waves, and varied and random currents that push and pull the waters through constant change.

The ocean is an example of a whole system that acts under the power of high connectivity and disturbances to produce a dynamic outcome. Sure you might get a perception of the storm's power by watching the size of a particular wave, but you will never know the connections of its contributing factors that happened long before it crashed. Likewise, we can't know any system or one person for that matter by examining one event, one team, one ideology, one comment, one moment or a specific condition. Instead, we must learn how to consider the intricate realities through high levels of connectivity.

It's Not Just One Thing

Open the books. Look at every chapter and every word as they connect to the whole of the story. As a teacher of English Literature for middle schoolers and high schoolers, I never let the student define an entire book by a single chapter or single theme nor were they allowed to define a poem by a stanza or a single metaphor. Sure a chapter in a book or a stanza in a poem might accentuate or highlight meaning central to the story, but it cannot solely define the whole by itself. The beauty of literature is in the layers as they combine and unfold. The multiple images in a poem helps construct powerful meaning and the syntactical arrangement is critical to understanding the significance of the piece. It's all the fluid, random relationships within the piece that help define the meaning.

For example, who can rightly look only at Upper Yosemite Falls and categorize the whole of Yosemite Valley by one static image? Although, for example Upper Yosemite Falls is spectacular and brings sheer wonder and amazement, to understand the grandness and immensity of Yosemite Valley and the total beauty of *its entire system* that was poured out in divine proportion, it is imperative that you view the *entire valley* and all of its splendor. The whole of Yosemite Valley as is possible to see, brings most people to their knees and humbles their hearts to something that is beyond themselves. Seeing the whole brings an awareness of an immense "Otherness."

Interdependencies

Similarly, like the wave, a chapter, or a stanza, as this change is pillaging our traditional mind-sets, we have to connect to this idea of whole systems thinking where *meaning is found in the whole thing*. "Seeing the major interrelationships underlying a problem leads to new insight into what might be done. [We need to see] interrelationships rather than linear cause-effect chains, and processes of change rather than [static] snapshots" (Senge, p. 72&73).

A leader's focus must become one of wholeness and how to connect to subjectivity instead of objectivity so that he or she can experience the whole of Yosemite Valley for example. We must understand interdependencies by seeing the whole system, reading every chapter, and looking at the wave as a culmination of unutterable amounts of connected iterations.

Rapid Change Disintegrates Disconnected Systems

I don't claim any special insight to the economic crisis both at home domestically and globally, but we are all hit uniquely by its force at some level and to some degree. I know that change is no secret nor is it a revelation. However, what is new is that the complexity in change is our new reality. It is the new constant, and it ushers an immediate effect that increases the speed and velocity of diversity. It reveals problems that aren't as clear cut as they used to be.

What I have seen first hand in business, read about in the papers, studied from academia, and watched on the news has only emphasized the reality of the wide spread need for a new type of thinking. The idea and practice of interdependence and interconnectivity does not alleviate all of the problems for leadership nor does it bring an absolute solution to the market, to leaders, to organizations, to the church, or the global landscape, but it does propose a new mentality that can surface dynamic probability. It can transform a typically reactive stance into a systemic, innovative response and alleviate the debilitating power of control.

That said, we need more than just new answers, we need rich creativity and dynamic innovations. We need to start conversations that have access to real data and real change. Like Twitter, we need immediacy, transparency and accountability. Yet we are stuck in an older perception that is guarded, calculated, divided, and splintered.

To break this, as leaders, we need to enable our systems to have value driven conversations at all levels through a flat playing field, and those conversations need to be driven by relevant, real information. And yet, currently the conversations we permit are usually manufactured, splintered, and filled with scripted rhetoric. People talk but don't produce anything of great value because the community is disconnected from each other and transparent information. It cannot direct change. Our organizations are frozen enterprises because of structure.

Just as the various systems in the human body (e.g., the circulatory, nervous, digestive systems) work together to sustain and enhance life, so too in all living systems the various elements in the system interrelate and serve to augment each other. Dysfunction is the result of a breakdown between various components or agents within the system. When each component operates at peak and harmonizes with the other components, the whole system is enhanced and benefits from synergy - that is, where the result is greater that the sum of the individual parts. When all are present and interrelated in an effective way...[we] will operate at peak.

Furthermore, in living systems theory, moving an organization into adaptive organic mode requires that we 1) develop and enhance relationships [and conversations], 2) cross-pollinate ideas from different specialties and departments, 3) disturb equilibrium by moving to the edge of chaos, and 4) focus information according to organizational mission (Hirsch, p. 174).

I found a common strand in my role as a teacher, church leader, and business leader. The human element is untapped because it is so splintered under molds of form and function. We are caged because an older era wanted tight efficiencies and control. In this framework, both leaders and the people were disconnected from each other, the system, and the conversation. Without the structure of a system being spontaneous, creative or connected, we only perpetuate our disconnectedness.

Although the world that I used to operate in as a teacher and the one I operate in now in the world of business seem galaxies apart, the common theme is this unrealized potential of people and organizations because the architecture disconnects us from a living system.

Today's Speed of Change

I believe that many of the following examples from the automotive industry show 2 specific things: 1) the speed of change, and 2) the depth of impact a disconnected system will encounter. Who would have thought just a few years ago that GM would be scurrying for a way out of the Hummer, Saturn, Pontiac, and Saab franchises, begging for a hand out from Congress, filing for bankruptcy, or that Toyota would be closing some of its truck manufacturing plants here in the US and posting its worst lost in decades, or that gas would be $4 a gallon? "Auto sales slumped to a 16-year low in July (2008) as automakers failed to keep up with consumers' growing demand for smaller, more fuel-efficient vehicles. General Motors, Ford, Toyota and other automakers said Friday that their U.S. sales fell by double-digits" (nadaheadlines@nada.org). Devastating news hit the dealer and manufacturer in every corner. As I read market reports, it wasn't shocking to see the industry down by 40-50% year over year month after month:

- Chrysler LLC dealers were stunned by news that they no longer will be able to offer leases through the automaker's captive finance arm, Chrysler Financial.
- With its dealers struggling to sell vehicles from a brand that might be sold, General Motors has paid Hummer dealers early bonuses and is in talks to buy out stores.
- Analysts were busy revising their forecasts last week. They now see North American output crashing to its lowest level since 1972.

- Sales of the compact [Ford] Focus were up 53.2% in May. Ford decided to close down its previously high producing truck plant in Michigan, and retool it to produce Ford's next generation of compact cars.
- US dealers only have a one day supply of mini coopers as the first half sales rose nearly 34% over 2007.
- The sudden escalation of gasoline prices to more that $4 a gallon has hit American motorists like a 2-by-4 between the eyes. Big pickup sales have cratered. Small cars are booming.
- Plunging values of big pickups and SUV's are battering the lease portfolio of Ford Motor Co.'s captive finance unit (Automotive News, July 28, 2008, 82nd year – No. 6318, p. 1-34).

The gas crisis and credit crisis hit and leveled the big truck market and Al Gore's global warming film was on the lips of everyone from politicians, Hollywood stars, to corporate executive, to local citizens. Big was out and Hybrids were in. Both hit a fever pitch overnight and took the market by absolute force, and before the manufacturer or dealer could say "small car, low emissions, or MPG" their inventories of big SUV's and trucks were instantly gluttonous at the factory and the local dealer. For the US market, the SUV and truck market almost but disappeared. The market moved almost instantly from a point where SUV's and trucks had a quick, dependable turn rate and held all the money to a place where they piled up far, high, and deep like 1000's of logs being sent down a river as wide as the Mississippi in flood season and suddenly got caught in a bottle neck 2 feet wide.

The reason I highlight this is to show how difficult it was for the industry on the corporate level down to the local dealer body to change or be prepared to respond nimbly during crisis. One of the reasons that change hit so hard and the response was so reactive was in large part its inhibitive, disconnected structure. The hierarchy and the bureaucratic sludge was prohibitive to the system being able to have any kind of intuitive or communal response. A stiff and top-down structure furthered the calamities as the market dumped out its realities to the corporations and the consumers without regard to their calculated forecasts and predetermined figures. Instead, the industry at a corporate level and a local level adhered to an older model. Instead of looking at this storm as an opportunity for edge thinking and bigger waves, the leadership and the system froze and stood still.

The surfer was no where to be found. You see, surfers instead of fearing change and upheavals when the storm arrives, look and wait for it with anticipation because we know what it brings. The best surf is found in these big, erratic storms because they allow for epic moments, but leaders stuck in an older way stay wedged on the shore. The newer mindset, instead looks for his board. It's not that this type of leader looks for calamity. Rather we think nimbly because *we are about the wave and not the storm.*

I saw managers and employees that were tagged by the older mentalities. They were dazed, trying to wedge into some make-shift barricade to weather the storm. They didn't like the storms because they didn't know "how to surf." They were never taught. Their thought process was linear and conventional. They saw the crisis crush jobs and cripple local stores and hobble industries. Instead of being encouraged to populate new conversations throughout their community to find ways out and around, understandably they limped forward. They anticipated more calamity instead of looking for opportunity. The structure set them to wait and to see what would happen instead of living in a structure that encouraged them to mix and mingle with the pandemonium, get pushed to the edge, to then innovate. They tensed up and waited for someone else to tell them what to do.

I tried to begin conversations about how we could innovate and create new profit centers, and how we should convert fear into a positive notion as it pressed us to the edge. I proposed to them that any new idea or product they (workers) generate from the conversation that creates net new revenue for the company they would share in a lions share of the profits. I hoped the edge would press us toward creative center. I hoped the lip of the wave would cause "edge thinking." However, because management and leadership in general is steeped in top down practice, the behavior from the community can only produce what it was taught to produce. Changing the conversation or even trying to create a newer one felt like picking up a newborn, setting them upright, and then telling him to run.

A Perfect Storm

I am not proposing that this mindset could have averted the magnitude. This massive collapse of the market and certain industries was a "perfect storm" and something we may never again see in our lifetime. However, if leadership set interconnectivity as a core component of organizational structure, it could have responded with greater flexibility and their interaction with the crisis might have been met with a more nimble and lucid response. Through networked communities and random relationships, the response could have been creative, unconventional and combined with collective wisdom from the people that might have helped wade through the mind field. Instead, the structure responded from top down, compartmentalized people, and micromanaged from the perspective of just a few.

Reactive and Haphazard

Because the conventional structure is typically disconnected, management deci- sions are reactive and often haphazardly spontaneous. When crisis hits, our struc- ture propels us to a standstill because shock, speed, and the type of upheaval occuring puts us in a state of bewilderment. Leaders are typically used to move- ment and reactions that were based on old practices and older mentalities, and because of this unique speed of change we are like deer caught in the headlights of an oncoming car. We can't move with the market or through our people because all of the decisions come from the top few and filter down to the bottom where compartments and functions tend to put things to a standstill.

Even though the jolt and violent gyrations of the markets were unprecedented, in general the leadership behavior and actions that followed were arid, stale, and ultimately disconnected. We were incapable of recognizing how to respond nimbly and be flexible. Instead of communities murmuring with productive conversations and brewing with innovations, the employees were corralled according to job descriptions and functionality and had to wait to be told what to do. Leadership didn't create or allow new hybrid communities to emerge in a setting of an interactive organizational response. In general, both organizations and leadership sat idly on their hands and fought for survival.

Leadership Held Captive

Fundamentally, leadership is held captive not by the market but by a mentality, by a fear of losing control. Instead, we must learn to understand how to connect the whole system both dynamically and unconventionally. We must anticipate radical change and react nimbly when it hits.

This example of a rapidly shifting market is not the primary point that I am trying to communicate, nor am I trying to use the market trend as the key and only factor that forces this mentality. This example does however accentuate the *speed of change* in this evolving, global market, but even this is not the primary revelation. Markets will always shift, turn, tip, recycle, correct, etc. Today, they simply do it faster and faster because everything is so connected. The point is three pronged: We must 1) learn to interact with indeterminate change and learn to live on the "edge," 2) be intellectually nimble enough to navigate a very diverse landscape through vibrant conversations in random communities, and 3) convert disruptions into a power that drives innovation. Instead of causing havoc, if we are empowered to innovate through total systems, these disruptions within this new reality will stimulate activity and produce mindsets that systemically evolve.

Too Thick

Change is inevitable while leadership is weighted down in our old, thick ways. When disturbances happen, we need to become not just nimble but nimble enough to use the change to innovate. We must learn to realize the benefit of dramatic disruptions, or the other side, the darker side of the random order and complexity will neutralize our progress.

Under the older traditions however, we repel disruptions because it's a threat to our stability. This linearity freezes the system, but under a new mindset, these same disruptions inspire innovation. They help to create the unusual. They empower the system if it is connected to push rapidly and then disseminate outward. Therefore, we must learn to change and move like the water floating down a river's bank. Conversations, information, and connections must become rampant and interconnected to promote the flow of information and ideas.

It's like looking at a network of rivers from a 10,000 feet above the ground. From up high, you can see all of the veins and legs of the river flowing and meandering along their course to connect and intertwine. You can also look back to see where they came from or how far back they stretch. At ground level however, looking at that same network from a single point, all you can see is right in front of you, only so far out, and only from a limited perspective. You cannot see any type of interconnected network or dynamic emerging courses that formed upstream. Everything in that river before you - the water, the current, the sediment, the speed of travel, the amount of water, the floating debris – can only be observed in front of you as it is and where it is.

Higher up at that 10,000 foot level however, all of those things are still the same thing when you were at ground level, but you can observe their connections from further up the network of rivers as well as their influencers from distant places. Those details – water, sediment, debris – now have meaning and value different from the isolated view you took in at ground level.

This idea of open systems and interdependence allows this perspective from a 10,000 foot level and delivers ideas and thoughts and conversations that could have never happened on the ground because your perspective is limited. More importantly, at this higher level, it allows you to witness and see a network of con- nectivity and its influences that network out and touch other developing networks. Recognizing these characteristics encourages us to think in a state of "otherness" and through a network of connections that has unconventional means to an unrecognizable and unpredictable end. "We must abandon the formal, static linear planning process…In the new nonlinear world, no predictions remain valid for too long" (Lewin, p. 202).

The Emerging Cocoon

We must become believers and connectors to this new reality and learn to intimately connect so we can not only survive but succeed. Because our new role in the future is to be more and more like a Wiki editor through these conversations, we really need to understand that what we are used to seeing and thinking is no longer sure footing.

For example, a larval caterpillar goes through a predictable and spectacular metamorphosis where it transforms itself from a voracious eating caterpillar, seals itself into a tightly wrapped cocoon, and emerges a beautifully speckled and delicate butterfly that gently floats through the air like the fog softly rolling into the bay.

However, in this new and crazy climate, for example, the same caterpillar wraps itself in its cocoon, tears itself free, and instead of a beautifully speckled butterfly, it has fallen heavy to the ground as a big, awkward elephant with horse legs, a lion's tail, painted in zebra stripes, and chirps like a sparrow. The shapes emerging from this climate are unpredictable and materialize often completely unfamiliar. Where we were used to anxiously wait and watch the caterpillar dawn its baffling colored wings, now we wait in vibrant and nervous expectation not knowing what may break the cocoon or even if the cocoon will tear open at all. Or perhaps in this climate, it's even possible the cocoon was the finale.

Therefore, it is imperative that we be nimble enough to tackle and dismantle the challenge. Who knows what's coming from the next cocoon - a giraffe-rhino with the legs of a black widow spider that can fly like an eagle?

What used to be measurable and predictable is now sporadic and indeter- minate. Predictions have now become hypotheses that forecast probable patterns and pos- sible shapes instead of calculation and precision. Today, it's most probable that some- thing unusual and crazy will emerge, and our current, linear, top-down mentalities aren't prepared for what we will see? There needs to be a chorus of interactions from communities willing and able to come together, discuss the implications, and find a way out or over. Like the ants, we need real time responses from communities in open conversations with intelligent, accessible data that can make a decision and act.

We will see more and more information in our world that will have emergent properties that bear little to no resemblance of their original properties. Like the wetness of water or the human heartbeat, the ultimate outcome of their newer properties will be result of macro levels interacting with the lower levels to create dynamic, unsuspecting outcomes. In other words, only when they emerge can we see what and then only can we begin to unravel it and find its alleged meaning and connection, and only then can we unpack the "thing." Caterpillars are still cocooning, but instead of turning into butterflies, they are turning into polka- dotted elephant-zebras that can swim like a fish or perhaps it is a purple hued alligator-leopard that hops like a frog and climbs trees like a monkey.

To forecast the future and plan for behaviors is like playing the slots of Las Vegas – you never know the outcome and the gamble becomes the only predicted constant. Because of these altering access points to change, it doesn't matter if you are a pastor, teacher, middle or senior manager, political leader, a well studied and practiced executive, or even a parent, there needs to be a fundamental shift of mindset to move with these drastic structural shifts.

Too Many Via's

Current models are stifled and filled with sludge. They are heavy to move, filled with arduous situations and set-ups, and they are about as nimble as a pair of feet cemented in two buckets lining up for a hundred yard dash. When drastic approvals must pass through a laborious, writhing chain of bosses and committees that are laden with the malignant mentality of command and control: Does it meet with our strategy? Did they follow proper protocol? Did they pass through the food chain? Did the subcommittees approve of the proposal? Did the committees meet and discuss the proposal with subcommittees? Did this pass through upper management? Does this meet our budget and the forecasted numbers? Are we on track with last years proposed agenda's?

Speed is the order of the day, but we have manufactured too many "via's." Speed equals power equals nimbler ways equals innovation, but if the system or the person is inadvertently set to slow things down it transforms a cheetah into a laborious three toed sloth. How can we move with innovation if we are befuddled with burdens, mazes, and roadblocks? The themed spirit of human element is shackled.

Take for example a snap shot of the car buying process. I have never met one person that likes the car buying process (in the business or out of the business) primarily because there are too many of these via's crated next to ambivalence and confusion. Whether they are in the business working the deal or a customer trying to buy a car. The process is laborious and cumbersome. The dealer and the customer compete in the process *because that is the understood system*. Its hated by the customer and tolerated by the industry because the mentality is "that is how it's done." The customer thinks the process is the only way to save their money

I get the philosophy of the sale and the necessary component of persuasion and manipulation for the customer and the retailer, and I am not at all advocating we don't fight for profit. Negotiation. We do it every day over and over. However, I think we can do away with several of the via's and make the system quicker to increase the power for the customer and the company. It needs to be flatter, more accessible for the customer and the salesperson, and ultimately efficient so that the customer is happy and the company can go on to sell again and again and remain profitable. And yet, the customer and the company, are stuck in the "via." Our creative spirits are cluttered and battered.

Trying to change it is like trying to move an ocean freighter with a couple of row boats. There is this entrenched mentality that the customer and the dealer encounter during the negotiation that is usually riddled with "back and forth." It starts with the sales person, then goes through the closer, then goes through the sales manager, then goes through the general sales manager, that is then reviewed by the bank, that is then ultimately approved or declined by the general manager. This then goes back to the general sales manager, that then goes back to the sales manager, that then goes back to the salesperson, that then goes back to the customer. And when that is all finished, if the deal is made the sales person then starts the process again between himself, the customer, and the F&I manager. It is pass off after pass off after pass off. The industry has its historic reasons and philosophies behind the maze of the sale, but ultimately it doesn't need to work like this. It needs a full bottle of Drano to unclog the pipes. I realize and understand the sales process of control and manipulation, but there must be simpler ways. There must be more natural ways.

[Dee Hock says] Purpose and principle, clearly understood and articulated, and commonly shared, are the genetic code of any healthy organization. To the degree that you hold purpose and principles in common among you, you can dispense with command and control. People will know how to behave in accordance with them, and they'll do it in thousands of unimaginable, creative ways. The organization will become a vital, living set of beliefs (Hirsch, p. 202).

Oz

All of this only creates an "Oz" behind the curtain flashing lights and ringing bells just like that scene from the movie. The customer is out of touch with their real experience except being kept in the dark while they talk in secret, and the sales person and management are kept from their customer while they talk in secret. There is no connection, no relationship, and nothing close to random inter-connectivity or transparency. And yet all of this goes on while we move forward faster and faster in a flat world. This process of the sale cannot change though unless our mentalities change first so that we can see a way around the older process and then into the new one. If we just change the process, it won't hold because our minds will regress back to familiarity.

These hierarchical roadblocks and micromanaging details put a cinch in the pipeline of creativity and innate talents of people. It strikes a subtle sense of fear into us and then puts control in the hands of the hierarchy. The system is sepa-rated, and we are separated.

However, in some places we are seeing systems erasing borders in order to come alive. To engineer collaboration and pollinate new thinking through trans-parency and immediacy, companies are opening conversations.

Cutting-edge companies take collaboration further, integrating opera-tions with vendors and suppliers in ways that give each party access to data that helps keep the supply chain flowing and inventories lean. Once such links are established, a manufacturer, for example, no longer has to guess at a ven-dor's inventories or future promotional plans; hence forecasts - and sales – are improving (Wall Street Journal, Jain and Covas, R10, Monday, July 7, 2008).

Instead of keeping things close to their chest, organizations are talking openly with business partners and vendors to build better forecasting and planning models and increase potential outcomes. They are looking through the eyes of *collective* wisdom and gathering input with "round table" discussions. By doing this, they take away the notion of secrecy and control and seek instead to collaborate new and unlikely resources to build new thought models. They then plan together and learn together, and although the results may not be always fruitful and completely lucrative, they will move the needle and eventually and more often grow the net result of the objective.

Listen to a conversation in the Wall Street Journal on Monday, July 11, 2010 with Mr. Dennis Nally chairman of PricewaterhouseCoopers titled, "PwC Chairman Aims to Keep Millennials Happy." He addresses how and why it is so important for organizations in the workplace to shift previous models of talent retention and create new tools that address a new community of workers with a newer mindset: sense of community, transparent conversations, and deeper level values other than mere "job security."

WSJ: What is the biggest challenge for companies when trying to recruit talented staff?

Mr. Nally: This millennial generation is not just looking for a job, they're not just looking for salary and financial benefits, they're looking for skill development, they'r looking for mobility, they're looking for opportunities to acquire different skills and to move quickly form one part of an organization to another. How you manage that sort of talent and how you deal with expectations is very different from what's been done in the past.

So, clearly articulating your people strategy, what you can deliver and importantly what you expect in return is key.

WSJ: How do you go about creating that connectivity?

Mr. Nally: The human capital agenda has to be driven by the CEO. It's so strategic today that you want to have great support coming from the HR organization, but if this isn't viewed as just as strategic as new products and services or research and development, [it] won't be successful" (Wall Street Journal, Marketplace, B4).

Instead of using such collaborative efforts mentioned above, the hierarchical pyramid puts a company and people at bay, specifically human capital. All of these layers and potholes suffocate innovation, stifle the system, and create rigid coworkers; it halts rapid movement and blocks potential fluidity. It slows things down. The lines aren't allowed to become boundaryless.

Stability, Superiority, Discipline, Predictability?

The current and typical structure roots itself in the ideology that stability, superiority, effective operational discipline, and the ability to predict calculable results translate to bottom-line performance. The derivative is that therefore if an organization for example can produce machine like precision with measurable results, the future is controllable, the unknown is minimized, and predictions are precise. Obviously I am being extreme to illustrate a point. However, this sounds like a "no-brainer" approach given these alleged controls and that this is really how people operate and how people as a resource are maximized, but is this how people are designed?

Is our total composite, humanly speaking, mostly utilized if we are ordered around and told what to do? Or are we bursting with resources unique, intuitive, and divine that can be opened up in random relationships?

As leaders, do we really only lead under this canopy of control? Are our potentials and those that we lead unleashed or encrypted? Is our natural organism designed to fit job descriptions and punch time clocks? Is our DNA like this historical and traditional DNA of an organization – operationally disciplined and precise? Do we really maximize their performance under this iron umbrella? Do we want such an arid environment where results are only a matter of calculation and our paycheck is the only end goal? Do we really get something out of the exchange that translates to value or meaning?

Instead, it's clear that the primal evidence of people's core and human nature's essential composite point to something totally opposite the mentality of mere calculation and precision. The needs and intent of the person are far, far greater than mere stability, superiority, discipline, predictions, calculations, and a highly productive output. These are important points in some circumstances; however, these all but erase the human factor, the real human factor that makes us unique in all facets, filled with bursting potential within the creative ingenuity of the heart, soul, and mind. We are highly unique beings with an intentional design; leadership must learn how to find this deep well of the human spirit in order to develop a highly productive team and therefore a highly productive organization.

- The organization must be adaptable and responsive to changing conditions, while preserving overall cohesion and unity of purpose.
- The trick is to find the delicate balance that allows the system to avoid turf fights and back-stabbing on the one hand, and authoritarian micro- management on the other.
- The organization must cultivate equity, autonomy, and individual opportunity.
- The organization's governing structure must distribute power and function to the lowest level possible.
- The governing structure must not be a chain of command, but rather a framework for dialogue, deliberation, and coordination among equals (Hirsch, p. 203).

If we were robotic in nature and born to be order takers, the command and control might be the most productive tool, but we are a living system. If we can agree that we are natural organisms with natural processes, why would we put natural organisms into an unnatural, machine like conduit. Sure, it worked at one time to the end that was needed, but it worked under a prescribed and perhaps maligned end game of mere productivity and output.

The Industrial Revolution produced tremendous amounts of productivity and efficiency and organized mass groups into confined and categorized units of production. However, it left us cold and never touched the central tenet of the person. It missed the creative, relationally based design, and it didn't touch anything of "eternal truth."

Indeed, one doesn't have to be a Marxist to be awed by the scale and success of early-20th century efforts to transform strong-willed human beings into docile employees. The demands of the modern industrial workplace required a dramatic resculpting of human habits and values. To sell one's time rather than what one produced, to pace one's work to the clock, to eat and sleep at precisely defined intervals, to spend long days endlessly repeating the same, small task – none of these were, or are, natural human instincts. It would be dangerous, therefore, to assume that the concept of "the employee" – or any other tenet in the creed of modern management – is anchored on the bedrock of eternal truth (Hamel, p. 130).

For example, an article in the Wall Street Journal dated Monday July 7, 2008 called "Misunderstanding the Chinese Worker – Western Impressions are dated – and probably wrong" from the Global Business Section by Kathryn King-Metters and Richard Metters contends that there has been a significant cultural shift in western companies understanding of what motivates Chinese employees. A bunch of research data gathered in the 1980's on China by Dr. Hofstede concluded that the paycheck was the primary motivation. Executives tended to say, "Chinese have zero loyalty to their employer. The most important motivator is money," but now today non-monetary incentives do a much better job at attracting and retaining Chinese talent for multinational firms. The mantra for retention has gone from the impression that money is all that matters to, for example taking pride in being a part of a team and creative problem solving. The cultural shift has exposed the fact that they want more than just a paycheck. They want to be perhaps a part of significance. They want to be a part of something that matters. The article said, "By focusing solely on salary as a motivational tool, they are giving short shrift to things such as training, time off and community building – incentives that could go a long way in a highly competitive job market…taking a star employee out to dinner may be a more effective motivator than a bonus or a plaque on the wall."

Gary Hamel, the cutting edge managerial consultant, in his insightful book about management innovation called the "Future of Modern Management" attributes the classical definition of the organization, a.k.a. bureaucracy to the renowned German sociologist Max Weber who gives these primary attributes to the typical and historical management structure:

- The division of labor and responsibilities were clearly delineated for every member of the organization.
- Positions were organized into a hierarchy resulting in a scale of authority.
- Members were selected for positions based on their technical competence or education.
- Manager worked for the owner of the enterprise, but were not the primary owners themselves.
- Everyone in the organization was subject to strict rules and controls relevant to their particular job. The rules were impersonal and uniformly applied (Hamel, p. 13,14).

Checks and balances are critical and I am not proposing a leaderless, purely socialistic model. I would be remiss to say that anything from the past models were only bad and generally fruitless. However, under the older model and under this climate, checks and balances have morphed into drones of control and power. They are perhaps dangerously close to company killers or hired guns. However, Hamel says that much credit is still due the early management pioneers for the innovation they authored and the principles they implemented that have stood the test of time: "variance analysis, capital budgeting, project management, pay-for-performance, strategic planning" (Hamel, p. 6) He said,

> Those intrepid pioneers developed standardized job descriptions and work methods. They invented protocols for production planning and scheduling. They mastered the intricacies of cost accounting and profit analysis. They instituted exception based reporting and developed detailed financial controls. They devised incentive-based compensation schemes and set up personnel departments. They created sophisticated tools for capital budgeting and by 1930, had also designed the basic architecture of the multidivisional organization and enumerated the principles of brand management (Hamel, p. 7).

However, he said conversely those discoveries from a century ago are more likely today to quell the necessary storm of creative management than fan its flames. He doesn't believe by any stretch of the imagination that management can survive under these stringent conditions. The traditional system of controls is currently set up from centuries past to be able to work with their pace of change centuries ago. Today, those models are akin to a household spray bottle being used to put out a forest fire. Or perhaps it makes as much sense as a Nobel Prize winner sitting down with a 6 year old to have an inspiring conversation about the future of professional soccer in the United States because David Beckham signed with the LA Galaxy.

Hamel says that the system worked at one time. It had its purpose and was *functional* under previous conditions, but it doesn't work anymore. Today we need dynamic interactions. Notice the date that he mentioned – 1930. That's a long, long time ago. I'm not saying, and it is my clear impression that Gary Hamel is not saying, that old or older is always synonymous with incapable or insufficient. However, in the current condition of leadership under this landscape of dynamism and upheaval, this style is antiquated and hinders the very critical creative, intuitive, and innovative means necessary to move ahead.

Except for Leadership, Everything has Changed

Consider this: "The Internet has upended how consumers engage with brands. It is transforming the economies of marketing and making obsolete many of the function's traditional strategies and strucutres. For marketers, the old way of doing business is unsustainable" (HBR, p. 65, Dec. 2010)

Even though, the world is flat (Thomas Friedman) and radical change has become an epidemic, *leadership* has stayed the same. The traditional, dated models haven't changed or deviated from their original architectural and hierarchical design of the science of management. However, big, radical change has happened everywhere else in organizations, world economies, private and public communities, religious denominations, global financial markets, technology, and the global landscape. With the borders all but disappearing in the global terrain and with the reality of the internet and decentralized industries, there is a tremendous free flow of information and shared intrinsic architecture. Aside from these older models of leadership and management, we have only seen rapid developments on all frontiers in most of the world. Even more startling is this change revolution that has taken the globe by force since the 21st century has only just rolled its oars into the messiness of the chaotic and undulating sea of change. Trying to fit the older management principles and practices into this era of essential and rapid innovation, is like trying to catch a great white shark with a worm, a piece of string, and a hook while paddling in a flat bottom canoe.

In his book "The World is Flat" Thomas Friedman elaborates on deteriorating "borders" and crumbling walls used to divide and splinter productivity. He says that centralized industries, localized production, and loyal communities have all been essentially demolished or at a minimal level spread abroad and dispersed almost like chaff in the wind. It has forced the hand of management to find erratic solutions to erupting developments, evolving entities, and emerging patterns so they don't miss the wave of revolution pounding the shoreline of the new frontier. And yet these newer solutions are still in large part only reactive, hip shot responses that generate little to no deep fix or flexible impact.

A Flat World Speeds the Depth of Change

We are all impacted by this change, because at a point, we are all somehow connected. This change doesn't have favorites and it hits at whim with uncanny reverberations. For example, one rapidly moving wave of change has been the global economy that has unfurled disaster faster than we can move and/or react. Because of this global "closeness," change is bigger, faster, and more complex.

The US Great Recession has been an epicenter in the global economy, its ripples have formed destructive waves crashing into economies all over the globe. Because the world is so much more connected and intertwined, our spiral adversely affected global markets quickly with a heavy hand. Our credit crisis rooted in housing market that festooned under the shortsighted vision and unencumbered greed, loose policy, mismanaged investments at home and abroad, gas at an all time high, and the implosion of the auto industry caused a horrific jolt to the global community. Here are some more examples of this speed.

Institutions like General Motors, Bear Stearns, Fannie Mae and Freddie Mac, Merrill Lynch, Lehman Brothers, and A.I.G. rapidly if not overnight fell into disarray and countries that heavily invested in our markets consequently felt our collapses through a rapidly developing global intimacy. The front page of the Wall Street Journal said Tuesday, September 16, 2008 in the headline "AIG, Lehman Shock Hits World Markets,"

- "The convulsions in the U.S. financial system sent markets tumbling across the globe tumbling, as two of Wall Street's biggest firms looked set to exit the scene and the insurance titan American International Group Inc., turned to the Federal Reserve and the state of New York for assistance."
- "With AIG now tottering, a crisis that began with falling home prices and went on to engulf Wall Street has reached one of the world's largest insurance companies, threatening to intensify the financial storm and greatly complicate the government's efforts to contain it."
- "The rapid demise of 158-year old investment bank Lehman Brothers Holding Inc., together with the takeover of 94-year old Merrill Lynch & Co., represents a watershed in the banking industry's biggest restructuring since the Great Depression" (Wall Street Journal, A1).
- "After on of the most tumultuous weekends Wall Street has ever seen, Americas are asking: How much bleaker is the outlook for the U.S. economy, especially where people live, work, borrow, and save" (A2).

And then on September 17, 2008, the very next day, the front page of the Wall Street Journal read, "U.S. to Take Over AIG in $85 Billion Bailout; Central Bank Inject Cash as Credit Dries Up,"

- "The U.S. government seized control of American International Group Inc., - one of the world's biggest insurers – in an$86 billion deal that signaled the intensity of its concerns about the danger a collapse could pose to the financial system."
- "Banks abruptly stopped lending to each other or charged exorbitantly high rates Tuesday, threatening to spread the troubles of American International Group Inc. and Lehman Brothers Holding Inc. to a broad range of financial institutions and the global economy" (A1).

As these examples highlight the speed and the power of global interconnectivity, companies and the individual similarly need to be prepared to innovate as fast or as nimbly when immense challenges collide with systems. The connection is that they need to consider how to create the efficiency through similar structural speed in order to absorb the impact.

I show these headlines to emphasize the speed of change. Days and not months altered the underpinnings of historic financial institutions and industries because the world is so highly connected. It is imperative that we are prepared to rapidly assemble the collective community and collectively respond.

111

To emphasize this connectedness, blurred boundaries, and the influence and integration of new global economies the economists and professor at NYU, Nouriel Roubini said,

> Leaving aside the fact that we are going to have a pretty nasty recession and international crisis, the global economy is going to grow at a sustained rate once this downturn is over. There are significant financial and economic problems in the U.S., and that's why I'm bearish about the U.S. But the emergence of China and India and other powers is going to shift global economies and politics radically, and the world is going to be more balanced in the future, rather than relying on one engine, which has been the U.S. There are big issues ahead: How do you integrate the 2.2 billion Chinese and Indians into the world economy? There will be transitional costs and the displacement of workers, both blue-collar and white-collar, in the advanced economies" (http://online.barrons.com/article/SB121763156934206007.html).

Through these global iterations, the borders are coming down and the emergence of massive populations and mingling mindsets will integrate into one global community. As a result, more disturbances are certain. We need to think globally with a nonconventional mindset so that we can innovate when these disruptions rock our perspective.

The Internet: Equalizing through Interconnectedness

The internet has transformed our mindset through speed, transparency, accountability, and accessibility. It has brought us to a level that forces our hand. It has exposed the secrets and put light on some of the disproportionate practices of capitalism as well as allowing access to certain but limited proprietary information. It has leveled the playing field. Through it, various venues have opened wide new channels and companies: advancing technology, outsourcing, open source software, Google, Microsoft, eBay, MySpace, Facebook, Twitter, Craigslist, Wikipedia, Search Engine Optimization, the World Wide Web. Such creations and discoveries have all helped to reshape our landscape with a globally textured mindset. It is this new shift that is fast and creative with limitless knowledge centers.

- "There are more than 170 million websites today, but in 1994 there were fewer than 4,000."
- "1998...Larry Page and Sergey Brin founded Google...by using computer algorithm...sent a spider into the Web that would index every page it crawled past."
- "The company started serving up ads in 2000. In 2002, it had revenues of $400 million; in2005, $6.1 billion; in 2007, $16.5 billion" (Wall Street Journal, September, 17, 2008, Stross, p. A25)

The engine behind all of this alteration is rapid, free flowing change through vast global interconnections. The world is flat:

> Outsourcing is just one more dimension of a fundamental thing happening today in the world. What happened over the last [few] years is that there has been a massive investment in technology, especially in the bubble era, when hundreds of millions of dollars were invested in putting broad- band connectivity around the world, undersea cables, all those things. At the same time, computers became cheaper and dispersed all over the world, and there was an explosion of software – e-mail, search engines like Google, and proprietary software that can chop up any piece of work and send one part to Boston, one part to Bangalore, and one part to Beijing, making it easy for anyone to do remote development. When all of these things came together around 2000, they created a platform where intellectual work, intellectual capital, could be delivered from anywhere. It could be disaggregated, delivered, distributed, produced and put back together again – and this gave a whole new degree of freedom, to the way we do work, especially work of an intellectual nature...(Friedman, p.7)

Because of this flatness, change happens virtually in real time, and trying to understand what is coming at you is like trying to hold a greased watermelon. That said however, I want to emphasize again I am not supposing that random relationships and open systems can immediately avert all crises of any kind and therefore be able to then hold onto the watermelon. Rather it is more probable that it can interact quickly with intelligence and respond thorough communal wisdom. It's clear that in many cases like the financial crisis or the auto industry fall out, many aspects are especially complex. Perhaps, if more of organizational life was filtered through an open system mentality from the beginning, the gluttony, greed, and under sight of some of the corporations could have been stamped out through transparent conversations, bottom up interventions, shared information, and performance benchmarks. In other words, the strict accountability and transparency of the system can maneuver itself through and beyond crisis because of a pliable, responsive systemic thinking. Friedman said,

> "Clearly, it is now possible for more people than ever to collaborate and compete in real time with more other people on more different kinds of work from more different kinds of corners of the planet and on a more equal footing than at any previous time in the history of the world – using computers, e-mail, networks, teleconferencing and dynamic new software... When you start to think of the world as flat, a lot of things make sense in ways they did not before. But I was also excited personally, because what the flattening of the world means is that we are now connecting all of the knowledge centers of the planet together into a single global network, which could usher in an amazing era of prosperity and innovation" (Friedman, p. 8).

A flat world that opens up this connectivity makes it easier to "travel" or explore and it creates unique options. The inhibitors have been almost all but pressed out of the mix and global communities now use collaboration to fuel the advance. Therefore, interdependence helps create a fluid organization so that when these things surge, when it needs to brace itself for the hit, and when opportunity knocks, it can flex its shape because the system is versatile.

Too Slow

Older leadership models however are too slow in this new arena to move. They can only muscle a reactive stance. By the time they respond, old problems or dilemmas have already morphed into multiple new subsets that have then again branched off to develop newer problems with arms that reach farther and deeper than before. All of a sudden you are in the eye of a hurricane and found solutions become yesterday's headlines. And because of this, the older model is like a stiff board that is inflexible, static, and capable only of its original form. The newer model is like a soft, pliable piece of clay that reacts to the elements and can be shaped and then reshaped. It moves with the hands of the potter.

Leadership must harness the power of the people through the catalytic, autonomous, transparent structure found in an open system. If ideas and creativity have to pass through the flooded tunnel of hierarchy, via's and bureaucracy filled with the sediment and debris of the last century, change will find its way around the tunnel and leave all those lingering in the puddles of the past - soggy, wet, and still. We must be nimble and limber enough to absorb and move with the current otherwise it will get stuck in its own mire.

Natural, Creative Organisms

This message may seem trendy and ideological, but I believe it exposes a vast treasure of unharnessed human potential that can be unleashed into a flat world.

Both the complexity and speed of the change today reveals the chasm between the older mindset and the newer reality of emergence. The future of leadership, must learn about the natural order taking shape in the world and implement it into the structure of the organization. Instead, we have created cultures with arduous decision making processes that quell the spirit of employees with innovative spirits. This forum has discouraged open, frank conversations.

We as individuals all have a burgeoning potential within our own governing principles located deep within our natural order. We are creative beings by nature. Leadership needs to recognize this, develop it, and then construct a culture that powers sustainable learning. In that vein, at the heart and soul of this, is an opportunity to breach the limits of the water's surface and plunge us directly into the intent of our design – to learn, to create, and to inspire through relationship.

Specifically, I see a need to develop organizations that are filled with adaptive, innovative people that can embrace this unfolding unpredictability. We need to affect real change in people and develop new learning capabilities in order to positively affect the future and create systems that adapt, learn and innovate.

It requires leaders to build systemic organizations where _interconnectedness is the one thing._ "Systems thinking show us that there is no outside; that you and the cause of your problems are part of a single system. The cure lies in your relationship with your 'enemy'" (Senge, p. 67). We need to teach change and learn by it as well. As a result of that we will _fulfill a central tenet in our design and purpose_: As humans, we were designed for relationship and conversation, and as leaders we are put in place to help our people learn the art of conversation and develop emerging relationships.

The art of surfing isn't about creating the latest bandwagon so that when the conversation turns to cutting edge trends there is something to talk about. This is about our design, this is about our creativity, this is about our freedom as living systems.

The point in tasking this journey is to put shape to a critical task in a turbulent and shifting climate. Our target as leaders is to author deep, lasting change that is entrepreneurial in spirit, laced with non-linear applications, and filled with natural reactions, and we can do this by eroding staunch, historical barriers. Instead of being stuck in a mentality that will only continue to grow old, we must develop systemic responses so we can interact with change as innate, unfolding, and exciting instead of dreadful, autocratic, and lifeless. "Yet our progress to date has been constrained by our efficiency-centric, bureaucracy-based managerial paradigm. Most of us are still thinking like dogs" (Hamel, p.14).

The Postmodern Mind, Emergence, and Interdependency

If postmodern is an impressionistic painting of blending and blurring colors and meandering images, then this interdependent, emergent wave is akin to the webbing network of the internet. "It's the spider's web in its trembling, a single touch on one strand setting all others resonating" (Tickle, p.160). Postmodernism is the mind-set and interdependence is the property. They both are evolving and defined more by the narrative than by parameters of linear logic.

Postmodern	Emergent	Modern/Traditional
Subjective	Subjective	Objective
Organic	Natural Tension	Industrial
Paradox	Evolving	Logical
Non-linear	Non-linear	Linear

Corporate management, religious denominations, individual churches, school districts, political systems, non-profits, and large organizations must take on this different stance when trying to move, grow, or stretch forward. We must be able to ebb and flow with the radical, seismic shifts in mentality, the global landscape, and encroaching, emerging discoveries. We can't operate within the parameters of the "boomer" generation for example because this new shift is a network of interdependencies that bypass an older, more precise order. There are three implications in this change, 1) globally we live in an interconnected landscape, 2) with it comes a dynamic, new reality of interdependence, 3) and the following generations already use a postmodern mindset as the basis for analysis.

The "Industrial" trend is giving way to an "emergent" trend while the modernist has given way to the postmodernist. "Emergents, because they are postmodern, believe in paradox; or more correctly, they recognize the ubiquity of paradox and are not afraid of it. Instead, they see in its operative presence the tension where vitality lives (Tickle, p. 160).

We are shifting away from precision to things that feel unorganized and messy. We identify more with subjectivity instead of objectivity because it pushes us out into the open. We look like a quilt speckled and littered with dissimilar patchworks of colors, just as postmodernism is akin to dissimilar colors with the random characteristics of interdependence, transparency, and subjectivity.

This shift in thinking - the postmodern and emergence - is not a specific age group or people group, nor does it have parameters that define a definitive movement. It is not a revolution or some extreme uprising aligning itself with anarchy. It is not that drastic, but it is potentially that powerful. It is not anti modern or nonmodern, but simply post modern or "after" modern. It is an emerging mentality that is popping up like a wild spring flower blooming in the meadows and speckling the landscape with dollops of different and co-mingling colors and patterns. It is a paradigm shift, and its transitioning personal and organizational life into an arena where things are defined in their evolutionary state instead of determinate, predictable values.

"...logic is not worth nearly so much as the last five hundred years would have had us believe. It is, therefore, not to be trusted as an absolute, nor are its conclusions to be taken as truth just because they depend from logical thinking. Very often, in fact, logic's fallacies result from logic's lack of a sufficient height or distance in its perspective. That is, logic suffers from the fact that it is human, not divine, and suffers all the limitations of humanity, including being irrevocably contained in time and space (Tickle, p. 160).

The world is redesigning itself with a collaborative landscape of a mixed and jumbled peoples, cultures, religions, ideas, truths, and world views in-part because logic as we knew it is "not worth nearly so much." What used to work is now more like a stain rusted engine that sputters, churns, and rumbles and produces meager results. This perception where things and people need to be calculable, determined, and controlled is essentially gone. There is a countercultural movement that is here now, alive and very active. It is entirely more messy, evolving, and unorganized in comparison to typical structures

> [We are a] band of people who are messy, have addictions and shortcomings, make mistakes, get rejected, and are screwed up...People who embrace discomfort knowing there is so much to be gained for all of us...It's a time in history when technology and global cultural shifts have made neighbors of all of us. We are surrounded by by people of vastly different and unfamiliar cultures, beliefs, and backgrounds. Our neighbors are buzzing with new cultural sights, smells, and sounds and a dynamism fueled by immigration and the fusion of ethnic people groups (Gibbons, p. 83)

If we hover in our current condition, the outcome will be lethal. If we don't innovate as leaders, we will get washed to shore like the inexperienced surfer caught in the impact zone of a set wave.

We need to be like the surfer that navigates through these crashing waves to get past the breakers, and then out and beyond to find the incoming wave. Once we are on the outside, we can sit, wait and watch for the next set to roll in and take the ride. Unless we figure out how to press and paddle through this confusion and what looks like a mess by understanding the undergirding of the oceans churning, we won't get past the messy and foam riddled whitewash of the broken waves.

The older way instead tends to linger in an equilibrium because of a dated, more *modern* mindset that waits for certainties which then prohibits flexible interactions. It is a mindset where control, objectivity and machine like precision are dominating themes.

Many would argue that we already live in a post-modern world. The babyboomers - the "last" of the modernists - are slowly exiting the workforce, and with their exit brings a massive influx of a generation that thinks differently. What's peculiar and particularly important is that this group is bringing with it this new mentality, a new work style, new emphasis on value, a new emphasis on the story or the narrative, the power of the conversation, and a philosophy that is like that patchwork quilt I mentioned above. What is forming is a mind blowing, global network.

> What is happening is something much closer to what mathematicians and physicists call network theory. That is, a vital whole is not really a "thing" or entity so much as it is a network in exactly the same way that the Internet or the World Wide Web or, for that matter, gene regulatory and metabolic networks are not "things" or entities. Like them and from the point of view of an emergent, [any organization or community] is a self-organizing system of relations, symmetrical or otherwise, between innumerable member-parts that themselves form subsets of relations within their smaller networks, etc., etc. in interlacing levels of complexity.

The end result of this understanding of dynamic structure is the realization that no one of the member parts or connecting networks has the whole or entire "truth" of anything, either as such and/or when independent of the others. Each is only a single networking piece of what is evolving and is sustainable so long as the interconnectivity of the whole remains intact. No one of the member parts or their hubs, in other words, has the whole truth as a possession or as its domain. This conceptualization is not just theory. Rather, it has a name: crowd sourcing; and crowd sourcing differs from democracy far more substantially than one might think at first suspect. It differs in that it employs total egalitarianism, a respect for worth of the hoi polloi that even pure democracy never had, and a complete indifference to capitalism as a virtue or to individualism as a godly circumstance...Rather, it is how the message runs back and forth, over and about, the hubs of the network that it is tried and amended and tempered into wisdom and right action...

[The emergent generation then is] "A conversation," which is not only true but will always be true...Furthermore, whatever else such a conceptualizing may be, it is certainly and most notably global, recognizing none of the old, former barriers of nationality, race, social class, or economic status. It is also radical...and it is predictably our future both in this model as the relational, non-hierarchical, a-democratized form of Christianity entering into its hegemony and a s analog for the political and social principles of authority and organization that will increasingly govern global life during the centuries of the Great Emergence (Tickle, p.153).

When I worked briefly in the financial services, I was told over this period of time will see the largest transfer of wealth in the history of our country. My generation (generation X) and the following generations will be greatly affected obviously in a tangible way, but what I think is the most interesting story is the shift of the global mind-set. True, we will see the great hand-off of wealth, but ultimately more important will be the transition from one mental, intellectual, spiritual place to the next. Listen to a quote describing the obviousness of ever-present change in every generation but the reality of a true point of transition in this emerging generation:

"You're right. Change is ever-present, and nearly all generations see themselves as generations of change. And they're right. But let me make a distinction between change and transition. Let's say I'm making an omelet. I mix the eggs with a little milk and put them on the griddle. A good omelet is cooked slowly, so I keep stirring the egg with my fork as it cooks, slowly, stirring, stirring, stirring, like this. But at some point, something happens. The egg that has been changing from raw to cooked rather suddenly transitions from a liquid to a solid. At that point, if I keep stirring with the fork, I will ruin the omelet. The tool that succeeded in helping me bring the omelet to this point now threatens to destroy it. The tool that I need now is not a fork but rather a spatula, so the omelet can be gently folded and then served, like this... all ages are ages of change, but not all ages involve transition...If you keep on doing the same old things with the same old tools - the tools you have inherited from my generation - you'll make a mess of things" (McLaren, p. 40).

At this point it might serve the discussion well to input just a bit of history to illustrate this transition as it corresponds with actual time line and its coinciding mentality. Originally, the time line reads like this: (McLaren, p.15):

Prehistory	Ancient World	Medieval World	Modern World
	2500BC	AD 500	AD 1500

If you notice this time line above the "Modern World" is in the present; we are living in the modern era. However, the newer proposition that accompanies this new mentality is that the time line should actually put the "Modern World" in a past era or past tense. The present time that we now live in is instead an era of a post-Modern World:

Prehistory	Ancient World	Medieval World	Modern World	Postmodern World
	2500BC	AD 500	AD 1500	AD 2000

McLaren outlines some general but understood assumptions of the Modern Era and the mentality that eventually became ingrained in the fibers of modernity:

• An era of conquest and control. Once something is conquered it also must be controlled. People, margins, expenses, variables, economies, policy, process, etc. all need to be constantly kept under total control.

• An age of the machine. Mechanization and precision was the targeted end goal of the modern world. Like engineers, people needed to figure things out precisely. Eventually, they became like small cogs within the greater machine.

• An age of analysis. Analysis was the superior form of thought. If something was to be broken down into its knowable form, the effects needed to be broken down into smaller and smaller causes until they were understandable through analysis. Therefore, when it is understandable, it is then knowable and then controllable.

• The age of secular science. Everything was put through a scientific process and analysis in order to be knowable. Anything that didn't pass through the analysis of science that couldn't be determined knowable and controllable through a cause and effect analysis was left as a murky insignificant blob. It was callously discarded.

• An age of absolute objectivity. This objectivity would yield an absolute certainty, an absolutely knowable entity. What was unknowable, or mysterious, or without exact cause and effect, therefore was left in the unknown. What human reason could not figure out was put to pasture and filed away into the abyss.

• A critical age. If you believe that what you know you know objectively, absolutely, and that you can prove through analytical certainty, you have to debunk anyone who sees your truth as subjective or relative. The pervasive mode of communication was a discussion that you either won or lost, versus a conversation where there is a mutual exchange and communal interaction.

• The age modern nation-state and organization. As the population grew in bulk with urbanism, so to did the need to organize the people into manageable masses. Man quickly became the man of the organization - factory line, political parties, religious views, etc.

• The age of the individual. With the need to organize, came the necessity of dismembering and breaking down communities and groups so that they could organize the parts and pieces (individuals) into functions, roles, descriptions for the purpose of streamlining the efficacy of the organization. The more isolated and independent people were on "their places" the better the institution could place them and corral them for their end purpose (McLaren, 16-18).

Remembering the illustration above of the omelet, the mentality is transitioning from a modern view where the controllable, knowable, objective, and absolute truth is giving way to a new paradigm of the unpredictable and unknowable and the subjective. Perhaps not as easily definable as of yet because the post modern world is in its infancy, but it is safe to say that, "In the postmodern world, we [have] become postconquest, postmechanistic, postanalytical, postsecular, postobjective, postcritical, postorganizational, postindividualistic, postProtestant, and postconsumerist" (McLaren, p. 19). It's not *anti anything* from the modern era. Rather, it is about the fact that we are *post anything* modern and transitioning from a bunch of loose eggs being stirred and tossed with a fork to an omelet being gently lifted and flipped by a spatula. The tools are different. The method is different. The product is different. We are different. Most important, the mentality is different. The story, not precision is the most important thing.

120

"Narrative, on the other hand, is the song of vibrating network...Narrative circumvents logic, speaking the truth of the people who have been and of whom we are. Narrative speaks to the heart in order that the heart, so tutored, may direct and inform the mind" (Tickle, p. 160).

However, there looms this hurdle that threatens to derail us in this transition. "Authoritarians cannot impose commitments, only commands" (Hamel, p. 91). Modernists tend to think of their point of view as THE point of view instead of just a certain view from a point. If we don't dismantle or at least tackle this, we will continue to hit our heads against the wall of objectivity and authoritarianism as the rest of the world starts to use a spatula.

The Piston Mentality

The older science and an older generational mindset is like the "piston mentality." First, like an engine of a car all the parts operate independent of each other with their own specific function. They only do what their design and components allow them to do. The engine works or performs only if all of the parts perform their designated and assigned function in unison. There is no crossover or interconnectivity where parts can exchange functions with neighboring parts, share workload or even innovate to perform better in a non-prescribed manner. The pistons only do what they do and only in their compartment. A piston can only and always be a piston like an axle can always and only be an axle.

Living systems instead tells of the whole picture and how the function of the unit is a result of overlapping iterations happening in tandem. For example, the common position that paralyzes this systems approach in an organization is "I am only the function of my role." Peter Senge says that such a view "misses the ways that orders interact with others' orders to influence the variables you perceive as external" (Senge, p. 49). In other words, your actions always have a consequence on those around you and on the total order of the system as does the interaction you have with the system. What you do matters. What you say matters. These actions or words positively or negatively affect the whole. Whether it is recognized formally, there is deep interconnectivity and systems are ultimately and totally affected whether by what is said or how the organization is structured.

Individual and corporate actions stretch out and ripple throughout an organization. If the system is to break the stagnation of the "piston mentality" or the "this is my space" I mentioned earlier, then the leaders must realize their roles, their influence, and their mindsets stretch much farther than they permit themselves to see. Even in a system under the older rule, there is a connectivity. Although slight, it still touches everything. Just as one's decisions affect multiple arenas and consequently as many people, so to have their decisions been influenced by the power of interconnectivity via the influence of others on them. The ripples are everywhere. Whether we like it our not, we are all connected to some degree and the world has made us all neighbors.

It's critical that everyone in the system participate in and comprehend their intricate connection to the whole. If one deviates from the core and panics, the whole system is adversely affected. For example, the familiar blame game unhinges connections and erects walls of dissension, "It's not may fault; it's their department." How the company or church for example is structured trains a way of thinking which ultimately influences behavior. "The long-term, most insidious consequence of applying non-systemic solutions is increased need for more and more of the [same] solution" (Senge, p. 61).

Leadership must realize that 1) structure influences behavior, 2) structure in human systems is subtle, and 3) leverage comes from new ways of thinking. Basic interrelationships control and manipulate certain behavior like in living systems for example where the cardiovascular and the neuromuscular interconnect and have subtle influences. How people make decisions is often a result of policies and processes and those policies and processes therefore have the ability to create certain instabilities if the system is corrupt (Senge, p. 40).

- Because they "become their position," people do not see how their actions affect the other positions.
- Consequently, when problems arise, they quickly blame each other – "the enemy" becomes the players at the other position, or even the customers.
- By and large, they don't learn from their experience because the most important consequences of their actions occur elsewhere in the system, eventually coming back to create the very problems they blame on others.
- The "teams" running the different positions (usually there are two or three individuals at each position) become consumed with blaming the other players for their problems, precluding any opportunity to learn from each others' experience (Senge, p. 51-52).

Leadership must expose shared destiny, accountability, and transparency. By enlisting participation in the creation of new ideas from the people and including them in the direction of the movement, the conversation will help teach us better ways to move. We must learn to focus on whole solutions for total systems thinking, dissolution of the "event," and finally interconnectivity.

We must learn to instill a cooperation that produces collaboration and connections so that more and more of us can take ownership of creativity and ingenuity and pass it on. We must participate in our future and help shape our destiny. I believe that if we can tap that innate desire to innovate and from that glean unique and wonderful advances, our ingenuity and productivity will accelerate and multiply. For example,

> More companies are improving their supply chains by adopting collaborative forecasting, in which different departments work together on planning. Some companies also integrate operations with suppliers and distributors to share data and so improve forecasting accuracy...More specifically, these

companies are requiring different departments…to share more information and work together on setting sales and production goals. They are regularly reviewing how close forecast come to actual results, and making adjustments in production and marketing as needed (Wall Street Journal, Jain and Covas, R10, Monday, July 7, 2008).

Autonomy, Accountability, and Tyranny

Running an organization through one mind of one leader in a small company or one concept from a select board of executives atop a large organization ultimately kills systemic innovation because others cannot participate in the solving or drafting of solutions. There isn't any conversation or autonomy. Instead, it's built on a platform of hierarchy and disconnectedness. The structure encourages them to disengage. It shackles collaboration and caps creativity.

Much like a dictatorship or tyranny, the people within the country are disallowed from participating in the shaping and making of the government and its ruling orders and laws. They collect the disseminated information and act on the laws set by the "top." There isn't any self governance because a very small percentage disperses the data and tells the rest what to do.

However, in collaborative environments where there is a lot of conversation, the checks and balances are set within the accountability of the communities if they operate in foundational values and core principles, and if the community disapproves of something the people can make the change. The people influence and ultimately decide the principles of ruling and organizing through their approval and or disapproval. They vote it in or vote it out. In other words, the leaders are subject to the majority and not the majority subject to the leaders. The leaders and the community members are held accountable. In a system where everyone is held accountable, a system can build on transparency and community. Without accountability in a system that also promotes autonomy through free forming relationships and networks, true chaos (disorder) will set in instead of self organizing systems.

One company that is practicing living this autonomy and accountability and encouraging this creativity is consequently reaping profitable rewards within its employee satisfaction and on the financial bottom line. This autonomy is a core principle in Whole Foods as it doles out new relationships of freedom every day to its teams:

> This exceptional degree of autonomy conveys a simple but invigorating message: it is you, rather than some distant manager, who controls your success. The fact that this freedom is matched by a high level of accountability ensures that associates use their discretionary decision-making power in ways that drive the business forward. Unlike so many other companies, frontline employees at Whole Foods have both the freedom to do the right thing for customers, and the incentive to do the right thing for profits (Hamel, p. 73).

The goal of autonomy and accountability is to help the organization learn within the community and therefore develop its people personally and professionally and thereby increase its market share for the company's profitability. Its task is to navigate through a complicated, traditional rhythm and undo years of habit and behavior in the old system. It's about bringing people together with people to collaborate within an arena of different mindsets. We must learn to disrupt typical behavior and realign it to new expectations, begin connecting systems, start conversations, solve the issue together, and allow a little chaos to pose new relationships.

We need shared responsibility in order to see out of an old maze and out of an older structure and open up to system thinking. "Systems thinking is a discipline for seeing whole. It is a framework for seeing interrelationships rather than things, for seeing patterns of change rather than 'static snapshots.' And systems thinking is a sensibility – for the subtle interconnectedness that gives living systems their unique character" (Senge, p. 68-69).

Top Down in a Bottom Up World

In this dated style of command and control, people and processes simply carry out orders and do not invigorate the community with creativity. Therefore the structure of command and control influences static, negative looping patterns of behavior. In other words, instead of learning from the influencers -circumstance, events, and people - this negative loop learning reinforces bad behavior and encourages dysfunction in that it begins with a negative stimulus, moves to a stifling causal influence, and then loops fully back around to a negative result and debilitating effect. It promotes disconnected, linear behavior.

I clearly understand that it is a huge undertaking to alter historic behavior, "There is nothing more difficult to carry out, nor more doubtful of success or dangerous to handle, than to initiate a new order of things" (Booz, Allen, Hamilton, p. 1). However, to therefore leave it untouched and unchallenged because of its enormity is just as catastrophic because times demand new solutions. It will ultimately yield fruitful results if leadership undertakes this alteration of landscape and holds its course, but it will similarly fall and crumble like a dry brittle leaf in if we leave alone that which must be changed.

A Fall

I know of an organization that recently went through a major transition, and it was a transition specifically with the fall of leadership that rippled throughout the whole community. The fall came at the top and affected the whole. It caused membership to significantly dwindle, resources to be in jeopardy, the reputation in the community to be severely damaged, and any remaining trust by those left in the community was deeply marred.

124

Yet the issue that emerged from the tragedy was the structure. In the fall, the people ultimately were disconnected from the system's community because like so many organizations, it was top-down. Instead of co-creating during the recovery, the structure drew lines between the members and the leaders. Instead of infusing them together to participate as a collective body, they set up distinguishing camps. This structure left alone and detached, will ultimately yield the same behavior. In other words, if leadership doesn't change the structure, the organization is open to the same potential collapse in the future.

The Blame Game

You could and should look at the leader that fell and say that his actions caused the demise. One could examine the board for improper due diligence, or the search firm that spearheaded the search for the new leader, or his previous organization that employed him, or why those in the community that noticed oddities kept quiet. All of these should be looked at and examined and ultimately put on the table for a sincere discussion. However, I think the issue is bigger and deeper than a few leaders, bad decisions, deceptive practices, and a judging and unforgiving community. I think it is more pervasive than just some people made some really bad choices.

If structure really influences behavior and linear realities (A=B=C) cannot provide a thorough explanation, then perhaps the structure and architecture of the community and its connection to its history, its relationships, its core, its behavioral characteristics, its programs, its social structure, and its leadership is the one that should be more closely scrutinized. Note here that the scrutiny of which I am speaking is not to jump backwards and delve into event mentality and the blame game. The purpose is to make the whole system healthier, responsive, adaptive and intuitive through interconnectedness and understand its underlying influences. Nor am I saying that the behavior of the individual leader does not bare its own investigation and does not carry heavy consequences, but what does deserve closer inspection is how the structure of the organization, *allowed and permitted* the senior leader to behave unnoticed, and therefore how the community allowed itself to behave under the influence of its own structure.

For example, perhaps the very structure ushered in the failure: 1) The chaff rooted in the fiber of ritual that secretly applauded a certain mentality, 2) the community that overlooked clear distress signs, or 3) the emphasis was put on corporate image instead of integrity, transparency, and honesty.

The key to seeing reality systemically is seeing circles of influence rather than straight lines. This is the first step to breaking out of the reactive mindset that comes inevitably from "linear" thinking. Every circle tells a story. By tracing the flows of influence, you can see the patterns that repeat themselves, time after time, making situations better or worse...In systems thinking it is an axiom that every influence is both cause and effect. Nothing is ever influenced in just one direction (Senge, p. 75).

Because the organization was under an board of directors, by definition it fit into a Newtonian mindset. Members sat and waited for the leaders to tell its them how the organization will operate in this time of transition. Too much was left to too few. For example, during the search for a new leader, the community was disconnected from the search process. The majority of the members didn't know who was considered, where they were looking, where they were not looking, or the parameters of the search criteria. Under the structure, a small group of unelected leaders directed the search for the high level leader. The congregation waited in suspicion to see who would be their next leader. They could only hope and pray that he/she is what was needed. However, their direct and even peripheral input was apparently put on the perimeter. Some might think a leader who is a Type "X" for example is needed while another group will think a Type "Y" is required and yet another group altogether might see the need for a Type "XYZ" and on and on and on.

My point is not that the board can only make a wrong decision. Rather, the potential to make a hasty decision through the flaw of structure and a few select voices is probable. That's why I believe structure ushered in the fall of the organizational leader almost as much as the leader. The isolated group of directors was under the strained structure that perpetuated top down mentalities and ultimately a system of failed behavior. Therefore, leaving the structure untouched will potentially keep the system from truly growing and deeply learning because it is strapped to the ground by a model of an anachronistic structure.

I understand that "...companies focus primarily on the structure and processes of the initiative itself, and not on showing employees a 'truth' that motivates them, at a very basic human level, to invest themselves in the change[,]" but this practice then creates a huge disconnect between the members, their organization, and specifically their leadership (Booz, Allen, Hamilton, p. 2). This exclusion of them in the process of the search and discovery forges a chasm that stretches across a very deep canyon between the cliffs where the members stand and the cliffs where the leaders are perched.

Typical Structure

This is a typical structure of most organizations : too few make all the decisions and the rest just wait and hope. I believe this batters the community, displaces synergy, and leaves everyone in the system utterly disconnected. The boundaries of the structure like the example above need to be blurred and messy to let more resources and people into the mix to collaborate and interconnect. "Simply put, in order to forge fundamental change in a complex organization, mangers must focus on the human side of implementing change – what we call 'change management' – as much as the hard analytics behind the change" (Booz, Allen, Hamilton, p. 2).

The organization before the wild swing numbered roughly 4000 members and quickly fell to around 1800 - 2500 after the leadership debacle. The members were hurt and wounded. To begin to heal and be apart of the mending process, they needed to feel apart of the change and buy into the meaning of its own membership once again.

Not only were the people wounded from the event and kept in the dark, but there was an air of exclusion and detachment, a clear disconnect. The process of finding a new leader was funneled trough a top down mentality. The general population had little to no involvement in the strategy, vision, applications, and operating policies of the place. There was little to no collaboration between the "corporate body," the selection committee, middle managers and support staff, and the board of elders. This caused separation and the people dispersed, "A logical and well-designed strategy for change, if not centered around people, is doomed to remain just an elusive goal described by distant management team" (Booz, Allen, Hamilton, p. 2).

Suggestions

Instead of moving around and frantically shuffling through a tap dance of hierarchy and elder selection for the next leader, perhaps the leadership should have completely undone tradition and thrown some chaos and complexity into the mix where the whole system began to intermingle. In this case, the goal of system thinking would be in understanding "the major interrelationships underlying a problem [that would] lead to new insight into what might be done" (Senge, p. 72).

I am not advocating an abolishment of the board of directors or a leaderless body of workers run by whatever the crowd votes. There needs to be vision based around priorities from foundational values that the leaders drive, but that then needs to pollinate with the people, the power needs to be shared, and conversations need to be transparent.

There needs to be a bit of Twitter thrown into the mix - transparency, immediacy, accountability. The people need to be a part of the change and included in the selection and direction of the organization in order to promote interconnections.

I say this to highlight perhaps the real need for organizations to open up, bring together, and then connect networks to breathe life into a living system. Leadership needs to reveal the "Oz" behind the curtains and expose the probability that most of it is smoke and mirrors. We need to illumine the power of connectivity and interlocking dynamic structures that bring freedom. No one person knows the answer, but we can grow to find dynamic possibilities under random relationships.

Meanwhile, the community in this example above hoped someone in charge would eventually bring the "right" person. Instead, they waited relatively ill

127

informed and in the dark. Perhaps "it" can be found together. I don't mean together like around the campfire with smores in hand. I mean together under a new order that births new ideas and new possibilities through a more open dialogue with the people in the organization and their leaders. This way the system works through an intercon- nected network. Take this example of Toyota and GM:

> Just like Wikipedia edits, each and every suggestion made by a Toyota line worker was implemented. In decentralized fashion, teams functioned like a circle, and whatever ideal employees had for innovation were put into practice. And in Wikipedia fashion, if someone's suggestion proved counter-productive, another employee would inevitably make a suggestion to undo the previous suggestion.

> This an entirely different way of dealing with employees. Rather than regarding line workers as drones who had to follow directions and be kept in line, Toyota viewed its employees as key assets. Imagine the line workers' feeling of empowerment. Their opinions mattered. But Toyota didn't stop there. It also flattened its management hierarchy and equalized the pay scale. Now everyone was in it together. The net result of these innovations was that the cars Toyota produced were of dramatically higher quality than the vehicles that left the GM plant...[In the Japanese hybrid organization principles] "Our team dictates what we do and how we do it. Our group leaders comes by about half-hour per week," recalled one employee. "I feel that the team members are what's most important. We can function without management."

> {But we need to be careful also to not decentralize too far] ...Toyota occupied the decentralized sweet spot in the automotive industry. Had it centralized its assembly line to mirror GM's, it would have taken power away from employees and reduced vehicle quality. But on the other hand, hd Toyota decentralized too far - doing away with structure and controls and, say, letting each circle work on whatever car it felt like - the company would have a mess on its hands. Decentralization brings out creativity, but it also creates variance. One Toyota circle might very well make a wonderful automobile, while another might produce a junker. (Brafman and Beckstrom, p. 186-187).

I think organizations like this need a living systems approach, and it can be realized by connecting itself to the reality of our global, interdependent landscape. The system could flourish if the structure is opened and allowed to become a little "messy" yet still utterly accountable under established lines of priorities and values. Organizations need a way to facilitate and promote participation.

> But as the Web grew and users became more sophisticated, Google's new, more decentralize approach was very appealing. The site's algorithms, which depend on user input rather than on editorial experts, produced more relevant results. Google replaced Yahoo's expert editors with a decentralized solution.

128

The sweet spot in the search industry is still fluid, and it's hard to tell whether it's heading in one direction or the other (Brafman and Beckstrom, p. 195).

Consequently, the ugliness of the above problem manifested throughout the organization in so many ways: staff turnover, budget restriction and cutbacks, deleted and under funded programs, an accelerating decline in attendance, congregational doubt and misgivings, nervous and jittery perceptions, crippled leadership board, and an overall "anorexic feel."

By not changing the structure and only trying to find a new leader, the system pushed back. The mentality became that more of the same solution is needed. It's like throwing watercolor paint over graffiti only to have the graffiti still show through and then think that more watercolor will cover up the problem. More is not the solution; instead it is often just more of the same failed attempts. Peter Senge calls this "Compensating Feedback:"

> When well intentioned interventions call forth responses from the system, |it| offset|s| the benefits of the intervention. We all know what it feels like to be facing compensating feedback – the harder you push, the harder the system pushes back; the more effort you expend trying to improve matters, the more effort seems to be required...Pushing harder and harder on familiar solutions, while fundamental problems persist or worsen, is a reliable indicator of nonsystemic thinking- what we often call the "what we need is a bigger hammer" syndrome (Senge, p. 58,61).

Leadership in any organization must devise a way within its operations and specifically in its organizational development that encourages and teaches leadership and the community how to bring about new, unlikely relationships within its viding interconnectedness within the system. "If management |or leadership| can ...provide a credible vision of a better company, show the benefits that will result, and alleviate the inevitable human fear, anxiety, and discouragement during the transition, then the chances of implementing successful change will be greatly increased" (Booz, Allen, Hamilton, p. 7). The task is to break out of a one time, historically unique and systematically productive structure with its roots in the "factory mentality" and embrace the messiness of global, corporate change.

Changing a Soggy Diaper

Mark Twain once said that the only ones that really like and appreciate change is the baby who gets his soggy diaper changed. Change is difficult whether you are the one authoring the change or whether you are the one changing. Maintaining equilibrium is comfortable. It's safe. Conversely, change is painful and can even feel metaphorically toxic, like a burning sensation in your soul as you try to alter years of good and/or bad habits and traditions that roll around inside your brain like billowing waves in a tumultuous, undulating stormy sea. Stopping the momentum of these patterns seems hopeless and daunting. Change may seem like and feel like rowing to England from New York harbor in a row boat with one oar. However, our future and the human spirit demand that we press forward with positive and dynamic solutions to innovate ahead of this mounting force of change.

Under this new revolution, equilibrium puts the company or the person in a terminal spiral. The goal should not be to rhythmically swing like a pendulum and set your pace to its mark. To do this is a death sentence in a world of total interdependence and interconnectivity. To be steady and stayed in a chaotic, advancing global landscape is to be on the road to termination. I don't mean to confuse "steady" and "stayed" with balance, but rather where mediocrity or perpetual, repetitive behavior has replaced innovation. The question then clearly becomes how do you motivate people and organizations to jolt themselves from years and years of sameness or from thinking that because it worked then that it will keep working today and tomorrow? How do you bring about lasting, deep change that transforms the roots of the person, the company, the church, the school while their mentality is like a flat, listless lily pad gently swaying under ripples of comfort in a slippery pond of green, moldy sediment? How do you change thinking and ultimately how do you change and influence behavior to bring about real solutions? We must learn to look at our humanness, our spirit, our soul and what it means to be a living system. We must learn that meaning is found in the whole thing.

The significant thing here is that the Great Emergence is doing so; and the theology that comes from that work will be the theology, in part, of society's reconfigured understanding of the self, soul, the humanness of being imago dei. It will impact everything from medical policy to moral theory as well as evangelism and religious formation (Tickle, p. 162).

Surfers Understand that Meaning is Found in the Whole Thing:

- Like a wave is a manifestation of multiple, random intersections, leaderships needs to understand interrelationships and processes of change rather than static snapshots.
- Under older regimes, disruptions confuse compartmentalized organizations, but using the natural laws of interconnectivity they evolve the system; they bring solutions.
- What used to be measurable and predictable is now sporadic and indeterminate.
- The linear organizational structure is murky, slow, and inhibits speed and creativity because it is too thick, stifled, and filled with mechanistic structures. This is an era of speed.
- It is no longer the case where leadership can depend on machine like precision and measurable results to create a future that is controllable, where the unknown is minimized, and predictions are precise.
- At a point, we are all somehow connected, we are all neighbors, and these blurry borders and crumbling walls of a flatter world accelerate change.
- The internet and platforms like Twitter have transformed nearly the entire organizational mindset through speed, transparency, accessibility, and immediacy.
- Through linear thinking and controlling mindsets, leadership at large leaves creativity underutilized, unrealized, and unshaped.
- We are in a paradigm shift, and its transitioning organizational life into an arena where things are defined in their evolutionary state instead of a determinate, predictable patterns.
- Like an engine of a car, leadership typically believes that parts operate independent of each other with their own specific function performing only to the capacity their design and components allow.
- Leadership should be subject to the majority and not the majority subject to the leaders.
- Too much in the organization is left to too few.
- Usually the only person that appreciates change is the baby that gets a soggy diaper changed.

Chapter 4

Find the Natural Principles of Living Systems

A Living System

"The system in which we work is full of expectations cast upon us from our first breath. Every degree of success is accompanied by an equal dose of bureaucracy. Any early success that you may have only breeds higher expec- tations and a burden to deliver. This burden is a weight that often obstructs vision and sound judgement."

(http://the99percent.com/articles/7074/Vision-Without-Obstruction-What-We-Learn-From-Steve-Jobs)

"...True the man [Steve Jobs] has always shunned the status quo, but I believe his rebel ways were only a consequence of his efforts to stay true to an original vision. Jobs didn't think different just for the sake of it, he just refused to conform to traditional expectations and limitations."

(http://the99percent.com/articles/7074/Vision-Without-Obstruction-What-We-Learn-From-Steve-Jobs)

We are programmed early in life to perform to "expectations cast upon us" usually at the cost of a burden that only continues to mount. The more we get recognized by what the mainstream represents as success, the harder we press to accomplish more of the same. As we take on what the world deems successful, this then acts as a blockade to our natural principles. It confuses our innate drive and ambition to create and build relationships. In other words, in a world that is historically hierarchical, our natural principles have been subdued by controls that restrict our design. Instead, we need to find the natural principles in living systems that can unlock the insane potential in people and organizations. Listen to how Toyota found natural principles in their system:

> Just like Wikipedia edits, each and every suggestion made by a Toyota line worker was implemented. In decentralized fashion, teams functioned like a circle, and whatever ideas employees had for innovation were put into practice. And in Wikipedia fashion, if someone's suggestion proved counter-productive, another employee would inevitably make a suggestion to undo the previous suggestion...'The Confucian concept, which the West shares, assumes that the purpose of learning is to qualify oneself for a new, different, and bigger job...within a certain period of time the student reaches a pla-teau of proficiency, where he then stays forever. The Japanese concept may be called the Zen approach. The purpose of learning is self-improvement. It qualifies a man to do his present task with continually wider vision, con-tinually increasing competence, and continually rising demands on himself" (Braffman & Beckstrom, p. 186-187)

Do you ever wonder how we work? Do you ever step back to be amazed at the complexity within our own bodies, our minds, our brains, and our conscious-ness and how it all interconnects, works in a surreal collaboration and continually propels us forward to push to better places? Do you ever wonder how ants seem to overcome and always continue on the their trail no matter the leaf or branch that falls in their way? Do you ever stand on the balcony of a crowded mall or a place like Central Station in NYC and watch people scramble, bump, and jostle in a crowd? They swerve, dodge, move, shoulder each other, and adjust their path of travel according to the influence of those around them. All of these things, seem to be a swirl of blurring movements. If you look real close, you might just see a mess, but if you really, really look close and into its layers, there is dynamic interconnectivity in the undulating. If you look beyond the scramble and into its layers, you will find a system, a living system.

If you watch the ants, a crowd, traffic, and even your own body, you will see this complex, interwoven, highly connected system that at a distant glance works autonomously within a maze of networks. All of these examples of a living system work because they can diffuse confusion and use it to make their system better. The ants, the crowds, the traffic, even you have a subtle governance with mutable laws, interactive agents, and a natural structure that encourages collabo-ration and high levels of communication. I know this like science jargon, but we will see why understanding these systems make these times we live in so fantastic.

In the examples above, there is a deeply ordered set of principles that govern their interactions but don't control or manipulate the system or the outcome. These laws quickly move an entire ant colony around a branch or leaf, constantly adjust the crowd in a train station, and ultimately move traffic on the freeway. All of these disheveled pictures are images of a living system - a natural and deep order interacting within a highly connected system that creates complex change.

It *looks* like a big mess, but its really important that you begin to see that it is actually propelled by mutually interactive agents and mutable or "soft" and changeable laws. In other words, one movement in a highly connected environment perpetuates a continuum of other movements that creates a swirl of activity and acts in chorus as a system. For example, because of this random connectivity like a crowded train station, you can't pick patterns or predict movements because if one person decides to move left, the person on her left may dart forward or to the side to avoid the bump and her move will affect those around who might dart left or dart right. A movement perpetuates movement but we cannot predict where or what it will be or to what degree the movement will affect the system.

One movement in a crowd by one person stirs activity because of the crowds proximity within itself and that's why we see the bumping and moving and jostling. Their closeness speeds other movements and potentially the bigger the crowd the more dynamic the ripple. Just because I move one way in a crowded Central Station, there is no way to predict the amount of movements that might come from my one movement. The only guarantee is that my movement will influence the system to some degree. The only valid prediction is that movement might beget dynamic or subtle movements.

How do you predict patterns like this? How can you forecast in a market that acts like a crowded train station? How can you make definitive movements in a world that is forever changing and restructuring because of its closeness?

We cannot control things, people, their speed, or much less predict what influence a movement will have internally. Nor does this reality make it easy to predict what is coming next or what an action or disturbance will have externally. Although it does make for some of the most exciting times to be alive, it poses problems because we can only really look at probabilities and proximity. The only certainty today is that there is an undisclosed order, and to unwind its web we need to learn to recognize its characteristics. Understanding these characteristics will help untangle things a bit, but the greater hope is that it will infuse leadership with a new wonder and excitement about learning the art of surfing.

A Close Scramble of Networks

The world is a close scramble of networks. Like these scenes - the ants, train station, mall, our bodies, the internet - even though they appear just as a random collection, they actually have deep underlying principles that govern the movements and create their dynamic interdependencies. We can't predict the outcomes but we can imply probabilities, and we can assume that connectivity speeds things up.

Complexity science takes the principles of a living system and applies them to life, markets, businesses, churches, companies, crowds, people and traffic to grapple with these confounding intricacies of change. It provides new insights and new rules for living that address the problematic nature of our world in complex and diverse flux. It helps to unravel patternless movements, unfamiliar structures, emergence, and a world that has grown restless with linearity. Consequently, the world is stirred with fascination over this growing and changing conversation, because if this is all true, then we can interact with mutable laws and actually change outcomes. We can move about in a flat world instead of becoming locked and fused in sectors.

- It has evoked wonder and excitement about the living world around us – how life surges and declines; how nature competes, cooperates, and thrives on change.
- It has whetted some managerial appetites for a new approach that might help to unshackle the potential of people and organizations and has begun to challenge the machine model as a suitable management platform for the information age (Pascale, p. 5).

We get to interact with life, undulate with communal discoveries, and surge forward on a wave that frees the human soul and mind to life as we peer down its unfurling line. Understanding these characteristics and wrestling with such intrinsic truths will help us develop into better leaders.

When we can learn to recognize the behavioral characteristics, we can better navigate. I am not saying we can draw out a blueprint if we get a hold of this, but it will begin to help us connect to our own design and therefore that of others within our organization and the organization itself.

In order for the leader, manager, pastor, executive, or teacher to navigate through this convoluted maze, we must all learn to recognize certain characteristics and behavior specific to our times and be okay with them. Things like:

- Emergence - things rising up from unusual places that are dissimilar to an original form or essence.
- Non-linear vs. linear thinking - seeing things other than A=B=C or 1+1=2 for example. Looking for the story through interdependencies instead of direct cause and effect.
- Unpredictability - incapable to exactly determine outcomes because we can't find dependable patterns that reproduce themselves in manner we can predict.
- Random couplings - unusual things come together to form unusual entities.
- Evolving patterns - instead of rhythmic patterns with dependable outcomes we have to wait and watch it evolve before we know what it will be.
- Uncertainty- we are more certain of uncertainty and probability than we are of predictability and precision
- Blurring boundaries - the lines, boundaries and fences of things typically penned and corralled within quadrants are blurry and blended.
- Complex *yet* adaptive - systems that appear chaotic really have adaptability because of their proximity and interconnectivity.
- Unlikely relationships - interdependence produces relationships that wouldn't and couldn't have formed otherwise in a compartmentalized system with boundaries.

- Odd looking systems, processes, and structures that break from traditional patterns.

Listen to what David Gibbons - a pastor that advocates what he calls the third-culture - talks about how the world is changing.

Western, sequential, how-to approach has not resonated in much of the world. And its not going to... It also doesn't find a receptive audience with most people in post-Boomer generations in almost any country in the world, including in the the West. But the ethos coming to life in our new world is requiring us to rethink how we approach and talk about [life and this world]... Some of the new forces at work include the democratization of the world; the flattening of authority structures in businesses and major social institutions; the appeal to grassroots values and methods in social-problem solving; the erosion of trust in leaders and intrusions; the shifting of economic and cultural power influence for West to East; and the movement from individu- alistic decision-making to tribal or corporate decision-making (Gibbons, p. 104-105).

He depicts in his chart the distinctive mind-set between the older guard and the vanguard and how the differences between someone, some organization, or some mind-set thinks in a more non-linear or chaotic fashion (Third-culture Rhythms) versus the traditional linear, more modern fashion (Typical Western Pathways). Look at how different they are and where the disconnect is between the new way and the traditional way (Gibbons, p.105).

Typical Western Pathways	Third-Culture Rhythms
Linear	Adaptive/liquid
Orderly Steps	Messy Journey
Individual	Community
Categorizes	Holistic
Teaches	Guides
Cookie-Cutter	Customized
Western	Eastern Fusion
Comfort	Painful
Programmed	Artful
Homogenous	Multicultural

A living system veers away from mechanistic applications of "command and control" and moves toward a whole systems approach where community and conversation is essential and authority is decentralized. The impact of a living system, or an open system and its spontaneous evolutions disrupts the traditional framework and introduces new patterns of indeterminate, interdependent behaviors.

In a decentralized system, there's no clear leader, no hierarchy, and no headquarters. If and when a leader does emerge, that person has little power over others. The best that person can do to influence people is to lead by example...This doesn't mean that a decentralized system is the same as anarchy. There are rules and norms, but these aren't enforced by any one person. Rather, the power is distributed among all the people and across geographic regions...Instead of a chief, the Apaches had a Nant'an - a spiritual and cultural leader. A Nant'an had no coercive power. Tribe members followed the Nant'an because they wanted to, not because they had to. [Geronimo was a Nant'an.] Geronimo never commanded an army. Rather, he himself started fighting, and everyone around him joined in. The idea was "If Geronimo is taking arms, maybe it's a good idea. Geronimo's been right in the past, so it makes sense to fight alongside him." You wanted to follow Geronimo? You followed Geronimo. You didn't want to follow him? Then you didn't. The power lay with each individual - you were free to do what you wanted. The phrase "you should" doesn't even exist in the Apache language. Coercion is foreign concept.

The Nant'ans were crucial to the well being of this open system, but decentralization affects more than just leadership. Because there was no capital and no central command post, Apache's decisions were made all over the place. A raid on a Spanish settlement, for example, could be conceived in one place, organized in another, and carried out in yet another. You never knew where the Apaches would be coming from. In one sense, there was no place where important decisions were made, and in another sense, decisions were made by everybody everywhere.

On first impression, it may sound like the Apaches were loosey-goosey and disorganized. In reality, however, they were an advanced and sophisticated society - flexibility, shared power, ambiguity - made the Apaches immune to attacks that would have destroyed a centralized society (Brafman and Beckstrom, P. 20-21).

Leadership needs to find new, unlikely connections that promote sustainable learning, nimble behavior, and flexible thinking to unleash the synergy quietly pulsating deep within the organization, the community, and the person. If we don't alter the system as it is today, the results will continue to be meager and static. "When placed in the same system, people, however different, tend to produce similar results. [This] systems perspective tells us we must look beyond individual mistakes or bad luck to understand important problems" (Senge, p. 42).

Push for Change

When I was an English Literature teacher, I used poetry to connect student's to their own undisclosed thoughts and their subconscious to stir up creative expression. I remember a particular poetry project that I assigned. Usually, the minute I assigned the work I was met with moans and groans of the young teenagers writhing in their seats, squirming like a worm exposed to the sun, and pronouncing their disgust with their familiar "Ahhhhhhh, Mr. Hansen..." Their pimply, zestful, ambitious faces would grimace and wince in pain as they anticipated - or dreaded in most cases - creating. I think unconsciously they feared the idea of original thought. I think they feared the disturbance.

I know most teenagers, adults for that matter like writing poetry as much as they enjoy weeding a matted hillside or getting a molar torn from their gum line, but the issue here is something more than writing a poem or doing creative work. It's the fear of disrupting familiarity and comfortable practices with something unusual and different.

But as a teacher, I know disruptions are good because they jar loose fragile, familiar patterns and make room for new movement. Although unpleasant, disruptions move us toward the edge. I used poetry like this in my classroom because it pressed our minds to become nimble and flexible and interactive.

This is how the assignment worked. They had to create the poem in class in about an hour's time. The assignment was given very little instruction, guidelines, or boundaries. They were to simply "let the poem materialize" through the provided resources (magazines), but namely they were to dig inside themselves, find and develop a theme, and cut out printed words from the magazines to arrange a poetic message. It was unique in that it was not a poem they prepared over a day, a week, or even for homework, and it didn't have to adhere to a formulaic pattern.

It went like this: I gave them a pile of magazines, scissors, construction paper, and glue, and they were to sift through the magazines and cut out only printed words within the magazines that resonated with them and a particular line of thought with a specific theme. They could use rhyme, rhythm, blank verse or no format at all, and make it any length they wanted. Of course the poem had to be clean, not too personal, and classroom friendly, but other than that they could create anything that came to their mind while they were sifting cover to cover and let new relationships "bubble up."

What I found every year was astonishing. Those poems without fail, for the five years that I taught were by far the most revealing, complex, imaginative, creative, and fascinating poems that my students wrote of any kind. The unparalleled freedom, moderate structure, and blurry boundaries within the assignment forcefully opened up their imagination, unlocked their creativity, and ignited free and spontaneous learning. As they explored and interconnected with emotions, thought, experience, and the looser structure of the assignment, they tapped into a vein that many students had no idea was even there. From the superstar student to the struggling, underperforming student, their individual poems were of stellar quality and filled with original, revealing insight. The poems across the board were more often than not just short of amazing. I believe this happened for 3 reasons, and these reasons coincide with the deep order of living systems. 1) I brought in a disturbance to their system of learning, 2) I took down the parameters that metered outcomes to a prescribed form and function, and 3) I opened them up to a learning process through new and unlikely relationships. The journey "enhance[d] [their]capacity to create" (Senge, p. 14).

The Edge

I don't do well with heights. Anything close to a roof ledge, the stairwell in my house, an unguarded mountain peak, or a ski mountain chair lift elevated high above the slopes, I get a twinge deep in my gut. I remember standing on the edge of a run while snowboarding in Mammoth, CA one winter nervously peering over the lip down a white wall of powder as the wintry wind flew along and up its icy face hitting me cold. I looked out and over the peaked landscape perched high above the snow covered valley and was immediately filled with a tremendous awareness, an almost alive but fearful sensation. The mountain's edge felt overbearing as though I was a helpless dot, like the tiny prey of an ancient behemoth about to be consumed. Everything was crazy and my head was spinning. I felt small and out of control as I leaned down and over the very lip of the mountain's crest. My senses were pricked and my awareness heightened as I dangled out and over. I was rushed with a trembling. I was afraid, but I felt also keenly alive and finely tuned.

If we let it, this flat world with all of its edges can bring a similar feeling of the edge as it dangles your mind and spirit over the canyon where your vulnerability is pricked. On this edge is where the senses and the capacities are heightened and awareness becomes the enlightenment.

Going back to my students and this dreaded poetry assignment elicits a similar response. The example of a black diamond run or global connectivity may seem exaggerated as compared to the poetry project, but the idea is to depict the notion that although the edge is scary and daunting for anyone in any stance and the emotional rush of the event seems out of control, the edge pushes change. It brings out the unknown, the hidden and the complicated and negotiates with things unfound. This is exactly the place this poetry assignment brought my students. Although they were brought in a small way to their "creative" edge, our world today brings us a similar edge. And we must respond systemically if we are to develop new patterns of learning.

Whether its a class assignment, the lip of a mountains edge, or the accelerating pace of a vastly connecting world, we need the edge. Although its perhaps scary, its necessary. Edge thinking is important. Listen to the process it brought to student learning. First, they got nervous, "How can I write this poem? How can I ever create a poem especially a revealing poem about me?" Second, they became afraid that they weren't smart enough and that it would look bad. Third, they hesitated because it challenged how they thought and the capacity of their thinking. "Why do we have to do stupid poetry Mr. Hansen?" Finally, their fear caused them to freeze. Their traditional mode and linear structures froze up the system. Instead of a disturbance encouraging new output, it actually put them in a standstill because of a mind-set.

We tend to see life in straight lines but Senge firmly believes as I mentioned earlier that life is made of circles of causality. Something is always being influenced by its predecessor and consequently it similarly acts as an influencer on what proceeds it.

> What we see depends on what we are prepared to see. Western languages...are biased toward linear-view. If we want to see systemwide interrelationships, we need a language of interrelationships, a language made up of circles. Without such a language, our habitual ways of seeing the world produce fragmented views and counterproductive actions. Such a language is important in facing dynamically complex issues and strategic choices, especially when individuals, teams, and organizations need to see beyond events and into the forces that shape change...When reading feedback circle diagram, the main skill is to see the 'story' that the diagram tells: how the structure creates a particular pattern of behavior (or, in a complex structure, several patterns of behavior) and how that pattern might be influenced. [For example, filling a glass of water] Here the story is filling the water glass and gradually closing down the faucet as the glass fills" (Senge, p. 74,76).

Creative thinking frightened my students, and frankly it frightens most of us. It pushes most of us to the edge only to freeze. But if we open up to a system that has a deep order of interdependence and probabilities, we can write that poem.

The poetry lesson is about breaking apart compartmentalization, and the lesson facing us now is that we need to open up the system. By connecting content to their found themes from their life experience, they were able to see connections to life that previously were hidden. Because I was able to see the connectivity in their own lives to the thought of writing a poem, I knew where to push them. If I thought linear, I would only teach toward completion and not toward the connectivity. How often do you fit the task to route application instead of breaking free and push into the learning? Leadership must understand the patterns and its resistance so that we can overcome the hurdles that keep our organizations and our people from learning.

Thinking from a linear view point, I might see a static snippet and mere resistance:

Assignment = Student Resistance = Poor Product Quality=
(Missed Opportunity)

However, if I were to map the circle of influence (Senge) using the assignment as the starting point, it might go like this: I would draft the assignment and post it to the class, which would typically and immediately get negative feedback because academia is performance based – widgets, factory mindset, and compartmentalization- which elicits fear of judgment, which brings fear of performance, which produces insecurity because society says, "You are as good as is your product," which blocks fluid and creative ability, which disallows interdependencies, which produces poor product quality, which brings them back to negative feedback from the assignment which brings them back to their perceived notions that they cannot create real and credible content.

Wherever you start in the circle, the loop continues on to the same points throughout the continuum. However, by understanding the circle of influencers, I was able to overcome the resistance because I understood their fear; by under- standing their fear and negative influencers, I was able to circumvent the resistance and teach to their insecurity and create a new confidence within the students that then allowed them to connect with a new and elaborate vein of creativity. They were then capable of interacting with real information and new relationships.

Now listen, I'm not saying that this one exercise contained the revolutionary answers to teaching and the means that forced the mind to critically think for the first time. I am not ascribing to some higher enlightenment that I alone have and I alone have found. Nor am I saying that as a teacher I found the key to unlock the kingdom, but I did find something very unique for me as I studied the learning process. This assignment and ones like it perhaps do press the minds closer to the edge by the very nature of their ambiguity and by the way they require the learner to manipulate and intermingle with unlikely relationships.

As they were pressed to spontaneously create under a new and vague paradigm, they were exposed to subjectivity and truly creative potential that under more restrictive guidelines might not have manifested. Sure they might have created a poem if the directions were more specific and the message was required to be strategically crafted – rhyme scheme, alliteration, metaphors, rhythm, theme, etc. - but the end result would have been less effective and less revealing. The assignment pushed change toward unfound messages where evolving discoveries fired like synapses on the brain.

Traditional Classroom

Both of my parents have been teachers my whole life. Whether it was their students in their classroom or being mom and dad to me and my sister, they were always teaching. In reflection, there are moments where I even felt like I was practically raised in the classroom. I was often at their respective schools after my school day was done waiting for them to finish up the next day's prep. I was either with my dad doodling on the construction paper or molding clay as he rearranged a multitude of student's work in his famous, highly interactive art room in F-2, or I was with my mom helping her pick lively stories and fun field trips for her jittery kindergarteners.

I grew up watching them be very successful and very much loved by the students. They learned how to illicit emotional and intellectual responses through innovation in their lessons, and by the very nature in which they interacted with their students they lavished them with respect and intrigue. They treated them all like creations full of potential and provided them the option and a means to discover intricacies and detailed revelations.

The psalmist in the Bible depicts how seriously they took the individuals that were entrusted to them in their classroom. They treated them with great care and an unearthly awareness of their potential like the Psalmist says in Psalm 139, "For you created my inmost being; you knit me together in my mother's womb. I praise you because I am fearfully and wonderfully made." They learned how to engage the student and help put actual shape to change by understanding that in order to obtain highly performing pupils, the very core of the creative, learning pupil had to be tapped.

For example, my dad annually created a lesson plan where the students had to collaborate and create their own full length animation film with a team of students. They had to create the story, design the layout, do the actual drawing for each slide, put it together and then film the project. His projects, whether they were the films they made or magazine collage they assembled, always seemed to push the student's creatively. He adorned his entire room with their projects, and the minute you entered his room you could see that they were dripping with inspiration like ripe fruit from ceiling to floor. Anybody walking in the room would have been creatively aroused and at least highly intrigued by any of the odd combinations of vivid colors, eclectic styles, unique expressions, and layered images. His classroom visually stimulated mental activity as their imaginations bubbled all over the room through their hanging projects. Colors mingled and popped while sculptures dangled into form almost coming alive; this visually chaotic display prompted unlikely artistic creations and combinations that put form to secret fields of expression deep within the student.

My parents helped shape their process of thinking by helping them explore new avenues of thought. I know there were other great teachers breaking from tradition as they continually saw the model become less and less effective, but I saw first hand the effect from my parents as they daily exerted their influence on the student's lives. They confounded the usual setting (nothing revolutionary but still important) with simple changes to seating with cluster, blocks, and circular arrangements along with lessons that were more interactive, intuitive, and subjective. My dad had unique and challenging flexibility with the art and photography medium with his middle-schoolers while my mom with 5-6 year old kindergartners was challenged with the limited attention span of a younger mindset. None-the-less, they both through different stages encouraged creative, critical thinking every day in the classroom that fostered thinking "up and out."

The students were challenged to mingle and uniquely process information and then respond with value that demonstrated original thought. This was different in that the more traditional model was in part based on the image of the industrial factory where the classroom was like the assembly line filled with students assigned to widget-like functions from teachers perched high above the factory floor in a distant office.

Picture this: Typically, the desks in a traditional classroom were arranged like rows in a factory. The students and their desks were in symmetrical, vertical rows from the top of the classroom to the back walls. The vibe was very stiff, sterile, and restrictive. Maybe a poster or two was hung on the wall to feign interactive distractions and break the sterility, but even then the images were lifeless and boring – a flower with a math equation scribbled over the petals, or perhaps a hillside adorned with a clever quip about never quitting, etc. It actually perpetuated the assembly line mentality where they were only permitted to view and "be next to" what the boss was thinking and not actually interact with the thought process of the community. The students like the factory workers couldn't interconnect and really participate with the plant's whole production. They could only be responsible for their isolated area of responsibility.

This physical set up of this traditional classroom didn't interact with the mind and force it to visually innovate and see anything other than what they saw facing forward (linear thought). The mind got stuck in a mentality through an image of the forward facing rows that then dwarfed into an ideology where the parts make up the whole. They couldn't collaborate or interconnect with other students because the environment was conducive primarily to disconnect from the whole system. The students were disjointed and removed from each other as well as the actual lesson's synergy. The conditions for learning generally were compartmentalized and the instruction was inhibitive.

I understand this example might be generalized, but as a teacher of 5 years I saw the routine and I saw the classrooms. I knew of some teachers who taught from the same lesson plans and from the same yellow, legal tablet of paper for many years never altering the content. Not only did they never recreate their own lessons for their own learning, they never recreated them to stimulate generative learning within their classrooms. They never pushed their students or themselves to the edge. Their walls were dead and the environment was as stimulating as a padded room. They exhibited the factory model of command and control and parts equal the whole all the while in the 21st century with sterile seating, objective lessons, route interaction, linear constructs, disconnections, and authoritative structures.

Don't Just Open Your Mind

I don't want to say simply that I like to help people "open their minds." It sounds too simple and in truth it's not the actual application I want exposed. In other words, it isn't opening your mind like a window when it's hot because you are looking for a breeze or opening a box because you want to see what's inside. I believe the activity is perhaps simple as we "let go" and allow connections to fire like synapses in the brain, but the concept is difficult because we have to unlearn and disconnect, relearn, and then be prepared to continually and always be reshaped.

The idea of systemwide connectivity doesn't simply provide answers but brings a dynamic setting that authors collective creativity. We are so used to siphoning information, putting it through a different spin, and renaming it to call it "a new idea." Where in fact, it is just recycled information that has been given a new curb appeal. Instead, learning through chaos and complexity is about allowing relationships and new combinations to emerge and develop through an often uncomfortable move away from the familiar and into brand new territo- ries. It's about personal and communal interconnectivity through making blurry boundaries that traditionally separate departments and disconnect people and discussions.

With blurry boundaries, we can interconnect and interact for example over details, ideologies, philosophies, beliefs, data, etc., and this encourages an inter-mingling of the minds so that unique and perhaps crazy solutions can be tried and applied. Unlike the piston mentality, there isn't one answer for a problem. There are perhaps many answers, or many combinations of old ideas that form hybrid solutions because people are allowed and encouraged to mix energies and intel-lect. For example, why should it only be a specific department that solves their issues? Why shouldn't it be the engaged employees from different departments that come together to solve an issue for the company because they are a part of the system seeking to better their community? Why is it just an elder board of a church or a pastor that addresses policy, sermons, structure, Spirit, or discipline? Why can't a cooperative and yet autonomous and accountable community author the change or address concerns or structure sermon direction?

An engaged employee connected to a community of engaged employees or an engaged church member connected to a community of members share in the participation because they are allowed to become a community through the inter-connectivity of the total system. Their autonomy and accountability produce a sense of ownership and belonging, and if they participate in directional decisions and vision casting then they become valued. The idea is to rid the mentality of the "paycheck" for example as the motivator and replace it with the truth that they are a contributor that impacts the significance of their environment and community.

Creating hybrid teams to solve problems is not a new concept I know, but what would be different is a leader who gives deliberate autonomy and authority to a randomly evolving group to evaluate and immediately make highly visible decisions for the community?

Traditionally, controlled creativity and select committees are allowed to meet under prescribed conditions to propose solutions if the "higher ups" approve of their findings. However, the solutions are usually old discoveries redressed and reformatted. Without truly innovative discovery and randomly connecting groups, recycled answers will continue to resurface and therefore more of same answers will be in demand because there are still no real solutions. The power is not found in control but in letting go and letting emergence spread throughout an organization. It opens up true potential.

A centralized organization is easy to understand. Think of any major company or governmental agency. You have a clear leader who is in charge, and there's a specific place where decisions are made. [We call this] organizational type coercive because the leaders call the shots...Decentralized systems on the other hand, are a little trickier to understand. In a decentralized organization, there's no clear leader, no hierarchy, no headquarters. If and when a leader does emerge, that person has little power over others. The best that person can do to influence people is to lead by example. [We will call this] an open system, because everyone is entitled to make his or her own decisions. This doesn't mean that decentralized system is the same as anarchy. There are rules and norms, but they aren't enforced by any one person. Rather, the power is distributed among all the people and across geographic regions (Brafman and Beckstrom, p 19-20).

There is a forest fire brewing within us all, but that very fire has historically been contained within a small campfire set to only warm a small pot of coffee. This natural configuration has been shrouded in thick, dense vines from an older mind-set. I know what is rambling through your mind and you are correct, autonomy unbridled, especially in a group setting with dispersed power, will produce a negative and unproductive chaos where it is just one big mess. But this interconnectivity and systemwide mentality is about autonomy with accountability and transparency.

We need to tear down walls that squelch true discovery. It transfers energy away from new endeavors and restricts the continuance of newly formed relationships. Fear, unnecessary tradition, or disconnected compartments block innovation within human development, but if the edge of chaos is carefully managed it can displace and disrupt the familiar into ripe, unique innovation.

Teaching

I am passionate about teaching whether as an English Literature schoolteacher, a youth leader in my church on the high school volunteer staff for 10 years, or as a business leader for over a decade. I see my role as a facilitator of development in the student at school, the youth at our church, and my employees where I work.

As a teacher, especially with young teenagers, I had to engage their learning (academically, socially, and spiritually) to increase their output and growth. Consequently, I see my role as a leader in a business organization akin to that of

145

a teacher and church counselor. In other words, I need to engage the employee's participation and contribution to the organization to increase our profitability while connecting a certain significance of their job to an intrinsic connection to value.

Teaching English Lit

Teaching English Literature did not make the task an easy journey. I mean let's be serious, who really likes grammar or even cares much about subject versus predicate? Who is remotely intrigued about independent clauses or adverbial phrases? Who wants to know the reason why it's better to say, "I feel well" instead of "I feel good?"

Unless I found a connection for them or pressed them for outside thinking, they were often nonplussed and disconnected from the subject and generally, like most teenagers, disengaged from an assignment, a specific task, or a reading. They might do the work, but they weren't innovative and their responses lacked ingenuity. It was a flat exchange.

I wanted more from them and I believed more was possible, but they were not challenged and their learning wasn't disrupted enough to generate creativity because of the typical educational structure they were used to drew them in instead of pulled them out. However, because I believed deeply in their development and in their own ability to accelerate their discovery, I tried to find new ways to liven the lesson and expand connections between learning and the student.

I initiated self and group discovery through lessons like emergent poetry, (mentioned in the previous example of magazines turned to poetry), literature based thematic discussions – love, fear, and courage in Romeo and Juliet; sacrifice, community, and justice in Lord of the Flies; power, insecurity, and betrayal in Julius Caesar - "living" grammar lessons where we walked the campus categorizing actual items into grammatical columns, – *trashcan* is a noun; *sitting* is a verb; *pep rally* is a noun; *running from the teacher* is a gerund phrase; *brown building* is an adjective; - and structured journaling where they would write about a theme, idea, or specific character to evidence an intellectual journey and a process of discovery that demonstrated new learning.

I wasn't always after the "right" answer. Instead, because literature and poetry allowed subjectivity, I pushed for new connections, new revelations, unique insight, key references to life applications, specific original thought, and new conversations. My goal was to connect bits or vignettes of their lives, characters in their own life story, and real circumstances in their various situations to themes in novels, messages in short stories, or diverse interpretations of poetry so that through inner connections they might learn and instinctively create. By extending the content to "marry" with their intimate and personal connections, they might better see messages I was trying to communicate.

In turn, conversely I was able to learn from them as they helped to open my mind and teach me how to continue learning. I wanted to encourage a learning that tapped into a natural human intuition through non-linear thinking. I wanted them to think beyond the classroom and a grade or mark that I might give them on an essay and move into a field of dynamic discovery where grammar made sense in a pragmatic application and where reading stories and poetry opened interpersonal comprehension.

In other words, I could simply assign exercise after exercise and expose them to parts of speech, grammar and syntax and force feed them like factory workers, but I thought if we'd walk the campus and connect what they see every day to what I was teaching about grammar it might produce a better "stickiness" factor. Therefore, they might find the journey of discovery enticing, and perhaps they might even write sentences with more syntactical awareness and understanding. Perhaps they might understand their particular situation better with their family or close friends by understanding a character like Ralph or Jack in Lord of the Flies. Perhaps they might communicate more succinctly because interaction with the content and its real life application provided a link from the classroom to the world in which they lived, walked, and breathed.

By digging into and plowing through themes and delving into the characters behavior and personality in literature, I was able to use stories and poetry to bring out real life issues in classic themes that would intertwine within the student's own lives. The connection became alive and real as they were able to indulge in the discovery of their own lives and behavior through other characters and themes. They began to see themselves with deeper comprehension and in turn communicate with those around them with better clarity.

Given proper boundaries within autonomous principles and constant performance accountability that rests on an operation of interconnections and creativity, people, productivity, and inspired output are prone to develop. If these conditions strategically teach to think up and think out of nominal traditional patterns, an innovative, natural learning will happen as the interdependencies become energetic. Relationships will develop between the learning paradigm and the people's adaptive response.

However, when entire platforms of learning or an organizational DNA are set up primarily with restrictions and controls as paramount, only so much can happen and only so much can "bubble up." It's like a shaken can of soda popped open and spitting everywhere versus a can of soda opened a week ago and left sitting on the kitchen counter. One is bursting with "fizz" and the other flat with a waning flavor.

For example, the traditional classroom model seemed to stifle this proposed engagement and the student wouldn't and couldn't own their learning until I disrupted their stayed patterns of discovery. They couldn't jump into their learning and "mix it up" with the processes and discovery. By changing the equilibrium through new teaching techniques that encouraged connections to the outside life and spontaneous insight, I caused a chaotic environment to prod development.

Similarly, the traditional leadership model within the typical hierarchical organization produced the same type of results as a traditional classroom – meager and blasé. Unless the stayed patterns are disrupted and the "widget" mentality is confronted, the results are moderate and the innovation will always be stayed, and the people will continue to work in their cubicle and remain identified as a part, distinct in only itself.

Transition to Business

As I've transitioned into business, I see the classroom much like I see the organization. Leaders, like teachers, need to learn new ways to engage and catalyze the spirit of their people.

As the traditional classroom has lost effectiveness and the student engagement is waning, the traditional leadership model is losing strength and we are suffering in productivity and performance. "Effective managers and professionals in all walks of life….have to become skilled in the art of 'reading' the situations that they are attempting to organize or manage" (Morgan, 1986, p. 11). In other words, in this charged environment and "clumpy" but increasingly connected landscape, unless managers and leaders learn to read the awkwardness of the chaotic model and encourage and foster increasingly random relationships from sales to service to production to distribution to marketing, the opportunity to reform the workplace into a place of learning, growing, and meaning will fade into the distance, potentially along with the organization itself.

Many components of traditional mind-sets are critical – metrics, performance benchmarks, accountability – but how it has historically pulled, or better yet manipulated, these aspects from the person versus how it needs to pull and propel these same concerns in this global, complex, fast marketplace is now becoming less effective. Many improvements have been put in place time and time again, but it has been to no avail. "The competitive pressures keep on getting worse, the pace of change keeps accelerating, and companies keep pouring executive energy into the search for higher levels of quality, service, and overall business agility… Results improve slowly or not at all" (Pascale, 1997, p. 127).

I have seen these traditional cultures, with authoritarian styles in education and businesses constrict performance in people and organizations. They are such that they are the opposite of natural organisms with intrinsic abilities that are always developing and discovering new performance levels through ingenuity.

They produce predictable, controlled outcomes that consequently have little to no flex in their ability to be adaptive. They operate in a continuum of fear.

Shadow of Fear

I have witnessed this shadow of fear and control emerge from these institutions like a dark, heavy fog in a Count Dracula novel sliding along the floor of Transylvania's town. It instills fear and creates an environment where people, like the townspeople in Transylvania, would "rather stay inside" than come out of the town and intermingle.

What happens then in the "Transylvania type" organizations is that this fog permeates the attitude and creativity of the people. They perform within a realm of specifications and restrictions where they can peek out of the small windows of their company like portholes in a battle ship to get a tiny glimpse of what is happening, but in that tiny porthole they also have no perspective of the whole operation or the total system. What they see and immediately have access to is a dot of the company's landscape that they then make decisions and derive certain perceived truths based on a very limited and restricted view. They have no real or true knowledge or connection to the other parts of the operation – financial or operational. It divides them into parts and pieces.

Coo Coo Clock

The traditional mindset is mechanistic, and like a machine, the parts make up the whole. "Consider, for example, the mechanical precision with which many of our institutions are expected to operate. Organizational life is often routinized with the precision demanded of clockwork" (Morgan, 1986, p. 20).

Remember those cartoons where for example a "tiny" person is running from something large and terminally evil and they hide inside a coo coo clock? From the outside of the coo-coo clock all we see is the face of "father time" telling the hour for example, and then at the tip of the hour it chimes and the little Swiss people come from within the clock and do their dance until the chimes are done. However, when we travel inside the clock's working mechanisms, we see a labyrinth of parts closely working together to produce a very precise and succinct product.

Watching the pieces work together with such precision is a thing of intriguing beauty. However, even though the workings tick and sway the clocks hands into accuracy and perform a myriad of duties, individually they are useless to the clock and without each one of them working precisely in unison the clock is mechanically unhinged. It doesn't work, and even though they are microscopic parts, their separateness from the whole provides grand implications to the functionality of the clock.

Many organizations and people think like this coo-coo clock, and this is why today so many people and so many organizations are struggling. If we unveil the layers of the idea, there is something specific to highlight - aside from the precision of the clocks mechanisms - the same two Swiss people dancing and twirling every hour on the hour to the same music, with the same movements, to the same tic tock of the clock. The observation from them here is threefold: 1) repetition, 2) precision, and 3) sameness.

First, the repetition of the "little Swiss people" is typical of our behavior in that we continually turn out repetitive cycles of thought, product, productivity, and process. It's always the same. We throw repetitive, same solutions at familiar problems that continually surface instead of evaluating the structure that produces underlying behavior. This is the "little people" problem in that our behavior is dependable, stayed, and common. Second, like the clock, our mechanics are based on precision, and therefore this format only allows for precise, regimented, and calculated behavior. There is no room for the exciting, potential and the probable. All that is allowed is what can be determined through careful study and analysis. Finally, all of these lead to sameness, where interactions, behavior, creativity, output, and operational philosophy are predictable and sterile. Ingenuity and spontaneity that can be pulled from the people that contribute to accelerated and exciting development are left at bay. They, the people and the company, like ships in a harbor, are anchored and still.

This type of traditional, Newtonian mind-set focuses on hierarchical, top down mentality where leaders dictate to "others" (departments and people) their "creative" ideas.

Certainly, the natural science discoveries of Newton and other in the past centuries affected our views of organizations. The organizational form we call bureaucracy reflects our knowledge of structural mechanics – a bureaucracy is intended to be a set of parts (people) with functions (rules) that follow accepted scientific principles (policies). This machine metaphor for organizations remains pervasive as we continue to try to determine, predict, measure, and evaluate all sorts of organizational phenomena" (Stumpf, 1995, p. 39).

From the commands and edicts, they predict the outcome through deterministic behavior, cause and effect linearity, and objective perspectives. These controls and ordered processes perform linear functions and leave little to no room for subjective possibilities. What if what a leader sees as the solution is only a part of the answer and something dynamic lingers on the lips of an employee or employees who are not allowed to have a voice? What if what the leader proposes is only half of what the outcome could be, or even a third of the potential? What if instead the structure of an organization was such that the voice of random communities was the pervasive force that shouted out through interconnectivity and autonomy? Yet this domineering mentality of control, stability, and discipline squelch that arena of discovery; it actually keeps hope and creativity stuffed into rigid controls. This is unfortunately how most of us think.

The idea of the WHOLE SYSTEM and what it is comprised of is changing. The older idea that the parts are the whole and that these parts are then designated pieces, separate and limited, is slowly fading. Instead, the WHOLE SYSTEM *and* the echoes and voices intermingle with current parts to form random relationships and then commingle. The WHOLE SYSTEM is actually a plethora of random "swirlings" and connections, relationships that converged together from all over to connect and reconnect. These parts in the traditional Newtonian format are fit betwixt walls and confined to cubicles and boxes disallowing evolving, unique relationships and transcendent, networking multiplicities. It is this "gooey" thick mentality that condemns fluidity and emergence.

Surfers Find Natural Principles of Living Systems

- Living Systems takes governing principles of living organisms and apply them to leadership and organizational life to grapple with the confounding intricacies of change.
- The key is to disrupt stayed patterns, comfortable relationships, and familiarity in order to make room for new movement.
- The edge pushes a state of mind that is keenly alive and finely tuned to the situation and the potential.
- Rows of chairs in a classroom were arranged like assembly lines in the factory and promoted linearity instead of collaboration and innovation.
- Like a teacher, a leader should develop people and organizations through exposing and connecting intrinsic learning capacities so the system can brew in non-linear, edge thinking.
- The leader must learn to teach and inspire catalytic creations.

Chapter 5

Recognize Light Disturbances to Highly Connected System Could Have Tremendous Effect

Living Systems

"Structures are needed, but they must be simple, reproducible and internal rather than external. Every living thing is made up of structure and systems. Your body has a nervous system, a circulatory system, and even skeletal system to add structure to the whole. The universe and nature itself teach us that order is possible even when there is no control but God Himself "(Hirsch, p. 186).

A wave is the result of disturbances within a highly connected system. Without the wind, storms, currents, tides, etc. where lucid connections abound, there would be no waves. Likewise, leadership needs to develop high levels of connectivity so disturbances can instigate innovations instead of topple organizations and the people within them. Leaders must find a different way of openly connecting their systems that is a distinct break from the more typical, machine-like structure. This will instigate the human soul to be more creative instead being splintered into routinized commodities. Like the ocean where inter- connectivity thrives, there is a newer place we must learn to lead that is not only more connected but resonates with the issue of our essence. It is organic. It is natural.

"...organic images abound...These images are not just verbal metaphors that help us describe [a] theological nature...; they actually go to the issue of essence. Therefore, they will need to be rediscovered, re-embraced, and relived in order to position us ... for the challenges and complexities facing us in the twenty-first century. We must find a new way to experience ourselves,

152

beyond the static, mechanistic, and institutional paradigm that predominates our...life" (Hirsch, p. 180).

From a surfer's mindset, it is these disturbances out at sea that bring the wave that we surf. Because the ocean is a highly, intimately connected system, a light disturbance can ultimately begin the process of a wave and see it through to its rising peak. These natural conditions of the sea and and its connectivity produce the wave and bring about its very essence. It's not a secret machine deep in the bowels of the sea that generate the swell to create the wave. It's the natural conditions, the natural movements, the natural rhythms of the ocean that can interact with disturbances that ultimately produce the "emerald green wall" that the surfer loves to ride.

Cosmology

Let's look at cosmology (creation) for example and briefly examine the natural rhythms within the fibers of life itself. When you look at the delicate lines of a leaf, the roar of a waterfall, the rustle of the wind through pine trees, the velvet rub of a rose petal, the intricate dimensions of a snowflake, the deep blue of the sky, or the majesty of the night sky pierced by the stars flicker; you will likely see an "otherness." By looking at what is right in front of us and sensing its dimension, perhaps there is a place where we can craft a way to live and lead that is directly related to our essence. In other words, what if this way of leading is ultimately connected to the very gentle purring of nature. Instead of the machine imagery or mechanistic view that is the current tradition, what if there is an "ecological and intrinsically spiritual view of the world rather than any of the other disciplines that have conventionally informed leadership and the development of organizations" (Hirsch, p.180). It is this idea of living systems that finds its root in the "Cosmology [that] must guide us in to a deeper understanding of ourselves and our function in the world" (Hirsch, p. 180).

Decentralized

As a structure, it is decentralized. As a mind-set of leadership, it is a flattening of the hierarchical grid that turns the pyramid of control upside down. As a way of thinking it is looking at the fingerprints of creation and finding "intrinsic vitality and intelligence...[where the] cosmos itself seems to operate profoundly intelligent; the more we find out about it from science, from the structures of atoms, the patterns of weather, the pattern of birds, the human psyche... From quarks to supernovas, the universe seems to vibrate with living potency..." (Hirsch, p. 180). In other words, the world nor our person is meant to operate as a machine. Instead, this concept of thinking and leading from our "essence" and more like a living thing in nature, will open systems so they can experience and live interdependencies.

Leadership in this frame can begin to scale the traditional walls that hinder horizontal communications. Under this new paradigm, the system encourages its agents to interconnect and use disturbances to drive progress and change, much like nature.

A cosmological view can switch entire organizations from a top-down world into a bottom-up, flat landscape, and it makes the ground fertile for unpredictable but exciting outcomes.

How It Looks

This is how it might look. The people in the system may be predictable or determinate in their nature and trained behavior, but when those same people con- nect with different people and form relationships, unsuspecting things will likely happen. Behavior mixes. People and relationships mix. The people individually don't change dramatically, but their interaction with other agents author change through relationships that is potentially dynamic. This evolves the system. In other words, alone they are what they are and will change to a degree through natural human development, but when let loose to freely interconnect, this action changes the structure and its outcome. At this point of inflection, the people and the system can dramatically change and ultimately shift. Its the relationships intermingling that bring the deepest change. They mutate the outcome into something unexpected. When the system opens and flattens and connects, people form relationship and alter the behavior of the system.

A Jungle

Lets take a vine for example, a regular plant vine. By itself a vine is just a dangling vine from a house plant simply stretching itself out along the living room, hard wood floors. However, take that vine, put in a open system with a bounty of other vines that then can grow freely together with millions of other vines and the condition changes; it's properties don't change but its ability to connect does. Together they bring change. On nature's floor these millions of vines sloppily tangle their gangly, gnarly ropes and octopus like tentacles around each other, twisting and turning, wrapping and slinging themselves around all things in sight. The vines alone are just vines, but randomly allowed to intersect they form a dense, complicated and dynamic outcome - a jungle. Their relationships to each other create something much different than their independently predictable structures.

A Person

Another example, let's take a person like you or like me. We will physically, spiritually, and mentally always be a singular, creative, and unique individual with a wonderfully complex design. We are each individually very special. However, we are limited by our own set of parameters innate and distinct to our person.

154

Alone, we are limited and can only develop to the limits of our personal abilities. Sure we will advance to certain degrees. We will mature, learn, adapt, grow, but in essence and by ourselves you will always be you and I will always be me.

However, through relationships that we have or that we encounter, whether they are physical, emotional, spiritual, or exist through mere proximity, the outcome of the relationships, the stuff that happen from that connection or because of that connection for you and for me will be very different, dynamic, and emergent versus our original, rather static structure. Whether it is a relationship to a situation, person, circumstance or event, if we let it the connection or "disturbance" to our system brings change. It's our interaction with it that will determine the outcome.

To stretch the example out of you and me even further, the outcome you have from the relationship will likely be very different than the outcome I have in the relationship, even if the person is the same or the situation is the same that we encounter. The simple reason is that you and I are different, our biological and intellectual structural components - our humanity - is similar, but our details hidden within our own peculiarities are different. Therefore, when we interact with the same person or situation, our outcomes will vary greatly or very little. As well, the "other person" or the "other thing" we are both interacting with, although the same person, may react differently to each one of us because he/she will have his/her own set of peculiarities that react uniquely to our own peculiarities. At once, even in this microcosm, the probabilities become quickly dynamic. The ripples from the interactions become a host of probabilities that will then effect and interact with and create more and more of emerging events. You see where this is going.

Now take an organization, a church, a business where you might have hundreds of like people joined through the common bond of humanity yet each filled with their own unique set of design components, if leaders allow them to connect and then allow them to contribute to the organization an actual value that gets implemented, the opportunities becomes staggering. The vines become a jungle. If you open that system or the business or the church or the organization and decentralize authority in the hopes to dawn new connections, things are infinitely limitless.

Natural Relationships

When a relationship happens through natural encounters that are drawn together through common values and foundational pillars that are not manufactured, where it is unusual, unlikely, and unpredictable, amazing advances will perpetuate themselves. Now I am not saying that anything whether a relationship or an organization that is opened up to randomness will always have positive and amazing outcomes, or even any outcomes at all. What I am saying though is the probabilities are infinitely greater and the disturbances to a degree will stimulate and shake stability and sameness. When the power becomes distributed and shared and the power grid is dispersed and jarred, everything becomes dynamically kinetic. Like when you touch a single segment of a spiders web, the intertwining threads reverberate throughout the whole web.

Sure agents that are alike will interact with those that might be similar, but each one of those unique agents have distinctions that the others do not, and if they select to come together through common values, the open landscape will reverberate like the spider's web. Organizational life then becomes a place where commingling relationships bring innovation to square, linear boxes.

Picture a Ball

Picture a ball sitting in a large room surrounded by four very tall walls with instructions set on the floor telling you how, when, and where to hit the ball (newtonian hierarchy, traditionalism) versus someone picking up that ball and then at whim hitting it with a racket to watch it bounce all over in that room off those four walls in random paths and unpredictable intervals.

Now picture the deeper order, the deeper significance. The more vivid image of a living system is much more dynamic and interactive than one ball and one person with one racket. Take that same room surrounded by four walls (subdued controls) and fill the floor with piles of balls, throw in a crowd of people capable of mass collaboration, each with their own racket, and then tell them to at whim hit any of the balls anywhere located in that room until the room is dancing and swirling with activity and energy. That is a depiction of a living system. There is overlapping, redundant actions, webbing, interdependent, independent and collective action all at once and in random order. In other words, this previously linear, static room is now a highly interconnected, collaborative environment. It has a high level of connectivity and proximity and energy.

One ball being hit in the room to watch it dance off the walls with unique trajectory is an interesting study in physics and a slightly random, more controlled order, but its not exciting and the probabilities are very limited and eventually will subside. The ball can only bounce so many times before it needs to be hit again by that one person. However, if the room is allowed to have multiple participants with unlimited energy and the power of massive collaborations, the outcomes from the interconnectedness will be unparalleled. Sure its a bit messy, chaotic, and seemingly unorganized compared to what our traditional structural mentality is used to, but because we are not used to it does't mean that it's wrong or ineffective or unproductive.

I am not advocating what you are seeing in your Newtonian mind right now. It's probable that all you are seeing just a ton of balls, tons of rackets, and tons people doing what they want and creating a blur of chaos that multiplies and spins into other mass confusion. I want to add two observations here that need to be highlighted.

1. Simple, reproducible, internal structures are needed. A living system requires loosely subdued controls and shared values centered on core foundational beliefs. It needs a center from which to spin from that direct and shape the advancing network. Look at Facebook, Myspace, Youtube, Twitter. They have a virtually wide open platform with imbedded rules and central core foundational values that gently rest over "how you can play in their space." Granted they are loose, open-ended, and sometimes even mutable, but they have structure intrinsically connected to their mission and foundational values and company purpose. There is a center that directs the outward webbing to relevant networks and that center, if sincerely and organically drawn, holds the networks in line with purpose. In my example, the room has 4 distinct walls. It doesn't depict a wide open space where people can take the balls anywhere, put piles of them in their backpacks only to walk off them and then hit them anywhere they wanted. Nor does it say how high the walls are or how far apart they are or how wide the space is. It simply has some structure specific to design. Sure some people may leave the space because the "doors" aren't locked. However, there are subdued controls and mutable laws within a highly collaborative environment beneath a designated, richly thought out purpose that promotes the system to expand and connect. This environment pushes the system to evolve while holding fast to their foundational values. Without a common, agreed purpose and mission along side stated and believed values, it will become a mess. However, if they are common and center, within its openness, unexpected things, things not yet known will emerge with rich new content and unlikely probabilities.

2. Order is possible, even with perceived limited controls. A living system produces an environment of high energy in a slightly structured space with potentially unlimited emergence, and a commonality and a sense of autonomy encourages the evolution. The more a system is allowed to connect, form communities, and build conversations that are pertinent to their immediate levels of interest around foundational values, the more the system will expand and evolve. Like Wikipedia, it will expand to continents and become an expansive network of communities adding, subtracting, and amending conversations of value.

Adaptive challenges and emergence: by constantly interacting with its environment, the living system will catalyze its built-in capacity to adapt to changing circumstances. Failure to do so results in decline and death. Emergence (new forms of organization) happens when a living system is in adaptive (and therefore learning) mode, all the elements in the system are relating functionally, and distributed intelligence is cultivated and focused through information (Hirsch, p. 183).

The New Jungle

Let's take a look at something that isn't an example or just an image. It's real and its shaping our new way of thinking. Technology. It's the face of our newer and very real "jungle" spreading its vines, its complicated, interwoven networks throughout the world. Consider these "vines" or networks of the Web that have tangled, overlapped, interconnected, spread out and intermingled that I mentioned above - Facebook, Youtube, Myspace, and Twitter. They all happened in just a few years and yet have caused tremendous shift. They have reshaped the way we communicate and connect. These entities are ripe examples of chaos and complexity. They are real, live, brewing entities that have a flattened power grid, incredible multiplication, and endless random relationships forming and reforming to extend their influence around foundational values and shared beliefs. And their systems are open and grow and expand when disturbed. Listen to this, "I am flying to New York, streaming music from Pandora, [checking email,] and watching YouTube videos via American Airline's GoGo Inflight WiFi on my iPad 2" (Transworld Business, August 2011, Opinion, p. 016).

In earlier chapters, I talked about how we have become a new society where technology is the engine and its byproduct is a new way of thinking. Social networking for example is a huge, audacious jungle that has overtaken how we communicate, market, and connect because its community is unparalleled in size, but more importantly they collaborate on a massive, yet simple scale. The numbers are staggering and their international collaborative effort is stunning, but the idea and application is organic. It is making the world flatter and flatter by taking a ton of those balls in that room and letting anyone, at anytime, hit the ball in any direction however hard or soft they want to hit it and as often as they want to hit it if it resonates with core, shared, stated values. There are more and more balls that then creates more and more communicative and creative input that therefore produce more and more output of expanding, random networks. It's like the parable in the Bible where Jesus takes just a couple loaves of bread and few fish and multiplies them over and over to feed thousands upon thousands upon thousands, with baskets left over. This is our new world.

From an Industrial Economy to a Service Economy

Consequently, as we have become a service economy instead of an industrial economy, largely through the advance of technology and the specifically through the spread of the Web. We have become a communicative, interactive, interconnecting global network with a loud vocal voice via the Web instead of a nation filled with large, obtuse factories and smokestacks producing widgets (both metaphorically and literally). This is a living system on a grand scale. As the shift in our national economy happens, we must shift from that same mindset locked in the industrial era of smokestacks and assembly lines to a network logged into Facebook. We are now in an era of "conversation" and "community" that feeds off of transparency and immediacy and is moved up by disturbance. Listen to Peggy Noonan in the Wall Street Journal in the Opinion section talk about our change:

> American culture is, one way or another, business culture, and our business is service. Once we were a great industrial nation. Now we are a service economy. Which means we are forced to interact with each other, every day, in person and by phone and e-mail [and Twitter and Facebook]. And its making us a little mad.
>
> I'm not sure we've fully noted the social implication of the shift from industry to service. We used to make machines! And steel! But now we're always in touch, in negotiation. We interact so much, [we tweet and Facebook so much that] we wear each other down. We wear away the superego and get straight to the id...(Wall Street Journal, A11, Peggy Noonan, August 14-15, 2010, Opinion).

Did You Know? (version 2)

Here is a updated version of the Youtube video called "Did You Know?" I referenced an earlier version in an earlier chapter. This is from that same series but is updated to 2009 stats and focuses on how this social networking revolutions has exploded on the scene to catalyze this new landscape and shifted our thinking. The growth is stunning. Here it is for reference - http://www.youtube. com/watch?v=hyZRS0BnpAI&feature=related. What follows is the text. Again, it is much more powerful when you watch it, but reading the text will clearly still communicate the impact.

> Did you know?
> Years to reach 50 million users -
>> Radio 38 years
>> TV 13 years
>> Internet 4 years
>> iPod 3 years
> Facebook added 100 million users in less than 9 months. iPod applications downloads hit 1 Billion in 9 months
> If Facebook were a country, it would be the 4th largest.
> Twitter played an unprecedented role in sharing information during the 2009 Iranian presidential elections.
> We no longer search for the news, the news finds us...
> In the near future we will no longer search for products and services,
> They will find us via social media.
> Social media has overtaken porn as the #1 activity on the Web.
> What happens in Vegas stays on Facebook, Twitter, Youtube, Myspace
> There are 100 million ACTIVE users on Youtube.

Users have their own channels to which others can subscribe. Americans
have access to
1,000,000,000,000 web pages
65,000 iPhone apps
10,500 radio stations
5,500 magazines
200+ cable tv networks
There are 240,000,000 TV's in the U.S.
More video was uploaded to Youtube in the last 2 months than
if ABC, NBC, CBS had been airing new content 24/7/365
Since 1948(which was when ABC started airing).
10 Million -The number of unique visitors ABC, NBC, CBS get every
month collectively. These businesses have been around for a combined
200 years
250 million - The number of unique visitors myspace, Youtube, Facebook
get every month, collectively.
None of these sites existed 6 years ago.
95% of all songs downloaded last year weren't paid for. Wikipedia
launched in 2001.
It now features over 13 million
articles. in more than 200
languages.
Cisco's Nexus 7000 data switch could move all of
Wikipedia in .001 seconds.
Does it affect you?
2009 US Department of Education study revealed that on average, online
students out performed those receiving face-to-face instructuion...

1 in 6 higher education students are enrolled in online curriculum. How
many text messages does the average American teen send
each month? - 2,272.
Above average: Brady James of Los Angeles, Calfornia sent
217,541 text messages in March 2009. Right now 93% of Americans
own cell phones.
The mobile device will be the world's primary connection tool to the
Internet in 2020
The computer in your cell phone today is a million times cheaper and a
thousand times more powerful and about a hundred times smaller
(than the one computer at MIT in 1965.) (Ray Kurzweil)
So what used to fit in a building now fits in your pocket, What now fits
in your pocket now will fit inside a blood cell in 25 years - (Ray
Kurzweil)

The End of Management

Its not just that a computer that used to fit in a building now fits in your pocket. Although this is amazing, the greater implication is what it means to how we think and live and communicate. The older idea of management and its very institutions for example - a definitive way of how we think - is no longer effective.

Yet in today's world, gale-like market forces - rapid globalization, accelerating innovation, relentless competition - have intensified what economists Joseph Schumpeter called the forces of "creative destruction." Decades-old institutions like Lehman Brothers and Bear Stearns now can disappear overnight, while new ones like Google and Twitter can spring up from nowhere... [These] market-leading companies have missed the game-changing transformations in industry after industry - not because of "bad" management, but because they followed the dictates of "good management" (Wall Street Journal, Sat/Sun, Aug 21-22, 2010, W3)

We are used to corporate bureaucracy. Although initially it was meant to control costs, harness mass production of product, manage large groups of workers, reduce heavy transaction costs and carefully study market trends, today this "good" management causes current, conventional leadership to miss "disruptive innovations that [open] up new customers and markets for lower-margin, blockbuster products" (Wall Street Journal, Murray, Sat/Sun, Aug. 21-22, 2010, W3)

Traditionally, the "top" control "the rest." There's no real collaboration because we were too busy controlling. But this "good management" shackled innovations and shielded us from break out ideas found within conversations of communities. Our minds, our organizations, our churches, our very persons are unaffected and under stimulated. They are route carriers of the cold commands of the few. It's hard for people to truly bring together their synergies because leadership confirms the structure and compartments that make it so limited and "rigid." We have been trained. We are all susceptible to the ills of "good management." We are inhabitants of distinct, cold walls with only one ball, one person, and a set of rigid rules.

Typical Structures

In a typical leadership structure, leaders, communities, schools, churches, and businesses dispense their edicts instead of a sense of shared power to the existing problems. Under this older mental model, we rely on the institution of compartments where the structure in our minds naturally corrals us inward instead of letting disturbances pushing us outward. However, living systems theory suggests under a canopy of open communication and interconnectivity, unique things are waiting to be formed and then applied to unhinge conventional approaches.

We must be ready and able to solve problems not yet formed with answers we do not yet know.

There are some that believe that corporate hierarchies will eventually disappear all together as the power of collaboration multiplies and converts our mindsets. We are quite possibly in the makings of a new era where it becomes the norm where people are empowered to work together and form communities and conversations that move the global landscape to networks of complex, mass collaborations. Some even think we might be headed for a new "golden era?"

That's heady stuff, and almost certainly exaggerated. Even the most starry-eyed techno enthusiasts have a hard time imagining, say, a Boeing 787 built by "mass collaboration." Still, the trends here are big and undeniable. Change is rapidly accelerating. Transaction costs are rapidly diminishing [The primary reason for the creation of the science of management]. And as a result, everything we learned in the past century about managing large corporations is in need of a serious rethink. We have both a need and an opportunity to devise a new form of economic organization, and a new science of management, that can deal with the breakneck realities of 21st century change (Wall Street Journal, Murray, Sat/Sun, Aug. 21-22, 2010, W3).

Another Problem

Another problem is that the Newtonian structure dictates orders from a potentially very shallow and limiting pool of resources. I say shallow in that the pools of existing relationships (ideas) and the potential of new relationships (new ideas) are usually only from a few experiences and few connections of a few people. Therefore, the ideas of others within the community are untouched and unrealized. A living system however presents an array of unique, unfound solutions that are located directly in the people from yet-to-be-formed communities. The rich resources of these people and their combined experiences become the composite that form the new and the "unlikely." Although the model is yet to be absolutely defined, it is clear that we must redo how we lead or it will be done for us.

This suggests we must create models of inner connectivity that push dynamic potential because the traditional setting leave us dry and wanting. These older command and control models illicit a practice of "repeating" instead of "creating." Although these type of structures are slowly waning, their roots and practices historically still have strong influence in current leadership circles.

If executives or middle to senior managers, church boards and elder boards, school boards and executive committees are the only resources, the organization and the people will ultimately lose out on value and outcomes that unite and build the organization. Because there is no sense of true collaboration, connectivity, or creativity, churches, businesses, and institutions act too conservatively and push back on disturbance instead of letting it shake the system forward. They gingerly allocate

162

their resources like people, money, and function in measured, careful, calculated predictions with little to no risk under a corporate notion of certainty. However...

Information brings change: all living systems respond to information. In fact, they seem to be able to sort out information based on what is meaningful or useful to them. Information is therefore critical to intelligence, adaptivity, and growth. The free flow of information in the system is vital to growth and adaptation (Hirsch, p. 183).

This flat world will no longer allow such slowness and deliberate calculations of people and resources in world clamoring for a free flow of information. We need to risk more and explore this unfolding landscape to find those "yet-to-be-found" solutions for "yet-to-be-problems." I don't mean to insinuate that we all at once need to embrace a rambling whim, but we do need to deeply explore a certain ratio of the unknown and not deflect interruptions or disturbances. Take for example Google's philosophy where they have a 20% rule for employees. They encourage their employees to work on Google-related projects of their choosing 20% of their work time outside of the scope of their assigned projects (An example of subdued controls like the image of the four walls and unlimited balls). Its that mentality that produced innovative out-croppings like Google News and GMail. They believe more in the "what might be" versus the "what is."

The new model will have to be more like the market place, and less like the corporations of the past. It will need to be flexible, agile, able to quickly adjust to market developments, and ruthless in reallocating resources to new opportunities.

Resource allocation will be one of the biggest challenges. The beauty of markets is that, over time, they tend to ensure that both people and money end up employed in the highest-value enterprises. In corporations, decisions about allocating resources are made by people with a vested interest in the status quo. "The single biggest reason companies fail" says Mr. Hamel, "is that they over-invest in what is, as opposed to what might be."

This is the core of the innovator's dilemma. The big companies...failed, not necessarily because they didn't see these innovations coming, but because they failed to adequately invest in those innovations. To avoid this problem, the people who control large pools of capital need to act more like venture capitalists, and less like corporate finance departments. They need to make lots of big bets, not just a few big ones, and they need to be willing to cut their losses (Wall Street Journal, Murray, Sat/Sun, Aug. 21-22, 2010, W3).

Therefore, it is alleged that too much is "left on the table" because the Newtonian leadership style boxes in creativity; it doesn't let minds truly create. This command and control style, the "my way or the highway" expels and separates people from the solution finding process. It instigates and downplays the human spirit. True discovery remains concealed until connectivity unlocks it. In other words, community members are not only excluded from participation and contribution, but their vast reservoir of gathered synergy is disconnected, never to connect and begin new, dynamic relationships, new ideas and radical, innovative answers. Discovery, true generative learning is left dead because organizations don't allow their people to participate in value adds.

Take for example an organization where the executive branch or senior leadership is seeking a solution to a process glitch where internal connectivity is breaking down causing a disruption to customer service, product presentation, and specifically the bottom line profits. Or look at the troubled network and community of a church staff where a pastor is the sole executive communicating the vision and the solutions while the inner workings of a church seems to continually exist in turmoil and conflict, disconnected from his/her vision. Perhaps the answer is lost because the leadership in an organization or perhaps the pastor in the church is unable to recognize the need to allow others in the community to discover different solutions through mass collaboration. Perhaps its a fear of becoming obsolete for both the leader and the pastor. They might be thinking, "If the people are allowed to produce value and progress in spite of me, what am I needed for?" Leaders are needed just as much as someone is needed to steer a ship and keep the network webbed from its center outward, but what is not needed is the ego of a leader that needs to be fed because his/her sense of control rules the organizational structure. This demoralizes inspiration in any community, person, business or church. As well, this style of leadership is from a position of insecurity, which is the worst place to lead. Instead, this new mind-set leads from a place of essence.

In addition to resource allocation, there's even bigger challenge of creating structures that motivate and inspire workers. There's plenty of evidence that most workers in today's complex organizations are simply not engaged in their work. Many are like Jim Halpert from "The Office," who in season one of the popular TV show declared: "This is just a job...If this were a career, I'd have to throw myself in front of a train."

The new model will have to instill in workers the kind of drive and creativity and innovative spirit more commonly found among entrepreneurs. It will have to push power and decision-making down the organization as much as possible, rather than leave it concentrated at the top. Traditional bureaucratic structures will have to be replaced with something more like ad-hoc teams of peers, who come together to tackle individual projects, and then disband...New mechanisms will have to be created for harnessing the "wisdom of crowds." Feedback loops will need to be built that allow products and services to constantly evolve in response to new information. Change, innovation, adaptability, all have to become orders of the day (Wall Street Journal, Murray, Sat/Sun, Aug. 21-22, 2010, W3).

What if the people of the organization or the congregants of the church were encouraged to connect and dawn emergent thought and discussion to "percolate up?" What if the energies drew or designed things never before seen or thought because they were allowed to connect and commune with others of like value? What if entire congregations were allowed to rectify turmoil and misguided groups or individuals by providing a communal solution through this collaboration and transparent communicaitons? Picture what might become of society and organizational civilization if we were allowed to organically interconnect.

Proceed with Slowness

Living Systems can transform command and control into participative conversations with peer groups as leaders and random communities that innovate. The model establishes an evolving environment of interconnectedness with its people, its processes, its management, its leadership, and its vision. Although the current state of change is circumventing traditional models, moving from a command and control style to a more a flattened hierarchy must be introduced with skill and careful attention, even a slowness. It is critical that the transition happens with keen oversight and pliable insight. It could shock the system too much because this type of shift is difficult and even startling. It needs gradual buy in and a period of adaptation and learning instead of a total and immediate overhaul. Even though it's about infusing resiliency into the system, management and even the people will have its fears.

> When talking with senior executives about the need to encourage innovation...they'd like their employees to loosen up a bit, to think more radically and be more experimental, but they're worried this might distract them from a laser like focus on efficiency and execution...There is an understandable fear...[that] if employees are given the latitude to flex policy guidelines, experiment with new methods, and incubate new projects: 'If everybody's off innovating, who's going to mind the store?' These sentiments reveal a persistent management orthodoxy: *If you allow people the freedom to innovate, discipline will take a beating* (Hamel, p. 135).

It's Not a Free-for-All

However, given those fears it's important to understand that this is not a free for all where anything goes and innovation is pursued at all costs and with any kind of structure that bubbles to the top from anyone that fogs a mirror. Remember the example of subdued controls. It still demands a code of accountability to keep performance targeted with measurable results that feed back and filter through the foundational (centered) values and mission of the person or organization. There is a center where all conversations and community relationships spin outward from it. It will flourish under a system of foundational accountability because it doesn't measure success only when it hits a predetermined, prescribed goal. It is measured instead by momentum, agility, innovative capability, and flexibility while connecting to and propelling from its center.

For example, Whole Foods has four conditions that must be met under their structure of a living system environment: 1) First-line employees are responsible for results. 2) Team members have access to real-time performance data. 3) They have decision authority over the key variables that influence performance outcomes. 4) There's a tight coupling between results, compensation, and recognition (Hamel, p 136).

In a company or organization for example, living systems provide not only a perceived notion of participation but a real value exchange, but it specifically structures the company so the people then *want* to participate with the output of the company's ventures. They are actually inspired. People are encouraged to be a part of what the company is doing, what the company is creating, how the company is thinking, what the company is, and even what the company is planning. They have a sense of meaning, they have a sense of worth, and they have an outlet of creativity that reflects their direct efforts and not just the output of an edict written in a company memo.

There is greater ownership where the people get to not only feel valued but get to literally see that their input is valued and potentially implemented, as opposed to the older models where control was the mantra and microscopic participation was a feigned effort to pretend that opinions outside the boardroom mattered, "With no more than a knothole view of the company's financial model, and only a sliver of responsibility for results, it [is] difficult for an employee to feel a genuine burden for the company's performance...And worst of all, [it] disconnected employees from their own creativity. In the industrial world, work methods and procedures were defined by experts and, once defined, were not easily altered" (Hamel, p. 141).

Under a living system, people have autonomy but are also held accountable. I know this sounds like an oxymoron ("jumbo shrimp, almost always") but to give someone self-governance around a centered set of foundational values, keeps the conversation pertinent and focused. This then allows the networks of conversations that spin outward to add and even increase intrinsic value to the system or the person. These few things will begin to help bring naturally spontaneous and emergent relationships, the place where things happen, without the hindrances of explicit boundaries. The real opportunity happens here when we are freed to create and experiment and stretch all the while being held accountable to prog- ress. "The problem is that the whole burden of change typically rests on so few people. In other words, the number of people at every level who make committed, imaginative contributions to organizational success is simply too small" (Pascale, 1997, p. 127).

This New Mind-Set

This new leadership mind-set is less about parts and pieces, boundaries, structures, and linear thinking – where A = B = C – rather it is more about dynamic connectivity and non-linear thinking. It's about finding the unfound talents, the unfound solutions, the unfound gifting, the unfound relationship, the unfound flexibility, the unfound idea hiding deep within our systems, in our essence. It's critical that we are not talking about undisclosed, pre-existing answers or solu- tions that are simply hidden like the diamond in a lump of coal or the treasure chest of a Spanish Galion. That might suggest that the answer is already there or that it already exists and is waiting to be uncovered, scaled back, or chiseled into clarity.

This newer idea implies in its theory that the discoveries have yet to be made and the relationships have yet to be formed that then give shape to the new solution. This type of alleged future is unwritten, and it can therefore be messy. It's not all so cut and clear. Here, the relationships and the ability to relate and connect evolve; they progress. Time, autonomy, and connections are the significant factors that then shape the results if proper accountability is in place. Whether they all work or not is yet to be seen, and whether they work or not isn't even the issue. Something will work at some point if minds are allowed to interconnect as a pattern of daily behavior.

We are talking about new discoveries, and even though they may not work, they produce energy toward something that at some point will. Google for example wants its people to fail in some ventures because they understand that innovation unleashed will inevitably produce a large percentage of failure. Let me rephrase that, I am not preaching failure will be the end goal of living systems. Google doesn't really *want* failure, but they understand that when they allow their people to search the caves of creativity and scour the floors of connectivity, they have to explore and experiment; they realize that not every shake of the gold diggers' hand on the water and sand filled pan will reveal a gold nugget that will lead them to the vein. Sometimes all that is found is just more sand. Many connections do not always equal successful innovation, but they do know that a failure, like a "No" in sales, is that much closer to success.

A Complex but not Complicated Paradigm

This new complex paradigm of leading through a model of living systems is a descendent of chaos and complexity theory (KT). Its goal is to understand what is called a *complex adaptive* system where agents interact with other agents and then these agents collectively interact with the laws within the system. In contrast, a more ordered system limits the behavior of all agents because they are confined by the immutable or unchangeable rules of the system. The rules and the agents do not interact and the laws are static.

However, where there *is* interaction between agents, the laws, and the system, modifications happen. It's here in this vivid interaction that we need to understand this unique relationship where agents and the laws of the system intersect, intermingle and change. When they engage, the agents alter the system by mutating and changing its laws as they see important or necessary to do so. They co-evolve the system, and they can only do this through interconnectivity. Therefore, a complex adaptive system is *complex* – layered and intricate - and *adaptive* – ever changing.

In a complex adaptive system (living system), there are rules but they are lightly implied. Because these rules are lightly implied in a complex system, they are modifiable as they interact in tandem to better the outcome and overcome disturbances. Agents then modify the system in a "real time" if they warrant the need. In other words, they don't have to deal with too many "vias" to process change.

This doesn't work in a typical, more traditional mind-set because it is too functional, isn't nimble enough to innovate, and won't let itself loose the grip of its control. Conversely, in a system that modifies itself, agents constantly convene on an issue, dilemma, problem, or disturbance, analyze or evaluate the data and move on an informed consensus. It's collective wisdom.

Understanding Natural Governing Principles

A goal then is to unwind what are the natural governing principles of how we think and interact and then their relationship to a community, to people, and to life itself. If we learn to understand these more natural ways inherent to most any system, it helps us become nimble and flexible. Wikipedia says that complexity theory seeks to *"understand the nature of system constraints and agent interaction and generally takes an evolutionary or naturalistic approach to strategy."* If we understand our own deeper, natural laws that when paired with interdependencies found in conversations and communities, we could really learn how to surf and connect to life in a more fluid state. We must seek to figure out how to evolve our living to higher states that transcend an older, more prohibitive way.

In life, it is about creating a new environment where our minds are encouraged to instinctively tap into patterns of discovery through community and conversation. We are released to delve into learning, encouraged to manipulate conventional solutions, and stray from linear thinking and typical answers to hopefully learn. This "messiness" brings optimization but conversely confounds the hierarchical mind-sets. In such opens system, the potential confusion takes time to unfurl as the system is always changing and even eliminating what used to seem to be the "right thing" or "the answer" while creating new opportunities.

Under this complex paradigm, given the principles of KT, the system will be intrinsically adaptive. However, the traditional model has been trained to be reactive and isolated, capable at performing only up to its limited and defined limits.

It is confined to its prescribed conforming behavior. This stands in direct contrast to a vibrant, living organism that is creatively unlimited as it discovers the power of co-evolution.

The Achilles Heel

Previously the argument for corporations and this older way of top down went along the line that they were needed to control transaction costs.

It was simply too complicated and too costly to search for and find the right worker at the right moment for any given task, or to search for supplies, or to renegotiate prices, police performance and protect trade secrets in an open marketplace. The corporation might not be as good at allocating labor and capital as the marketplace; it made up for those weaknesses by reducing transaction costs (Wall Street Journal, Murray, Sat/Sun, Aug. 21-22, 2010, W3).

The current management belief, from Fredrick Windslow Taylor's book *The Principles of Scientific Management* published in 1911, operates under what happened over 100 years ago and unfortunately it is still the achilles heel that planted in and took root after the Industrial Revolution. It is the plight of "good management."

1. In pre-industrial times, farmers and artisans enjoyed an intimate relationship with the customers [but industrialization began to build barriers to direct feedback. Information became secondary].

2. As companies [grew and] divided themselves into departments and functions, employees also became disconnected from the final product. [They became cogs in an industrial wheel.]

3. Size and scale also separated employees from their coworkers…they no longer had system wide view of the production process [and no means to know if was broke, if it needed to be fixed, and who or what could fix it].

4. Industrialization also enlarged the gulf between workers and owners [and more often than not workers had to report to junior supervisors who had no authority to affect change or direct real influence].

5. Growing operational complexity fractured the information that was available to employees. {Employees might learn how they are doing in their job but little to no knowledge how they actually authored change in the company and how the company at large was truly doing. It was all contrived]. (Hamel, p. 140).

If we eliminate those patterns of centralized authority that reach back to command and control, we can encourage random, unconventional ideas to percolate up and out through blurry boundaries (decentralized authority) and collaboration.

If we give people the evidential truth that they count, that they matter, that they are needed, and then open the system to decentralize its authority, our minds, our organization, our churches, our schools might become fresh places of innovation and change willing to take on disturbances and use their impact to become more flexible.

[And now]...The ability of human beings on different continents and with vastly different skills and interests to work together and coordinate complex tasks has taken quantum leaps. Complicated enterprises, like maintaining Wikipedia or building a Linux operating system, now can be accomplished with little or no corporate management structure at all (Wall Street Journal, Murray, Sat/Sun, Aug. 21-22, 2010, W3).

A Surfer's View of the New Horizon

Allow me to describe a brief narrative that might serve as an image of what living systems might look and feel like metaphorically through an experience I had one morning surfing. We went out early on what we call "dawn patrol" where surfers hit the water early to avoid the crowd and commune with the unspoiled, unpopulated sea. We knew there was a swell but weren't sure how well it was holding out or how big it might be. We were just "stoked" to go get wet.

The sun was gently lighting the morning and trying to shine through the thick blanket of clouds hanging like a canopy over our heads from a late spring storm. We checked out the surf from inside the warm car and shielded ourselves from the patchy drizzle falling, almost cascading like snow from above. It looked and felt good from inside the car with the heater blowing warmth on our feet as we pondered the billowing surf. The comfort, the heat and lack of caffeine almost made us cathartic as we checked out the water churning with the white wash from the breaking waves, and just a few guys were out. It looked pretty big. In fact we didn't calculate its size until we opened the door and heard the pounding roar of its crashing waves thundering onto the shore and stepped down from the parking lot into the cold morning sand. It looked even bigger. I hesitated and watched the water swirl and move.

It wasn't however until we reached the water's edge with our boards in tow and our bodies stuffed in the wetsuits that we realized how big it was really was. It was powerful and the waves seemed to be in a class all their own. The waves reared up large and glassy with big faces crashing down with hollow barrels that morphed into several feet of thunderous white wash. We stood at the shore and gazed at the ocean and its power, a bit surprised by the power and the churning.

The whole ocean was moving like it was being stirred from beneath by a tumultuous power wreaking chaos on the surf and this particular break. I've surfed this break many a day and I love how it peels right and peels smooth from start to finish. It's one of my favorite rights because it rolls from the top of the point and beautifully funnels itself all the way into the bay. There's lots of hang time, ample room to carve and dig into the wave, and even throw in a snap or two. But this day was different; the wave was different. With respect, we jumped on the board and paddled in to the surf and became mere specs on the landscape of an incredible, almost palpable storm of power. We were instantly small and felt that we were a part of something completely "otherly."

As we waited in between set waves on what felt like the back of a giant heavily swaying and floating on liquid power, the anticipation began to build. The water was churning, the whitewash foamed and billowed like the clouds in the sky, spray from the wave's backside and mist from the storm blurred the horizon, and the ocean's undulations put us in a chaotic, transcendent state. Information was all around us feeding our senses – cold water, stormy seas, misty drizzle, off shore breeze, churning water, powerful surf, and an unnerving surge beneath the water's surface. The storm altered the ocean's landscape and the resulting surf disturbed our typical expectations; *we felt a loss of control.* The waves were different, the break was heavier, and the water was even more aggressive. We couldn't predict a pattern or sense the wave's behavior. It was sporadic and crazy. What was puzzling was this point break, this wave, and what I was used to here was typically clean and predictable.

None-the-less, I anxiously waited in the line-up for my turn and undulated on top of the moving and churning sea. A wave began to mound up and emerge in the horizon. It rolled toward me like a behemoth mass. I scanned the form, with commitment flipped my board around, and paddled into its momentum. It pitched itself up steep, I snapped up on my board, careened down the face of the wave, and sunk into its cascading, right-peeling shoulder. As I dropped in, something strange happened: the chaos dissipated; I fell into an emergent rhythm where I began to blend with an unfolding dynamic relationship with my board, the ocean, and the wave. The churning became the thrust and power propelling me forward into the wave. The chaos that engulfed me originally only seconds before transitioned into a pattern of dynamic unfolding, and it became the discovery. The chaos in the water now became a new and strange order under my board. As I carved the wave with a new tenacity and a fluid motion, I began moving within the ocean no longer hovering nervously above. I was in the cauldron and yet rhythmically I was creating and unfolding with its shape and within its power.

The Edge is a Condition not a Place

The edge of chaos is a condition, not a location. It is permeable, intermediate state through which order and disorder flow, not a finite line of demarcation. Moving to the edge of chaos creates upheaval but not dissolution. That's why the edge of chaos is so important. The edge is not the abyss. It's the sweet spot for productive change (Pascale, p. 61).

Without the chaotic environment brought by the disturbance of the storm and a willingness to charge into something unusual, the moment would have been lost for me that morning in my surf session. It would have been just another day at the beach. That morning felt and looked like what Pascale described as the edge of chaos (2000, p. 61), "Edges are important in life; in fact we are drawn to them. They define a frontier that tells us we are about to venture farther than we have ever gone before. 'As long as one operates in the middle of things, states science writer William Thompson, 'one can never really know the nature in which one moves" (Pascale, 2000, p. 67).

The edge of the wave – the shoulder – is where I want to be for the ride, and its where leaders need to be in a living system. If I drop in on the center of the wave, the tumbling white wash, or too far out on its mound I come up empty and befuddled. On the edge is where all of the momentum is, and to ride that prime spot I have to find the peak of the wave, the edge of its lip just before it breaks, and charge it. If I am too far forward or too far back, I miss it entirely or get pummeled by its force. When I catch the edge and ride its crumbling shoulder carrying me all the way down the line, I hover just at the tip of the barrel and peer out of the tube forming rapidly just ahead of me; it is also the place where you have the biggest rush and the greatest opportunity to really perform on the wave, commune with its power, intermingle with its shape, and understand a radical calm. However, all of this is only found on the edge. To really find that place and take that drop on the wave, I have to be on the cusp of its form and in the tip of its break realizing this is the place where it happens. It is only here where the wave emerges almost at the tip of my toes where I "carve the wave" without any presupposed plan. You simply lock into the surge, the form, and the rush and create connections out of displaced and indeterminate energy.

This living system is similar to this illustration in the sense of its appearance of chaos and disorder. The ocean that morning was disheveled and cantankerous. We could see the "emotion" of the surf and we were nervous to surrender to the power and the chaos of the waves and the water. When we hit the water we were impacted directly by its nature and had to conform to a large degree to its unfolding. It looked and felt like we were in the right place but the wrong time because the conditions and circumstances were pushing us from our base knowledge, comfort and familiarity. What we saw was not what we were used to and not what we even necessarily pictured in our minds as we rolled out of bed that morning.

Similarly, with KT, the patterns are unrecognizable, unpredictable and random while its behavior is erratic, but what appears to be churning and disorderly is actually under a storm of unique "chaordic" (chaos and order) organization with indeterminate manifestations. In other words, the patterns are crazy and in their confusion they can even be daunting, but not therefore necessarily only chaotic in the sense that they are out of control. all of the apparent and seeming mayhem, there is a discreet and unique emergent order that waits to be found. However, this order cozily hiding under the appearance of disorder, won't disclose itself until you or I enter into its cauldron. I can be in the middle where it is safe, steady, and still, but I will always only be safe, in the middle and unchanged while everything else is churning and changing. However, once inside of the caldron and *on its edge*, I find the unique relationships that emerge over and over again to form new and distinct patterns. And like the example of the surf that morning, the wave is always recreating itself indeterminately through disruptions. A wave is never the same. The genius and excitement then, like surfing, is that things are always going through alterations and reforming uniquely, and to catch the momentum I must be in tune with natural principles that I share with the ocean, nimble, anticipating and recognizing undulating disturbances, perched to 'drop in" on the wave.

One of the key discoveries of complexity science is that computer models of complex adaptive systems often evolve themselves to a critical point poised between the chaotic and static states, the edge of chaos, where the emergent response is most creative. There are strong indications that the same is true in nature [and organizations]. Order emerges at the edge of chaos- this is the phenomenon of self-organization. The order that arises is not imposed from above; it flows from distributed influence through the inter- actions of the system's agents. It is hard – and often impossible – to predict in detail what emergent order will look like, but it is certain that order will emerge (Lewin, p. 201).

I see the ocean, like a person, like an organization, like a company, like a church, as a living system that the complexity science of KT seeks to unravel through recognizing its governing principles and then press the system to the edge for creative emergence. As leaders, we must find out how the thing works at its core and in its essence. We cannot continue to simply and only redesign organizations or rearrange the corporate boxes, fire alleged underperforming staff, shift around intellectual capital, hire new bosses, and look outside the boundaries of the existing walls. We will have to do some of these for certain reasons, but the key is that these are not core moves. They are ancillary.

The answer may reside underneath and within the very system that is seemingly displacing the most chaos. Perhaps the answer is entering into the safe, stayed middle ground of the structure, pressing back some layers, and pushing it then to its edge to find unique and yet undiscovered relationships by lowering pre-disclosed boundaries. The edge is where the scary chaos takes on exciting possibilities and scintillating forms. Here are some vivid images living systems:

- Swarms. Lots of individual buzzing around, taking collective and independent action.
- Jungles. Connections are messy, overlapping, webbed, and redundant.
- A mad scientist's lab. Lots of half-finished prospects exhibit serendipitous connections, evidence of false starts, and occasional break- throughs (Pascale, p. 68).

It's change, uncomfortable, unrelenting, and indeterminate change. For this very reason we need to look for "positive deviants that defy the norms of conventional wisdom. Anomalies defy logic. Anomalies are discomforting. Their very existence is an affront to conventional wisdom" (Hamel, p. 187).

Similarly, to understand the changing conditions of the global, flat landscape, market variance, and the shifting demands of human and intellectual capital, it is critical to leverage the characteristics of a living system. The idea connected to leadership, our mind-sets, and surfing is that things are unpredictable and unstable, and disturbances and undulations, if managed strategically with delicate insight are good for the system. "KT is an image of a dynamic, living organism filled with different fields that influence its behavior. Quantum physics and [KT] have given us new insights how to understand organizational dynamics. For an organization [or person] to stay vital and competitive, in the present chaotic world, it must be constantly willing to learn and develop new skills and behavior" (Gyllenpalm, 2003, p. 10).

Surfers Recognize Light Disturbances in a Highly Connected System Could Have Little or No Effect

- Very light disturbances can have little to tremendous effects on a highly connected system.
- Understanding a living system can transform command and control into participative responses that produce a unique level of evolution and adaptation.
- Command and Control inspires repetitions instead of creations.
- Leadership needs to understand what is called this living system where agents interact with other agents and then these agents collectively interact with and modify the laws of the system.
- I was in the cauldron of this huge wave and yet rhythmically I was creating and interacting with its shape and within its power.
- The edge of chaos is a condition, not a location.

Chapter 6

Seek to Uncover the Deeper Order

Systems of Dynamic Interrelationships

"The main stimulus for the renewal ... will come from the bottom and from the edge, from the sector[s].... that are on the margins." -Harvey Cox, Religion in the Secular City.

"...[T]he most probable assumption is that no currently working business theory will be valid in 10 years hence...And yet few executives accept that turning a business around requires fundamental changes in the assumptions on which the business is run. It requires a different business." - Peter Drucker, "A Turnaround Primer"

It's poignant how Drucker said this years ago, and here we are in the middle of shift. The future of life in this new mind-set is about the bottom and the edge, not necessarily the top. It is about a place of margins. As we will see with living systems, discovery, true discovery lives and breathes in those places. Living systems theory (Hirsch) or whole systems approach (Senge), or its scientific term chaos and complexity (KT) by implication leads us to think it is "a state of *utter confusion and disorder*" (Rosenhead, 1998, p.3), but what we are talking about is *uncovering a deep organic order that is governed by a set of natural laws woven through the fibers of all systems, of all people, of all life - a living system approach.* Like Drucker, this discovery and its implications require a *different kind of living, a different kind of thinking, and a different way of acting.*

What we are talking about is how life organizes itself as a living organism and how its very nature is structured around a living, breathing, organic system of pulsations versus an artificial, mechanical intelligence. What we need to look at is already within us. It is *us*. I don't mean religiously or spiritually necessarily, nor do I mean to pick a particularly religious bent, but I am referring to how we are literally wired and designed in our essence. We are made to walk in the margins because that is where we find life. Life is made on the edge where change and risk is forefront because it pushes creativity, just like the edge of a wave for the surfer.

"A living systems approach seeks to structure the common life of organization around the rhythms and structures that mirror life itself. In this approach, we seek to probe the nature of life, we seek to observe how living things tend to organize themselves, and then we try to emulate as closely as possible this innate capacity of living systems to develop higher levels of organization, to adapt to different conditions, and to activate latent intelligence when needed (emergence)" (Hirsch, p.182).

This order is imbedded into the central core of organisms, in the very rumblings of life itself. Its the order that calls us to be more than ordinary. For our purpose, its relationship to forming our newer leadership mind-set is concerned with uncovering this *natural, deep order residing way beneath our* surface layers where we traditionally hover. As leaders, it's the place we need to search. This is where "the surfer" has learned to connect his soul to the unsuspecting, rumbling undulations of the tumultuous, enchanting emerald green sea. He lives and he creates in the margins and on the edge in order to optimize his relationship to the water. The draw of the sea is a connection to life, and for the surfer it reveals an otherness.

The living system is a discipline to see a new randomness with deeply imbedded but mutable laws. 1) equilibrium is death, 2) innovation is at the edge of chaos, 3) self-organization forms from interconnectedness (ants and traffic), 4) non linear thinking and migration. If we interact with these mutable or bendable laws through others also interacting and doing the same, we can then change the behavior of the whole system. As a practice, we must understand a complex structure of pulsations that perpetually begin to learn on their own — an innate intelligence - and then unwind it to its simplest forms. Together you take them into the underpinning of a new way of thinking. Here, you learn the way of the living system.

... All living systems seem to have innate intelligence. Living systems, whether organic in form (e.g., a virus, a human being) or systemic organization (e.g., the stock market, a beehive, a city, or a commercial enterprise, even crystal formations), seem to have a life of their own and possess a built-in-intelligence that involves an aptitude for survival, adaptation, and reproduction. This capacity for developing higher life forms has been lined with what is called "distributed intelligence" by theorists in the field. When applied to organizational behavior, the task of leadership is to unleash, harness, and direct distributed intelligence by creating environments where it can manifest" (Hirsch, p. 183).

Practically speaking its about finding an undisclosed rhythm in life, in business, in the organization that is a natural pulse distributing random surges of intelligence versus controlled and precise movements. Listening to theorists, it's evolving, emerging, messy, and even erratic, but when actually applied and unwrapped it is natural and deep in our core. In this beautiful mess is where is we find the Art of Surfing.

Its tough to just explain its theory and concept. I can tell you all day "how" to surf. I can tell you about the currents, the pull of the waters, the bubbling of undercurrents, the surge of a wave, the emergence of a wave's peak, the position of the drop, etc. but until you actually get wet by feeling and intermingling with all of these things in the water and experience that sensation on the face of a wave, it's all gibberish.

Something Hidden and Unfolding

This is about leading from the edge. It's not necessarily introducing a new blueprint for structure because a living system does not have a blueprint, instead it's about unveiling something *hidden* and *unfolding, a latent, intrinsic order that is within life itself.* It's about finding natural rhythms and systems of learning. It's about connecting to dynamic interrelationships. It's about surfing on the edge of big wave on a steep drop with two immediate but parallel emotions: 1) the fear of falling straight over your board and getting pounded by the wave, and 2) the exhilaration and surge of adrenaline as you rush the edge of the wave constantly creating and moving.

Concerning our more traditional mindsets, there are four distinct facets of the living system that stand in contrast to our usual ways: 1) The dethroning or leveling the typical pyramid, hierarchical structures of leading where only a few make all the decisions and authority rests at the top, 2) establishing a mind-set that helps funnel us forward toward the edge of an emerging pitch of an ever-changing wave, 3) transitioning ourselves into passionate evangelists of people so they can become relieved of the linearity of function and centralized authority and be infused instead with purpose and divine, creative value, and finally, 4) random, free forming dynamic interrelationships that develop meaning within the foundational values and purpose of a system.

A Waterfall

For example, in a top down model things are highly mechanized and broken down into specialized and separate parts. Usually the authority is hierarchical and the system is run by many rules and processes to keep things working tight and trim like a machine. I came across a great analogy of this application from one of my students presentation where I teach Organizational Development and Theory in an MBA program. She was comparing and contrasting systems of process in software development. She said the prevailing method of software development was a process referred to as the waterfall approach, very akin to the machine like precision of an assembly line. In the visual, you can see that in each phase or box, a team is designated to only complete that stage or function for which they are responsible only when they feel it is tested and perfected from their vantage point of task. Only then are they allowed to "hand it off" to the next team down the line. Very much like the factory floor where people assemble the pieces of the widgets in accordance to their task and specialization and don't interact with anyone outside of their position.

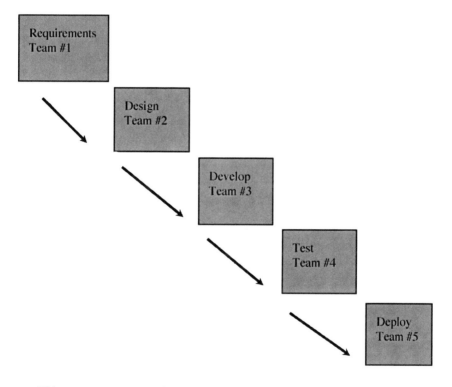

This process does push for perfection and attempts to present finalized steps, but more importantly it disconnects the teams interaction and collaborative efforts so that each box only interacts with its specific assignment. In other words, each team has to get it right the first time instead of going through a process of mutual, interdependent, interactive discovery stages. There is little reflection, revision, and it is difficult to go back.

Sue McKinney, VP of IBM's development transformation discovered that this rigid process was not working for her team. "What we had to do was modernize the corporate process, to move them away from being rigid [with] no transparency, very waterfall-ish, into something that allowed some flexibility" (http://agile.dzone.com/videos/sue-mckinney-agile-2009).

My student continued and displayed this diagram that shows a highly iterative process that coordinates ongoing collaborations with mutual discoveries and mutual revisions. Instead of a waterfall where process stages are only in specific assignments, here we have a circle of actions that loop back on each other to interact over and over again with the purpose to evolve the whole process of discovery into one big collaborative, interactive movement. It became a bound- aryless developmental phase with multiple iterations. What they did at IBM is a monument to the iterative and collaborative processes that humanize and simplify the ability to change, interconnect, and quickly adapt. It created improved com- munication across horizontal channels, team ownership, better workflow, trans- parency, increased collaboration, and elevated response rates. In the stages, you can see how the steps of the process interact and are simultaneously encouraged to collectively and quickly adapt to discovery, then make changes, and then do it all over again. "By replacing the traditional processes and culture with lean and agile practices, IBM's Software Group has transitioned its 25,000 engineers and the entire development leadership team to a new management and engineering style" (http://www.sqe.com/conferencearchive/agiledevpracticeswest2010/Summit. html).

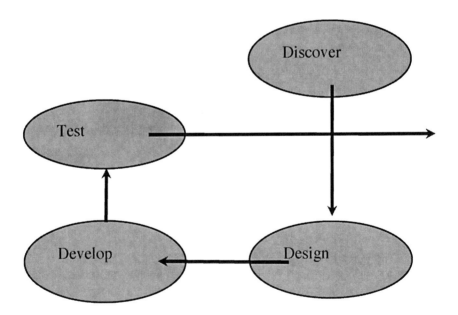

This more agile process breaks down the walls of communication in the "waterfall" and creates interdependencies where a waterfall-ish process strictly isolates movement to tiny and tidy boxes of limited movements before anything can move on. It's slow, perfect, inflexible, individualistic, and linear. McKinney put forth the mantra, "Short, time-boxed iterations with stakeholder feedback...

So I didn't have to tell the development teams what to do. Just by that one simple sentence [and process] they knew they had to change in order to be successful" (http://agile.dzone.com/videos/sue-mckinney-agile-2009)

For example, if we work in an organization that subscribes to a living systems approach, as employees we actually play a part in shaping the system instead of being cogs assembling widgets. A church that allows individual communities to form "cells" or house churches of micro-communities where they grow at their own pace, style, and methodology while adhering to foundational, core values of the whole body of believers. Your own life that is break from safe, stayed, typical functions where everything is ordered, mapped, scheduled, and the same. It's about bringing the bottom up through to the top where change and disturbance pushes things forward that then causes the system to mutate and alter in line with core assumptions and values.

Under this new way of thinking, we get to participate and contribute real input and emerge with the forces of change instead of route reactions. As leaders, we need to encourage our teams and people to become innovators and "creatives" through conversations and communities, like open source software. Like Wikipedia. In this model, we are released from our "duties" defined by command and control imposed on us by other people. Instead we determine solutions collectively by interacting within a loosely defined structure that encourage collaborations as a means to find what works best, or at least try to see if it works best in order to advance the whole system. Here, instead of autocrats and command and control personalities and precise life movements, we become guides, an unchartered course. In a living system, we get to interact with and contribute real change with real impact in real time.

Old Mechanical Precision is Nearly Unusable

The mechanical precision of the early 1900's, where management as a science maximized the efficiency of the organization and put into play precision and determinate outcomes like a machine, is today nearly unusable. I'm not saying its obsolete, but it is difficult for it to do what it used to in the 21st century with its perpetual, random forward motion. Instead, under this newer thinking and flatter landscape, we can create unusual, innovative movement, learn to dynamically perform in tandem with natural instincts, and produce outcomes that emerge. We can do it better, faster and cheaper than before, over wider terrain, and with fewer controls.

The living system approach provide results in a collective chorus or crowd wisdom instead of simply fulfilling a job description, a title, a function, a predictable. It's a new way of thinking, of working, of living, of producing because it humanizes the system. Like the Kaizen philosophy my friend and colleague recently spoke of in the magazine Transworld Business:

The Kaizen Philosophy is a wonderful Japanese business practice. It's basically all about taking your time and working together, in a positive and more efficient manner to plan smart business strategies. Then checking and rechecking those ideas for long term success. It is also a process that, when done correctly, breaks down the hierarchy of capitalistic titles like CEO, CFO, etc. It truly humanizes the workplace, eliminates overly hard work, and teaches people how to perform better and learn how to spot and—most to alternative and creative means of operating your brand, or store, can dramatically help you grow, especially in a trying economy. (Ken Perkins) (http://business.transworld.net/50009/features/upstarts-nemaki-industries/)

The Zone of Instability and Stability

I am not saying to let a system or its people run wild. I am saying that we need to bring freedom and creative energy to systems so that people can be ushered into their intrinsic, innovative design. Living systems encourages this through natural structures of autonomy and accountability that presses to the edge of innovation. However, like I said before it may make for a little perceived instability because it puts power into the individual, but it then holds him accountable to his actions, performance, thoughts, and ideas as they relate to a systems center. It's not a free for all or anarchy. It does allow self-governance but keeps the subdued control of theoretical walls erected by measuring your influence on the system and its related mission and values. It is a covenant instead of a contract.

This non-linear flow brings fluidity in a world historically layered with a "thick and gooey" bureaucratic ooze. Technically, however, it is defined as the place between the zone of instability and stability where the systems operate in a "phase transition or the edge of chaos- unpredictability of specific behavior within a predictable general structure of behavior" (Rosenhead, 1998, p. 3). Confusing right? Not really.

A Peek into the Transcendent

Looking at the technical definition only, by itself as a theory can seem complex and dense like the dirty, disheveled lab floor of a mad scientist riddled in endless scientific formulas, but as applied to a newer mind-set it can take on a lighter form with intuitive, intrinsic applications. However, the science of it needs to be broken down to bite size pieces. Otherwise, if we hover in the formulas of the parent science it just sounds like gibberish that theorists and lab rats love to chew and pontificate over during lunch and afternoon coffee, but this has real application for every one of us in the very foundations of how we think and live. It is about increasing our effectiveness and our outcomes by understanding a deep current of unconventional but novel order.

Complexity science [living systems] has may different avenues of study, but the one most relevant to understanding organizational dynamics - within companies [and life], and in the web of economic activity among them - is the study of complex adaptive systems. As we have seen, complex adaptive systems are composed of a diversity of agents that interact with each other, mutually affect each other, and in so doing generate novel, emergent, behavior for the system as a whole. The system is constantly adapting to the condition around it, and over time it evolves. Business organizations are also complex adaptive systems, in which the agent are people, and the interaction are relationships among them. In todays fast-changing business environment, companies will survive only if they are able constantly to adapt and evolve through operating optimally as a complex adaptive system" (Lewin, p. 200).

At the very core of its essence is this deep order. It's a peek into transcendence. However, to get to it we must peel back the surface and middle layers, the obvious and visible, to reveal the subatomic levels of this unexplained, unchartered natural order.

Unfortunately, what makes it a little tough to grasp is that this unfound order of living organisms doesn't come in a neatly packaged box with defined boundaries, directions, a cute bow, and scripted formulas. It can be messy, hard to find, seemingly impossible to shape, and incapable of predicting. However, it is also not as crazy and complex as it may feel. You have to discipline your mind to think differently and transform your behavior into a different way of interacting. In its nature is randomness, emergence, evolution, non-linearity, and complexity. You cannot think that it only sounds unruly, filled with uncanny theories that help it to "float away" with the first breeze. It is more than theory, and it is, although at first more complex, aimed at uncovering a simpler way of living.

From Bureaucracies to Disturbances and Random Connections

The goal in this leadership endeavor is to inspire people (and organizations) forward to creativity, build interconnecting communities, dismantle "thick" bureaucracies, and amplify our deep human truth. It mobilizes our adaptability and unleashes creative flow as a natural element in all that we do. A living system then can build on this invigorating functionality and minimize the stifling hand of control will unfurl our potential.

The first bit is that it performs these measures through some unfamiliar tactics. It uses the inertia from the unorthodox power of *disturbances, random connections with no recognizable patterns or predictable behavior, and unusual rhythms within emerging relationships.* Let me say that again. It uses disturbances. It accentuates these distractions brought about by change and uses its inertia to confuse the familiar out of sameness.

The second bit is that it potentially moves an older, stayed mentality that is typically disconnected from a system's movement to a place where they learn to interact and flirt with its laws. It scrubs duplication and replaces it with new, vibrant conversations and creativity.

The third bit is that it addresses the wrestling we have as we navigate our very survival in a new landscape now characterized by odd, unruly patterns of flux:

> The very struggle to survive, to adapt to the small and large changes of one's coevolutionary partners, may ultimately drive some species to extinction while creating novel niches for others. Life, then, unrolls in an unending procession of change, with small and large bursts of speciations, and small and large bursts of extinctions, ringing out the old, ringing in the new. If this view is correct, then the patterns of life's bursts and burials are caused by internal processes, endogenous and natural" (Kauffman, p. 15).

It also allows the unconventional to emerge while it quells the unproductive, stayed structures of the factory mentality. Things here are not neatly defined nor confined. Therefore the Newtonian bureaucracy and the newer indeterminate living systems sometimes will butt heads. The very nature of their opposing paradigms most likely will battle against each other, and like the theory of evolution proposes, the strongest most effective survive. If we are 1) open to a living system and its dynamic and challenging potential, 2) willing to distribute and flatten our centralized systems of control, we will be changed. We will learn how to surf and adaptability and creativity will become paramount.

> By contrast, complexity science implies that CEO's and managers must give up control - or, rather, the illusion of control - when they are trying to lead their organization to some goal. But they do need to create the environment in which creativity can emerge. The message of complexity science is not simply to stand back and wait for the right solutions to emerge. Too little control is just as misguided a business strategy as too much. Some structure is necessary. The degree and nature of control that CEO's establish in their companies strongly influences what emerges, in terms of culture, creativity, and adaptability (Lewin, P. 200).

These times demand innovation in order to stay ahead of the unrelenting, unknowable pressure of a connected global landscape. A living system alleges through its very nature these "bursts of speciations" or new and unlikely combinations and relationships to bring about richer, more creative, and fuller responses. "The order that arises is not imposed from above; it flows from distributed influence through the interactions of the system's agents. It's hard- and often impossible - to predict in detail what emergent order will look like, but it is certain that order will emerge" (Lewin, p. 201). In other words, these "speciations" as they imply, bring about completely new, hybrid situations. It requires us to think differently, behave differently, respond differently, and move under different impulses along side of each other. It puts to pasture the certainty of the predictive and brings to life the odd, yet innovative impulses of the natural and inspiring. It makes things a little crazy, but that "craziness" brings us to the edge of chaos and the brim of continual innovation.

Random Collaboration

What if the power to train the employees - from production to sales to fulfillment and everything in between - was put into the hands of other employees instead of a training organization or vendors outside the company? What if the most knowledgeable employee(s) in their respective work area was responsible for holding training sessions for the other employees? What if the employee then built the content around things he/she thought strategic and critical for effective communication to the customer drawing from the company's core principles? What if hybrid teams from different departments randomly formed and they were mandated to spend 15-20% of their time at work (like Google, 3M, and Semler and Co.) dedicated to creating new innovative suggestions for the company outside of its typical platforms, and then if the venture turned profitable they would share in a portion of the net new profits? What if all of the company employees were allowed to know the "secret" financial statement of the company so that they would know where and what to watch when it came to controlling costs and decreasing expense structures? What if employees got to share in a portion of the company's savings that they themselves generated from knowing what expenses to cut because of their detailed knowledge of the company expense structure? What if employee teams decided what to pay each other and their fellow coworkers and who to bonus and who not to bonus? What if they also decided who to hire and who to fire? What if senior executives, team supervisors, team leaders, floor managers, directors were hired by the very people they were elected to supervise, and what if then they "underperformed" and those same supervised employees could turn around and fire who they hired? What if when a critical issue surfaced, anyone in the company interested in the outcome would come to an immediate meeting, analyze the issue, vote on a resolve, and implement? What about implementing mass, random collaborations?

What if your organization or church or school became this living system? Could you handle the spontaneous innovation, rapid movements, unusual and unlikely undulations? Could you or your company embrace such relentless and nonconforming disruptions to typical activities? Could you handle this level of change? Could you handle expelling the illusion of control?

To tap into this in a company, an organization, a church, a committee may seem presumptuous, but the core of a living system is about creating meaning through relationships, undoing stereotypes that inhibit change, and leveling restrictive borders that altogether stop integration and interconnections. So the impetus in the company for the employee is that they would get to provide real time contributions and reap real benefits in intellectual and economic capital from the improvements to the bottom line. A living system creates a community rich in meaning and value. It all may sound a bit organic and kind of like a cultish compound, but I assure you that it is about creating rich outcomes with fewer resources that bring deep, sustainable impact.

A Machine Vs. A Living System

It is not enough to simply adapt or survive because there is nothing afterward of lasting value that remains or that becomes positively entrenched in our evolving. The older way simply get us through "the thing" and keeps us moving forward. We never really innovate. What I believe to be critical is for people to continually learn over and over again in such a way that they become capable of producing and creating on their own. Our innate ability to learn enhances our design to create which increase outcomes beyond what a traditional mindset of top down control can produce (Senge). I believe this level of learning is not only an important function of stimulation, but it is a critical human component that inspires both people and entire segments to ingenuity.

Reality as The Great Machine	Reality as a Living System
Separate Parts	Wholeness/Relationship
Power and Control	Co-Create and Participate
Objective/Knowable	Subjective/Probable
Entropy	Evolving
Order into Chaos	Chaos as Order
External Causation	Self Organization
Scarcity	Abundance

So although it may seem like it's a place where huts are built, the community plants staple crops, and they build their own villages, I assure you that the application is much more unfolding and dynamic. It isn't simply about sustaining life and sharing a workload. It is about innovating with life and creating a system capable of deep, meaningful change by tapping into resources imbedded within our fibers. A living system operates under the practice that true innovation needs blurry boundaries to move freely and create new realities through new relationships.

Chaos and Mayhem?

It would appear that such a structure that distributes power, shares sensitive information, and allocates resources via the influence and voice of the individual would encourage chaos, fuel the fire of mayhem, and then lead straight to demise or violent take-overs. What if we actually succumbed to the potential of a living system's new mindset? Would it fail? Would it succeed? Yes! What if the structure distributed the creative energy to the leadership, the company, the organization, the church, the school with a new savvy agility and streamlined energy into a balanced state between chaos and order?

"...From ecosystems to economic systems undergoing technological evolution, ... avalanches of new goods and technologies emerge and drive old ones extinct. Similar small and large avalanches even occur in evolving cultural systems. The natural history of life may harbor a new and unifying intellectual underpinning of our economic, cultural, and social life...I suspect that the fate of all complex adapting systems in the biosphere- from single cells to economies – is to evolve to a natural state between order and chaos, a grand compromise between structure and surprise. Here, at this poised state, small and large avalanches of coevolutionary change propagate through the system as consequence of the small, best choices of the actors themselves, competing and cooperating to survive" (Kauffman, p. 15).

Patterns of Crazy Randomness

Although a living system doesn't have traditional order with defined boundaries, patterns or outcomes, it does bring a newer more random and natural order that is sure to dawn a new creativity and innovative spirit to both an individual, a team, or an entire organization. To lose the structure of traditional order isn't a bad thing. It is likely going to be tough to uproot familiarity and things that are comfortable, but it will be a journey well worth the transition for those who have the spirit of discipline to both navigate it and see it through.

This living system does have patterns of their own sort but they are difficult to grasp. However, if the system is opened up, like a surfer senses the surge and pull of a wave's rise, so to can we find that in this randomness and craziness that unique patterns emerge.

"The indeterminate meanderings of these systems, plotted over time, show that there is a pattern to the movements. Though they are infinitely variable, the variation stays within a pattern, a family of trajectories" (Rosenhead, 1998, p. 4). Living systems possesses a place where "chaos is that unlikely occurrence in which patterns cannot be found nor interrelationships understood" (Pascale, 2000, p. 6).

A Pyramid of Hierarchy

Much of our life's paradigms operate under a pyramid of hierarchy and precision. At the top are the elite, the idea makers, the fire starters and at the bottom the rest of us who implement. Why is that? Why do we think so much of life is made up of the things relegated to those that have and those that don't and to those that are positioned well and those that aren't. I believe its because we all think the world is that proverbial factory where much of us are the workers and only a special few get the upstairs suites. Our mindsets put us there. We put ourselves in the assembly lines because we have been taught with a philosophy that is linear, static, sedentary, and filled with functions and slots.

Seth Godin recently spoke at a conference I went to and he gave a talk about how we are likely at the end of an era where the J.O.B is becoming obsolete. He wasn't talking about unemployment rates, al though they are high. He was talking about the flattening of the world through the creation of the laptop and the the era of the artist. Everything is now out in the open and we all have access to information, piles and mountains of information. With this access exposed to the world, we are no longer potentially captive to the pyramid mentality or imposed structure. We can now all create. We can now all innovate to the limits of our vision and discipline.

Don't get me wrong. I am not saying we all can "will" ourselves to a better place simply by choosing to muscle our way to the top of life. I am saying however, that there is a choice within where we all must travel the road we journey harder and deeper. We must seek with our souls, our minds, and our spirits to find this natural order existent in life that rumbles deep beneath the surface and then create. A living system will dynamically create and innovate depending on how hard we press into these natural, untapped fibers of our core that are underutilized and ignored. The living system allows those that will to be as Seth Godin says, "Artists."

We Get Stuck in the Layers

There are layers of layers, stacked on top of more and more layers where we have insulated our lives from disturbances. We protect ourselves from the spoils of the indeterminate movements of our curious, richly created souls. We shield ourselves from this perceived fear because it feels safe. We feel unnerved by the probabilities of imprecision and cling to familiarity.

I think we feel that to get out and try to "live up" is like trying to swim upstream in the Colorado river with no flotation devices, rafts, or paddles, or motors as it fiercely rages thorough the Grand Canyon. Surely, you know if you try such a swim you will never make it, and at worst you'll drown. Trying to influence this type of thinking or living in our own lives is daunting for sure. So much is against us, and actually so much of our own thinking is against us. We have trained ourselves to think in the assembly lines and we live under manipulations instead of striving to find a natural flow. We have trained ourselves to live in the box.

Living systems suggests turning the pyramid upside down. It changes our thinking to a "bottom up" flow where the majority becomes the influence and accountability within the community drives fruitful change.

A living system in essence consists of flat playing field that horizontally shifts the flow of information through interconnections, and this produces an open, collaborative flow of communication. There would be a slew of new and possibly odd variant patterns that might not makes sense, but the system would have to find its way through it. In this, the the system is prompted to interact differently, more often, and communicate in real time instead of through a labyrinth of mazes and approvals and committees. More conversations lead to greater possibilities, greater innovation, and a new pitch of discovery. And yes there will be a failure rate as the system repositions itself and relearns. Not every new idea will work. However, when a specific need or issue arises, a living system by its design is prompted to quickly respond, learn, and adapt.

For example, in an organization, the synergy will be driven by critical and real information that addresses immediate needs. The system can adapt and be immediately flexible with change. It will use change as an instigator to catalyze new creativity instead of a trigger that usually and typically freezes a system. With the community unencumbered with a boundaryless landscape, new and spontaneous interactions will be endless. The community will act with and understand the heart of the organization, be able to drive change through the mutual values, and create an adaptable environment.

Instead of the few telling the many, the many will now perform with the few. For example, departments are typically set within silos and operate under their own needs and specific goals defined by job descriptions and divisional departments. They have to apply for approval on anything they design whether it is process, product, or service. Instead, communities in a living system are encouraged to cross pollinate and problem solve dynamically and immediately instead being stuck in the mire of a parts and pieces mentality.

The outcomes, sometimes successful and sometimes not, will be filled with randomness and unusual connections because we will have turned the pyramid upside down and hybrid relationships will emerge and pollinate. Unusual outcomes will manifest, and confusion, to some degree, will happen. That is the nature of a living system, but the confusion does not go unmeasured or ignored. Instead it is evaluated against the "movements" of the organism to see if and how it adds or takes away. Ultimately, it will lead to new radical channels that open and circumvent crisis or allow a quicker recovery. Like a surfer positioned unexpectedly in the impact zone of a wave, he quickly paddles out to it and then over it so as not to get wrecked or pummeled by the wave. So the organization can learn to use a measure of change to its advantage or quickly "paddle over it." You must realize that the initial randomness of the system will feel out of control and uncomfortable, but until the older mindset is set to pasture these will be the growing pains.

Natural Principles

Because we have been run for hundreds of years under mechanical precision that manipulates outcomes, we have forced a natural world to fit into mechanized processes by interfering instead of innovating. We have missed a set of natural principles: edge thinking, decentralizing authority, autonomy, innovation, community, random relationship, emergence, co-evolution, disturbance, connectivity, etc. I am challenging leadership to seek this *deeper order of things* and discover its power to alter a static mindset. Underneath the alleged chaos is a set of naturally governing principles that run through the veins of the natural world, communities, economies, and organizations. As this obviously implies, if we can find this order and *tap into* how it runs, how it operates and how it functions, the potential for significant outcomes is very likely.

Let me use a slightly over simplified example to demonstrate some potential principles. Here is a question: If you take the flow of a creek, a river, or a stream and measure its efficiency, is it greater through a manufactured trench and a predetermined end or the natural law of gravity that moves it to a random end? The answer depends on your mentality. However, the variable that the water hinges on is where *you* as the "director of the water" believe the end should be that then determines how you apply the means. The filter of this older thinking is a mechanical precision focused on the functions of predetermined outcomes. Therefore, we build canals and aqueducts to direct the flow to where we want. We historically build structures– organizational charts, 5 year business plans, departments, job descriptions, clever titles - to direct the water to the end we think most important. Instead, a leader in a natural system would ultimately allow the team or the organization to innovate toward its natural end by leading, coaching and guiding it forward as a catalyst developing collaborative communities, horizontal communications, lucid structures, transparent conversations, non-linear thinking, adaptability and flexibility.

This is not to say that leaders let happen whatever a community wants. A natural system or a living system does not release mayhem into the system to run its course. Leaders are still needed and are essential at keeping thing moving and undulating like the ocean's tide. However, a living system knows where it needs to go better than an isolated leader alone set in his or her perch. If there is transparency, open, and accountable interdependent exchanges within the context of a clear vision and mission, the water for example will be directed with creative and effective intent through its natural currents. What if someone carves a path and the path is ultimately wrong? Intuition and collective wisdom under an autonomous and accountable structure will stir its momentum and collaborative effort back to "course."

The top-down operating mentalities of a past management age are contrary to how human systems think, act, behave, interact, and live. It is the science of management that was created to drive mechanistic precision. This is contrary to our natural world and therefore the world of a living system. A mechanistic device cannot operate under a lucid, interconnecting framework; its needs a platform of literal function and precise design to produce an expected outcome. The Industrial mind-set was designed with a need to control where the water flows. It assumes a false notion that that a linear path with determinant "canals" directing flow is the best way to direct the water. "The long-established reductionist approach has produced a substantial understanding of the world, both in science and in business. But in the new economy, as in the new science of complexity, the limitations of the mechanistic model are becoming inescapable" (Lewin, p. 197).

A Bureaucratic Maze

The older way tends to be a bureaucratic maze that winds around and then past a natural order. It contradicts the complexity of the human organism and a living system, e.g., the large corporation, the local church, the town educational system, the local company. Instead, let me quote the renowned scholar Stuart Kauffman. "It is our quest to understand the emergence of this ordered complexity around us, in the living forms we see, the ecosystems they construct, the social systems that abound from insects to primates, the wonder of economic systems that actually deliver us our daily bread..." (Kauffman, p. 19). In other words, the deep, natural order in complex organisms need closer inspection and understanding to reveal the workings of this natural world.

"Statistical mechanics demonstrates that we can build theories about those properties of complex systems that are insensitive to the details. But the statistical mechanics of gases [for example] is relatively simple, for all the gas molecules obey the same Newtonian laws of motion, and we seek to understand the averaged collective motions of the gas molecules. Familiar statistical mechanics concerns simple random systems. [However,] organisms [people, corporations, churches, schools] are not simple random systems, but highly complex, heterogeneous systems...Discovering the existence of key biological properties of complex living systems that do not depend on all the details lies at the center of a hope to build a deep theory of biological order. If all the properties of living systems depend on every detail of their structure and logic, if organisms are arbitrary widgets inside arbitrary contraptions all the way down, then the epistemological problems that confront us in attempting to understand the wonder of the biosphere will be vast." (Kauffman, p. 18).

In other words, like an engine of a car, the engineer must understand the details of each of its parts and all of its pieces in order to design it so it will work as a single, whole unit, and likewise the mechanic must understand the same details of its parts and pieces that the engineer designed to fix the car so the whole thing works in tandem with its parts. Each piece must perform its function so the whole can work, and a singular piece cannot perform a different function outside its design. Unlike an engine, a living system itself is an indeterminate order that is understood only in the revelation of its interconnections and interdependent communities. It's different. It is not in the parts but in the random relationships that constantly recreate themselves through an ability to freely interact.

If you watch an ant colony, they interact and intervene for the sake of the system. If they encounter an obstacle, they find a work around and communicate to the other agents. If they come across a leaf, they don't call the "leaf movers." They move it. When there is a disturbance to the system, they intervene and become interdependent. In contrast, a typical organization under the typical management structure is defined by the number and function of its roles, job descriptions, and organizational chart. There is very little blend or overlapping. The people only perform in that function defined by their prescribed expectations and report to their supervisors who measure and discipline against the script. Improvisation is a virtually non-existent, and it if exists it is usually an exaggerated anomaly.

Therefore it is near improbable to understand a living system's details like an engineer does an engine. Actually, to distinguish every component of a living systems meanderings and the inner workings like people, a corporation, a church, an educational institution, or even life itself would be to miss the whole point. And moreover, even if we find some of the details, it would still leave us with an inaccurate snapshot, because its very nature is random and only takes on shape and innovations as relationships multiply, diversify, and extend their complexities.

The "mechanics" of a living system aren't found in the details but the random things that come from the interconnections. Finding and pinpointing details will only intensify an inaccurate snapshot and foster a misperception of its wonder because that snapshot will have emergent properties that might only manifest that one time in that one spot from a one time connection. We can learn so much more if we systemically let the water run its course with a special blend of accountability and autonomy.

However, that said, I also understand that water running freely can cause grave damages with heavy consequence be it a garden hose or a raging river. A living system is not about wild unencumbered freedom without restraints. It is however about allowing the strength and natural principles of the internal workings of the system to manifest and propel itself forward instead of manufacturing a prescribed structure. In other words, let the water flow, but do so carefully.

Transparent, Spontaneous Conversation

These principles of a living system are cross-pollinating into the world of organizational life and individual living. By recognizing that there are principles governing organisms like you and me and large and small organizations, transparent conversations are beginning to take place that can birth a spontaneous order. Like a wave crops up from the deeps of a vast ocean through unencumbered connectivity, so to can creativity and innovation come about with a clear open bandwidth of conversations. For example, a living systems approach proposes through constant and transparent conversations communication can flow quickly and more often thereby minimizing delays, increasing possibilities, driving efficiency, and decreasing inaccurate information (Gary Hamel). If we stay stuck in compartmentalized thinking, we will stay stuck in a "part" mentality.

It's important in this discussion to rid ourselves from the "parts equal the whole" or the "whole is the sum of its parts." There should be no "parts" discussion. A living system is about relationships multiplying into networks of networks through conversation. To be effective is to always be in conversation, a conversation that has no real beginning and no end. It cannot of course be random and filled with talking just to have conversation. It must be centered around a purpose, a mission with common values, but it will be one with a moving line and ever changing themes.

Therefore, to have these conversations be effective, they must be boundary-less. They must be transparent and powerful enough to move change. When this happens, "bursts" of creative discovery emerge and fall to the bottom line of the company's financial statement, a church's tithing baskets or innovative programming, a student testing scores, or our own life endeavors, we can begin to unhinge these anachronistic, or outdated structures that keep us bridled.

Fantastic and Pragmatic

Kauffman again brings the scientific principles of a living system into the arena of the fantastic and the pragmatic. The allusion is that we cannot linger in the idea that specific individuals are, for example, limited to corporate boxes in an organization's DNA, or that once a worker always a worker, or that departments are limited to job descriptions, or that executives are the only idea makers, or that the few control the many, or that the best and most creative ideas come from the chairs at the top. Instead, a living system is a collective gathering of environments and communities that gather and create and solve and perform and innovate, like a surfer on the edge of a wave. The power then is in collective, interactive wisdom. In his following quote, once you get past the "science," he is alluding to an intimately interconnected system and its ability to unleash the potential and the power to surprise.

"Life, in this view, is an emergent phenomenon arising as the molecular diversity of a prebiotic chemical system increases beyond a threshold of complexity. If true, then life is not located in the property of any single molecule – in the details [in the parts] – but is a collective property of systems of interacting molecules. Life, in this view, emerged whole and has always remained whole. Life, in this view, is not to be located in its parts, but in the collective emergent properties of the whole they create" (Kauffman, p. 24).

Notice here how he emphasizes the collective properties of interactions- all the "matter" of the organization- all people, all departments, all levels, all locations, all energies. There is no hierarchy or top down mentality. He is speaking of a strict bottom- up, highly interactive organism. He points specifically to the familiar, "parts equal the whole," and says that instead it is a connection to the matrix. There is not a part or piece but rather a system of granular details pushed beyond its threshold through living in and through multiplying relationships; it is their conversations and their interconnectedness that enable the power to surprise, that then enable bursts of innovation. It is a chemical reaction that produces new outcomes that establish fortresses of sustaining change. Transparent conversations ignite and crystallize the new horizon and create new perspectives.

Like the surfer that listens and connects to the emerging waves by engaging in the patterns of the water's movement to then converge on the peak, leadership must learn to connect to his/her own community and encourage this type of transformative power of convergence. They must step back and set up organizations in such a way that continuous conversations catalyze the community and their power to innovate. In other words, those leaders have to relinquish their power and distribute it to the community; they are then held accountable to the community by their ability to lead, teach and inspire them toward the innovative conversations. We cannot operate from the perch anymore with linear, prescriptive thinking. It is a leader's job instead to prod an autocatalytic environment – self propelling, self igniting. He continues:

> "I propose that much of the order in organisms may not be the result of selection at all, but of the spontaneous order of self-organized systems. Order, vast and generative, not fought for against the entropic tides but freely available, undergirds all subsequent biological evolution. The order of organisms is natural, not merely the unexpected triumph of natural selection" (Kauffman, p. 25)

Traditional Assumptions

The traditional mindset generally oppose a mentality of transparency, emergence, spontaneous and self-propelling activity. Their argument goes something like this, "It is unlikely that a community that is free of traditional supervision and restraints will subordinate their wishes and aspirations to that of the betterment of the organization, the "conversation," or to that of the whole." Leaders typically argue that systemic approaches to such radical proposals are inherently "dreamy and starry eyed." The allegation goes that to entertain such a convention of conversation miss the ugly realities of autonomy and self-governance. The typical and historic belief is that people instead must be controlled within an environment of discipline and precision so that results can be maximized under a strict hand. A living system proposes that the opposite is true.

It replaces control with accountability and autonomy and precision with innovation and surprise. Instead of girding an organism with strict controls and functions to thwart off disruptions, a living system uses disturbances to propel the organism forward through adaptation. By creating systems that are agile and produce a nimble response versus a reactive stance, you create an organism that can thrive forward. You create someone that can surf.

Leaders that are stuck in an old era ask questions like, "How can and why should we give up our power and influence when time has tested the stamina of the model? What is our motivation to let the community innovate collectively while we sit in the perch? What systems of control and regulation are going to be there that will ensure that we don't file for chapter 11, all because followed this "great conversation?"

Whole Foods

I used to work just down the street from a Whole Foods Market and often I walk down the street to the store for brief and relaxing inhale where profitability and innovation intersect with grocery shopping. I loved to go there and just walk the isles to digest the precise and decorative order on the shelves, the ingenuity of the diverse and dynamic product, the eclectic atmosphere brought about by lively employees who adorn themselves in their own stylistic street clothes, the scintillating aromas that lightly hover above the aisles and command your awe, and the experience that it gives my psyche a lift on my lunch break. I never would have thought that a grocery store could recharge my batteries. Today, however I believe that it was my attraction to this living system manifested to certain degrees in the evidence of the Whole Foods conversation. They created a business model that continually generates a unique and intrinsic draw to the thousands of shoppers that dawn its aisles.

I usually go to buy one of their hand prepared sandwiches, freshly rolled Rainbow Sushi rolls, or taste a slice of their thin crust pizza smeared with pesto sauce and decorated lightly with tomatoes and cheese. Even though it is more expensive and I have to dig a little deeper in my wallet for a sandwich, I don't hesitate because I am drawn to their conversation.

I ask myself every time I go for my hand prepared ham and Swiss on whole wheat with fresh cucumbers and olive spread, "What motivates the employees to consistently provide fantastic service and make sure that I am taken care of?" I know they don't know me from the guy next door because no matter the employee or the day, the service I seem to get is consistent. The trend is seamless whether it is the bakery, the produce, the Sushi, the salad bar, the sandwich stand, or the checkout counter, the customer gets treated with surprises – excellent customer service, motivated employees, and a dynamic environment. They appear to be driven by something to enhance the customers experience. Maybe they are paid better than the guy or gal from the competition, but money alone is not enough of a motivator to provide a sense of greater purpose or common mission. They don't appear to be mercenaries who fight for for wages but won't invest in the cause or the plight of the people. Conversely, Whole Foods employees appear to operate under a burden of fulfilling the goal, "mission completion."

As a previous General Manager and minority partner of a company myself, I am always highly intrigued by an atmosphere charged by the energy of its workers through its innovative practices. I am always looking for dynamic ways to increase value in three specific places - the workplace for the employee, the experience for the customer, and the bottom line of profitability. Whole Foods, seems to clearly depict something higher than a job for their co-workers; they are able to create a place where they can subscribe to something higher. They appear to operate under a greater mission than a mere paycheck, a punched time clock, or corporate targets.

Take for example, although seemingly insignificant, the clothes they wear. No one is in a uniform. No one dresses the same. They look like college students dressed for class and then a lounge and coffee at the local pub. I'm not saying they are sloppy, but each employee expresses his/her own style in their dress. From their hair – trimmed and tight, long and braided, perfect pony tails, multi colored locks, Mohawks, or disheveled with style – to their choice of tee shirts, they exhibit personal preferences and styles. They clearly are allowed to be individuals in an arena that is typically corporate, stuffy, and same.

This sometimes overlooked visual of employee appearance plays out in their work forums and team driven performance objectives. For example, each store gets to pick several of its products to put on the shelves that is specific to the local markets and local tastes of the community as long as it meets the company's stringent quality standards. Each store individualizes its product. Teams of employees decide, not executives or boards of directors, what to display and what to sell. Similarly, employees vote on new hires to see if they will be compatible with the team. Mind you, this vote is not based on a simple like-ability factor, it is based on 3 factors: 1) how will the new hire help and contribute to the team's innovation and productivity, 2) how will the individual contribute to the individuality of the team system that is driven by creativity and performance, and 3) how will their addition increase team profitability? Because each store is so rigorously inspected and held accountable by corporate standards, tools of measurement, and benchmark performance, employees are motivated to work with and work for a team that accentuates individuality while increasing team productivity. "Whole Foods' approach to management twines democracy with discipline, trust with accountability, and community with fierce internal competition" (Hamel, p. 72).

At Whole Foods, when I peruse the aisles at lunch, my experience is not bound only to this particular location. The business model makes the philosophy paramount at every store. Even though my local store near my business may house a specific tea from a local provider and the store closest to my house 15-20 miles away may house an entirely different tea, does not mean their is a disconnect. It highlights individuality and innovation that bursts up and through the employees.

The teams have a stake and a say in the final product and are ultimately held accountable for their decisions and labor productivity against profitability.

Although Whole Foods set out to make grocery shopping distinct and create a grocery store that celebrates the individual with healthy, organic, unique foods, they ultimately are set up to turn a profit. As a matter of fact, they are a company that is very profitable as I write this, and one that does charge more than the commercial grocer for its product. The customers still pay the premium in part because of the "aromatic" experience and eclectic product choice. Yet, the under belly of the company and the very foundation of its platform design has a much higher purpose built around a very unusual model. The very successful and profitable company is based on one of those disputed and uncanny "dreamy and starry" philosophies that is difficult to imitate because it comes from the unorthodoxy of rebellious and contrarian management principles. They hold sacred the following

196

cores: "Love. Community. Autonomy. Egalitarianism. Transparency. Mission... A management system this comprehensive, this evolved, and this different doesn't emerge fully born. And it certainly doesn't come from benchmarking industry incumbents" (Hamel, p. 79).

Accountability

However, as Whole Foods has proved and demonstrated with a real business model based on human autonomy and profitable ventures, a strong and overarching accountability puts to rest many of the typical management arguments. Accountability is the hand that controls utter chaos and brings about innovative techniques. Accountability is center to a purpose, a common set of foundational values, an epicenter of mission. According to the argument of natural organisms, there is a pragmatic and dynamic fundamental in the system that thrives under such autonomy and accountability. It permits things to be monitored, quickly corrected, and then redirected. A living system will create and produce generative results if it finds this deep current of a natural order, of natural laws that governs existence.

For example, Whole Foods operates under the paradigm that "It is you rather than some distant manager, who controls your success. The fact that this freedom is matched by a high level of accountability ensures that associates use their discretionary decision-making power in ways that drive the business forward. Unlike so many other companies, frontline employees at Whole Foods have both the freedom to do the right thing for the customers, and the incentive to do the right thing for profits...[Newtonian mindsets are competing against more than just a philosophy.] They're competing with a community, a mission, and a dramatically different management philosophy" (Hamel, p. 73).

The mountain that the older thinking has to conquer is whether they *want* to change, whether they *will* change, and do they have the stamina to maintain the discipline to change. Let's face it, the paradigm shift that a living system approach proposes is nothing less than revolutionary to current and historic models, but its difficulty does not rival its revolutionary tones. The concept is simple, but the process and discipline of holding firms is the challenge. First, you have to become an historic management anarchist like the founder of Whole Foods. He unhinged the typical, canned formula and built his business not around an MBA equation but around an internal passion from a natural order. He took accountability and internal competition to guard against chaos and complacency and put it into a model that allowed the people to shape in its design (Hamel, p. 80). Second, you have to delve into the realm of the "dreamy and starry," unorthodox, and ill fated philosophies that sound unfettered and unruly. Then you have to tenaciously chase them and pursue a more pragmatic understanding of the natural underpinnings of the organism. You have to inspect and perhaps author philosophies that MBA type classes and typical management guru's would quickly dispel. Like

Whole Foods in the following chart (Hamel), you have to practice the unconventional and combat traditional structure:

Management: Innovative Challenge	Whole Foods Distinctive Management Practices
Empowerment, Managing less, and retaining discipline and focus?	Provide employees with discretion, information for wise decisions, and then hold them accountable.
Company where the spirit of community binds them together.	Manage and believe stake holder interests are interdependent; high degree of financial transparency; limit compensation disparity.
Build enlarged sense of purpose that merits extraordinary contributions	Make "Whole Foods, Whole People, Whole Planet, as real and tangible as the pursuit of profits (Hamel, p. 81).

Companies that build such a dynamic platform with distinctive practices, as this chart shows with Whole Foods, will build a living systems approach into the infrastructure and the soul of the company. As evidenced by how they build an enlarged sense of purpose, the company is not merely building an organization; they are defining a way of work-life and a way to build soul into a mission. It's not just about the profits, although clearly that is what keeps a company going and its employees employed, but it must also be about an enlarged sense of purpose that is held accountable with measurable results.

Watch the Ants

Have you ever sat and watched a community of ants? They are amazing workers, always working through dynamic situations, like moving obstacles exponentially greater than their body weight. Their solid lines of activity are akin to miniature freeways transporting and scurrying jobs to and from a destination. On closer inspection, they seem to always be communicating randomly and constantly. I'm not saying I sit and "listen" to them, but you can see it in their movement. Say a leaf falls in their path. Instantly they will converge their nearest forces around it and move it, or those closest will immediately convene and communicate backwards and forwards and start a new path around it or over it. They seem to improvise and act instantly through each other with creative solutions. They move together and appear to *selflessly attend to the community* and *improvise through a network of connectivity* and unconventional movements. Watch the ants and you will see the natural principles of a living system.

It Will Create a Resilient Brand

A living system has the foundation capable of building a resilient brand in most any organization as it creates a deeper understanding of purpose and existence and can add to the bottom line of a company. An organization that becomes a living system needs to be like the ants communicating effective change at the point of impasse through a labyrinth of interconnectedness and communal commitment.

How does this create a sustainability? In part, the fierce competition of capitalism and/or accountability is inherent in a living system, while the sense of community, conversation, and relationship create adaptable and flexible structures. For example, in an organization, your work group or your team measures your contributions to the groups results. Watching the ants, if you put your hand in the way of an ant trail, they will quickly self organize and find a new way around or over the obstacle. They will immediately readjust their patterns and communicate the change to the rest of the system. They are always sharing information, communicating change, and directing totally new patterns of movement on the fly. The community directs the community through the community.

Instead of this open and transparent conversation from a living system like the ants that encounter and communicate change immediately, information in a traditional organization is usually spaced out in tiny unimportant parcels. These parcels then are distributed to functional divisions as bits of disconnected data. The only "really important" bits are then only shared at the top.

An organism is effective only when the information is transparent and accessible to the whole system. First, in order to share the information effectively, it needs to be valued and its systemic connection to the system understood. We need to be educated and trained on what is important information and what isn't. For example, the organism needs to understand where the information comes from, how decisions significantly influence the bottom line, how the numbers connect, where the money needs to be allocated, how the budgets are decided, how to look for trends, what is the value of payroll, assets and liabilities, gross profit, net profit. This will help an organization to see where to peel back layers to expose potential wild fires. People within a living organization must understand the whole system so they can speak and contribute with intelligence, provide insight, and understand the greater implications of their suggestions. I am not proposing a free for all. I am suggesting an informed *conversation*, an open and insightful conversation that is held around open and real information where the ideas are put to the test and those proposing the ideas held accountable to their suggestions.

Be Like the Ants...

Employees, need to be like the ants who encounter the "hand" or leaf or branch in their way that then communicate back the information to the receivers;

they need to be the agents that collectively decide how to act an overcome the challenge. They are the ones immediately impacted by its challenge and they know first hand its bearing on the community. For the ant colony, it's not that there is an "executive ant" that is dispatched for intel from the front line at the obstacle, which then conferences with the corporate offices, who then decides in a secret room what to do for whole the colony.

Instead, ants act in real time with real and immediate results that generate real consequences for the whole. They communicate to the rest of the ants what is really going on and what to expect. Whatever ants first meet the obstacle, challenge, or barrier, acts and then communicates the finding to the rest and back into the colony lines until the collective receivers act as agents and move on the information. The authority is not in the "appointed executive ant," the most decorated ant that has proven himself over and over to the colony, or the one who has politically moved himself up the ladder. The community receives the information from whoever first encounters the information. The first ant(s) disperse the information to the agents behind them, who then adjust their patterns according to the data, and finally communicate the change to the rest of the community. They self organize. There are no committees for approval and no wasted time waiting for the senior ants to get back to the colony stuck and waiting at a juncture. They decide to go over, go around, move the object, or go entirely to another path. Under this system, communication thus flows quickly so there is no lag, misinformation, or corporate sludge to heavily traverse.

> "It turn[s]out that receiver-based communications is roughly this: all the agents in a system that is trying to coordinate behavior let other agents know what is happening to them. The receivers use it to decide what they are going to do. The receivers base their decisions on some overall specification of "team" goal. This, it is hoped, achieves coordination...The US Air Force had adopted this procedure to allow pilots to coordinate mutual behavior largely in the absence of ground control. The pilots talk to one another and respond preferentially to those nearest them, and achieve collective coordination in a way loosely analogous to flocking behavior in birds" (Kauffman, 1995, p. 267-268).

A living system, as elaborated, can be see in ants, but also in bee swarms, termite colonies, traffic, businesses, e-commerce, the stock market, the US Air Force, and organizations. "A complex adaptive system is formally defined as a system of independent agents that can act in parallel, 'develop models,' as to how things work in their environment, and, most importantly, refine those models through learning and adaptation" (Pascale, 2000, p. 5).

Traffic Ahead

I hate traffic, but it too is a living system. I think about it every time I get stuck in Los Angeles traffic because traffic like a living system is dependable, rapidly adaptable, and highly interactive with unique, random, patterns emerging from independent agents - the cars. Living in LA you just accept that traffic is a part of every day. However, no matter if it's West Coast, East Coast or the Midwest, traffic is essentially the same. It symbolically is akin to a clogged river, and physically it feels immovable and it ultimately looks like one big mess.

Again, a living systems approach has similar notions at initial glance. The surface appearance is congested, confusing, and obtuse, but if you got up in a helicopter to look at the total unit or the total system from high above, you would likely see a myriad of communication nuances popping up erratically all over creating an array of odd movements and unpredictable patterns. Traffic, like an organization, like an ant colony, like surfing is a complex adaptive system where the agents act independently and communicate information in parallel and adapt with responses from the other agents. It is an interdependent and inter connecting system.

Let's look at briefly at traffic. It is dependable, the patterns are unpredictable and probable, and it usually develops rapidly. It is caused by many things from the littlest of things to the most major. It might be the infamous "lookey loo" traffic observing the accident on the other side of the divider, the blown tire in the middle of the road, a stalled vehicle off the side, or the major 5 car pile up. None the less, its patterns are unpredictable, its behavior is indeterminate, and its likelihood is highly probable.

When traffic happens, it happens all over the freeway in almost all of the lanes in almost an instant. The independent agents (cars and drivers), like the ants, act according to the information in front of them and conversely dispense information backward. The reaction time is fast and the results are immediate. Traffic, like ants, self organize, respond to those nearest to them, collect and coordinate information, and then respond in the moment. Brake lights fuel the dissemination, and like the hand in the middle of the ant path, the brake lights communicate back to the others what is ahead and conversely the group responds. Through interconnections and intersecting relationships, traffic in the freeway system comes to constant emergent decisions with no traceable pattern. Actions from one driver will potentially affect all or most of the other drivers of the system, and at minimum that driver's action will probably affect someone at some point somewhere. The question isn't necessarily *will* it synchronize move- ment backward, but *when will* it synchronize and what affect will it have on the other drivers.

Drivers react quickly. They swerve. They stop. They slow down. They take side streets. They readjust. They crash. Each one of these actions cause emerging patterns that create reactions from the other agents which then effect the whole system. Traffic adjusts and refines activity, and like traffic in this example, we need to learn to similarly innovate as fast and with as much agile mobility.

201

Organisms like the traffic, if allowed to be continuously interconnected through chaotic principles will likely have a similar spiral outward from single to multiple actions. And again, like traffic, when the patterns unfold they will be probable and not deterministic, chaotic and potentially dangerous, difficult and hard to manage. However, the system ultimately will become flexible, adaptable, nimble, and mutual. Because of this, it is imperative that open conversations are encouraged, and that those conversations be transparent and relative. Unfolding issues and new relationships are bound to occur because "bubbling" probabilities and combined synergies create new connections.

What We Say and Do Have Profound Consequence

We need to realize that what we say matters and what we do matters because a living system allows other agents to be an intimate part of whatever is happening. One thing affects another thing affects another thing and so on. Like brake lights in traffic cause drivers all around them to respond and react, so to will our words, conversations, and actions in an open system have similar effect. Looks carry value. Words carry value. Conversations carry value. Unspoken but communicative actions carry value. If the system is intimately and carefully interconnected, there will be reverberations throughout the system on every minor or major movement and conversation in the entire system.

Small Pebbles

Whether you drop a pebble in a small body of water like a still pond or an immense body like an undulating sea, its impact will ripple across the pond or the ocean until it reaches its opposing shore. The pebble will disturb the system to a large or small degree and cause new behavior to the body of water. Like Pascale describes later as a key elements of a living system, disturbances excite a highly connected system and cause dynamic effects that author new behavior. Likely, the small pond or the big ocean would invariably be affected by the pebble. However, if you constantly dropped *multiple* pebbles in the pond or the ocean *intermittently but constantly* and *varied* the points of entry, those ripples would interact and intermingle with the other ripples to form indeterminate patterns and emergent directional "bounce." It would look a mess to the traditional mindset, but the patterns would soon form new behavior on the water's surface and therefore to the water's system.

More Pebbles Mean More Conversations

Such open, whole systems by their very definition carry value because the transparency and broken down barriers encourage and explicitly imply that more is at stake than just the voice of the few, but that all of the players involved are significant. The more conversations will invariably sprout an array of new conversations which will generate more dynamic activity, and this then will draw out a cross pollination with a greater probability of new hybrid outcomes. Sure it might at first be messy, but greater things are more likely.

If a broken down hierarchy or a pyramid structure is turned bottom up where more people interact like ripples in a pond, the total system will ultimately perform with greater effectiveness. Through collective insight, a church's spiritual core, the educational performance of a classroom, or the product of an organization will develop an evolutionary advantage. Because things are autonomous while strategically accountable, community quickly develops and shapes unchartered innovation. And because the community is strategically connected, rapid discovery and real time implementation are highly likely.

Gary Hamel authored an article called "Management a la Google" in the Wall Street Journal on April 26, 2006 in the Opinion section where he talked about a rapid ability to be strategically and rapidly adaptable, like the ants, bee swarms, traffic, etc.

"The ultimate test of any management team is not how fast it can grow its company in the short-term, but how consistently it can grow it over the long-term. In a world where change is relentless and seditious, this demands a capacity for rapid strategic adaptation...In many cases, companies have not been changing as fast as the world around them. What the laggards have failed to grasp is that what matters most today is not a company's competitive advantage at a point in time, but its evolutionary advantage *over* time" (Wall Street Journal, Hamel, April 26, 2008, Opinion).

Like the traffic that adapts its actions to avoid collisions, we must be as nimble and able to innovate with change and not be hindered by a hierarchical thinking "Accidents" (or failure) will happen in business, like they do in traffic, but it does not ultimately stop cars from driving nor should it stop organizations from innovating and risking. Accidents are likely when you put a bunch of cars together on a freeway, as is when you put a bunch of people together within an open system mentality of a company. Yet, just as accidents on the freeway don't stop people from driving, nor should failures shun the structure of an open system. Likewise, organizations need to be built on a living system and the realization of risk within interconnecting, but this will drive adaptability and flexibility. The community, like the ants, find a way around "the hand."

Employee Ownership (ESOP)

Another example of a subdued complex system can be seen in an Employee Stock Ownership. They can demonstrate characteristics of a living system with similar end goals, but they often lack the organizational "flatness" that openly distributes information and a highly connected network. They are built for the similar purpose of developing mentalities where individual, egocentric mindsets turn into active engagement. Employee ownership (ESOP) has a purpose to build such "independent agents that can act in parallel" and refine behavior and better the organization.

Under ESOP, it's alleged that less supervision is required while productivity is said to increase because employees become "owners." The purpose in ESOP distribution is that employees will develop an attitude that will lead to a new "owner" behavior from the idea that they can participate in the net results of the business. For that to happen effectively though, two critical setups need to happen for a living system to develop: 1) Build a new structure (structure directs behavior) of multiplying, highly connected networks and bottom-up mentality and 2) continually educate and train on the new mentality of living systems.

An article in the Wall Street Journal dated Thursday, February 7,2008 talked at length about "How to Get Workers to Think and Act Like Owners." Owners have a wishful tendency when they implement ESOP, and I suppose rightly so, that employees *automatically* should think like owners do and understand certain aspects of the business. There is a perception that because they grant this privilege of ownership, automatically an employee will alter his/her behavior and become more aware of critical components like expenses, inventory, gross profit, payroll, and net bottom line results.

The stock certificate is distributed with the intent to *automatically* impose an ownership mindset. The obstacle however is that although a principle is set up and a "tangible" goes along with it like employee stock that, the structure hasn't changed and a command and control mentality is still structurally in place. One business owner in Cedar Rapids, Iowa at the 100% employee stock owned company, surprisingly realized that they "'didn't know what stock was, didn't know what an [employee] owner was,'" he recalls. 'I made a mistake of thinking that everyone thinks like me'" (Wall Street Journal, Feb. 7, 2008, B6).

> "...Just establishing an ESOP [Employee Stock Ownership Program] often isn't enough to get employees to think like owners. Companies that want to create an ownership culture need to make an explicit effort to teach employees about their stake and keep them focused on increasing stock value...To that end, they should give workers the freedom to take initiatives to cut costs and boost a company's bottom line. Companies should 'push decision-making down'" (Wall Street Journal, Feb. 7, 2008, B6).

This new mentality of a living system has to be restructured into the organizational DNA and then that mentality has to be trained and continually promoted until it becomes the new way of thinking. The system and the people need to be educated and taught to recognize the change and "refine the models through learning and adaptation" otherwise the principle falls to the ground dead before it's even out of the gate.

Implement the Natural Principles

We can't just make a living system happen. We must learn to implement the natural principles of a living system and then constantly teach to it, and until both leadership and the people are adept at seeing it for what it is we cannot make the leap or the connection. Until we tap into this deep order more often, we will just get more and more confused and frustrated and then ultimately reach back to Newtonian behavior. We likely will revert to control, precision, and predictability to have a perception that circumstances are once again in our grip.

There are core elements and natural principles of a living system that we need to learn to recognize: 1) equilibrium is death, 2) innovation is at the edge of chaos, 3) self-organization forms from interconnectedness (ants and traffic), 4) non linear thinking and migration.

1. Equilibrium is a precursor to death. When a living system is in a state of equilibrium, it is less responsive to changes occurring around it. This places it at maximum risk.
2. In the case of threat, or when galvanized by a compelling opportunity, living systems move toward the edge of chaos. This condition evokes higher levels of mutation and experimentation, and fresh new solutions are more likely to be found.
3 When this excitation takes place, the components of living systems self-organize and new forms and repertoires emerge from the turmoil.
4. Living systems cannot be directed along a linear path. Unforeseen conse-quences are inevitable. The challenge is to disturb them in a manner that approximates the desired outcome (Pascale, 2000, p. 6).

Surfers Seek to Uncover the Deeper Order:

- The new leadership frontier is poised to search out this deep order of things. A living systems seeks to uncover a natural order that is governed by a set of innate, mutable laws woven through the fibers of all systems.
- The very struggle to survive, to adapt to the small and large changes, may ultimately drive some species to extinction while creating novel niches for others.
- What if senior executives, team supervisors, team leaders, floor managers, directors were hired by the very people they were elected to supervise, and what if then they "underperformed" and those same supervised employees could turn around and fire who they hired?
- In the randomness and craziness there is a deep natural order, and "the indeterminate meanderings of these systems, plotted over time, show that there is a pattern to the movements."
- Through constant conversations developed with open channels, unencumbered communication will flow quickly and more often thereby minimizing delays, increasing possibilities, driving efficiency, and decreasing ill- informed moves.
- The ants move together and seem selflessly to attend to the community and improvise through a network of connectivity and unconventional movements.
- The surface appearance of living systems looks congested, confusing, and obtuse, but it is a myriad of communication nuances popping up erratically all over creating an array of unpredictable patterns.
- Multiple pebbles intermittently dropped into the water will produce more ripples and therefore the more probabilities and patterns will intersect and manifest.
- Employee ownership is designed to build such "independent agents that can act in parallel" and refine behavior and better the organization, but they often miss the "flatness" that builds collaborative networks.
- Core elements of a living system: 1) Equilibrium is death, 2) innovation is at the edge of chaos, 3) self-organization forms from interconnectedness, and 4) non linear thinking and migration.

Chapter 7

Understand Interconnectedness is the One Thing

"Network thinking is poised to invade all domains of human activity and most fields of human inquiry. It is more than another useful perspective or tool. Networks are by their very nature the fabric of most complex systems, and nodes and links deeply infuse all strategies aimed at approaching our interlocked universe" (Hirsch, P. 200).

Linearity

Let's define linear: A linear equation accounts only for cause and effect answers. The plant is wilting so it probably needs some water. My stomach is growling so I probably need some food. But such strict thinking cannot account for interdependencies or things that are highly connected because it's only focused on isolated, static events and cause and effect relationships. For example, the car in front of me on the freeway hits the brakes and I respond by hitting my brakes because I want to avoid an accident. The attention is on my reaction that will impact only my scenario.

Instead, non linearity found in a living system is centered on interconnectedness because it sees that diverse connections are likely and very probable, and these then connect and influence the whole system to random varying degrees. It considers a larger, grander system that is most intimately connected through a maze of networks like traffic. In this case, when I hit my brakes I am immediately aware of the interconnectedness of the cars on the freeway that stretch out before me, behind me, and on the side of me. When I hit my brakes, I know I am com- municating to someone immediately behind me and to someone potentially numerous miles behind that I will never see. Therefore, when I hit my brakes I still don't want to get in an accident, but I am also aware that my response connects and communicates in someway to the larger system. I am still concerned with my impending likelihood of an accident, but I am also keenly aware that my situation exists within an intimately connected system that extends far beyond just me and my actions will most probably affect the movements of the whole system.

I talked earlier about the "piston mentality" where just looking at an event limits the ability of the leader to see outside of it and into the stratosphere of interconnectedness. Typically, we as leaders limit the scope of a situation to what is only before us or what perhaps was immediately said. We decipher the moment and unpack the event and usually miss looking backward and forward to other contributors and unique connections. By doing this we will always miss systemic issues that find their roots in the structure. A living system on the other hand accentuates random connections and a deeper order that push our perspective out to look at the traffic right in front of us but also to consider all of the traffic behind and on the side and what then our actions communicate to the whole system.

Life seems to be profoundly interconnected. The primary operative idea is that of relationships arranged in a dynamic network - a web of life and meaning. Living systems theory recognizes that we are always part of a larger system; we belong to an ecology composed of internal and external systems with which we are constantly relating. Disturbances in one part of the system set off a chain reaction that affects all the elements in a system. Capra calls this "the web of life." Some of the implications are as follows: 1) Small things can have system-wide consequence, sometimes called the "butterfly effect"...We should never underestimate the power of seemingly insignificant things to affect a system even if they seem unrelated at first. 2) A system is functional or dysfunctional to the extent that all of its parts are healthy and relating to each other in an organic way. 3) The way to develop a healthy learning/adaptive system is to bring disparate elements into meaningful communication with each other (Hirsch, p. 183).

Thinking only in this linear cause and effect stream hinders natural innovation because it creates immediate limits. It disconnects the system so things cannot communicate freely or openly. We tend to get stuck and take a snapshot and emotionally react and form conjectures without considering other random relationships. And then even worse, we make predictions from that stance. We discipline, reward, fire, hire, forecast, rebuke, etc. instead of looking at the roots of the system to study its behavior. Strict cause and effect linearity ultimately restricts learning and discovery.

At some point or even at all points, the actions of an organism are a result of someone else's response to someone else or something else, and therefore if such an organism is static and stuck in this linear thinking, their learning structure will be flat and disconnected from innovative creations. A system set like this will likely not organically grow because linear thinking keeps the system tied down. It is a listless exchange where selfishness and egocentric behavior dominate. Instead, a living system opens things up because "your success is not just influenced by your [actions]; it is influenced by the actions of everyone else in the system" (Senge, p. 50).

Non-Linear

Now let's define non-linear: A non-linear equation is not simply cause and effect. A butterfly flaps its wings and London and causes a tornado in Chicago or Wayne Gretzky rapidly skating down the rink and hitting an incoming hockey puck from a lightening speed pass while dodging defenders (I'll explain later). Nonlinearity provides dynamic, unconventional discoveries to a system because unlikely elements are brought into meaningful communications through organic means. When I hit my brakes, I know that someone, somewhere on that freeway will be affected by my actions so I act with the system in mind. I communicate immediately backwards when my taillights light up, but like the ants I am communicating with the system knowing my actions affect the local and global communities within that system. "What is most exciting about this approach is that things seem to flow effortlessly, because one is not going against the grain of the universe. The resultant ambience of the ... community is one that feels natural and therefore closer to the actual rhythms of life" (Hirsch, p. 185).

I don't merely act with my end in mind. I am also aware that I too am responding to someone else miles ahead of me that is lighting up their taillights and in some way we are connecting. You see, in a living system it's not that you can plan specific innovations or dictate certain conversations, rather they simply emerge. Someone taps their brake in front of me, then I tap mine, and someone behind me will likely tap theirs. And because these innovations and conversations in the system are highly varied and unpredictable, it's easy to imagine such a structure being just one big mess using our older, mechanistic mindset. Actually, that opposite is true. This indeterminism or randomness doesn't make the system so complex that you can't understand it, rather it makes it more interactive and dynamic because it works together (Kauffman, 1995, p. 17). The system "exchange resources with the environment, and they are systems because they consist of interconnected components that work together (Anderson, 1999, p.1).

If we act under the premise of interconnectedness where things work together for the sake of the system, we are acting in the belief that the entire system is preeminent to the selfishness of an individual. "Most theories about congregational life are flawed from the start because they are based on an institutional and mechanical worldview... [This view] is fatalistic and self-serving because the goal is to fix and preserve the institution for as long a life as possible. Such a worldview allows one to focus on mere organizational and institutional survival [rather than looking at our communities] as the roots and shoots of an organic movement that goes far beyond organizational survival" (Hirsch, P. 186-187)

Whatever decision we make in the moment or the situation, in a living system we are keenly aware of our neighbors and the notion that our actions ripples

209

throughout life and constructively and dynamically interacts with the other ripples already rolling across the water's surface. In a living system, we are acutely aware that random relationships that communicate constantly will likely create unparalleled but extremely simple innovations. Non-linearity seeks to build on what science calls *"emergent mutations"* or creative bursts instead of *"reactive jolts"* from management. "Event explanations are the most common in contemporary culture, and that is exactly why reactive management prevails" (Senge, p.52).

Interconnectedness

In a living system, non linear interconnections become the most important thing. The system itself becomes the key variable while we then learn to become a systemic thinker and purveyor of its behavior. This way, like a traffic officer, leaders can direct critical conversations and aid the flow of movement by helping to direct the traffic.

The system then is less confusing ultimately because it is lucid. When I am surfing and in the water waiting for the next wave to emerge, I am tuned to the horizon as I undulate with the erratic waters. I am flowing with the never ending, always different movements of the water so I can spring forward to the next wave. A lucid, adaptable structure allows many things to percolate up and out because there isn't a formula or script dictating a cause and effect mentality. Things "bubble up" and get evaluated based upon their contributions to the system. It is less about being someone who knows everything or how to control things. Instead, it is about how we transform into someone who is involved in many conversations by understanding the matrix of connections.

The Hockey Puck and Wayne Gretzky

Gleick uses the simple example of a hockey puck and friction. Without friction, a linear equation for a hockey puck will determine the amount of energy needed to accelerate a puck, but if you add friction to the same equation it creates a dynamic connection that adds complexity. This friction now is a disturbance because you have to decide *how much* energy to administer to a puck that is already moving (Gleick, 1987, p. 24).

Linear thinking would be similar to a static hockey puck on the ice slapped into the goal by a player with no distractions while dynamic, non linear thinking is one that has an accelerating puck passed to it and has to decide with how much strength do they then swing to score the goal. A static puck is simple - aim and shoot, but a moving puck involves much more probabilities and careful evaluation of many different variables with many potential answers. A static puck you just hit straight into the net, but a moving puck will potentially have more possible solutions and probable results. The two different puck situations however still both need to score a goal like we all need to perform and measure contributions to the system, but in today's society and today's market of unrelenting change, the moving puck is much truer to the actual climate. Therefore, decisions are made on issues that involve more complexity, more speed, and invariably more unpredictable influencers. Therefore, more is needed to solve today's unrelenting change – more voices, more diversity, more conversations, more probabilities, more interconnectivity, and more creative and unlikely ideas.

Imagine the hockey great Wayne Gretzky standing static, mid rink with hockey stick in hand and puck motionless on the ice square before him. He has no defenders, an open net, and clean, smooth ice. He is still on his skates before the net. He steps back, arches his swing back in perfect form, eyes the standing puck like an eagle glaring at an unsuspecting fish, aims with elite form for the upper right of the net, and lets loose a ripping shot that sails across the ice just above its surface. It hums with a blur and almost floats with speed and precision. He hits it so hard and so quickly that from the point of where it is launched to it striking the upper net square, the whole movement is a blur.

If he stands still and swings at a sitting target, the ability to predict where it will go and how much power the swing needs behind it is rather simple – point, aim, and shoot.

Now, figure Gretzky skating down the ice full speed, getting shouldered by defenders, dodging fallen opponents, and while in this rapid motion he gets a blinding pass from across the rink. He realizes he gets one shot, one slap to get it in the net. He cannot "catch" it, skate to a favorable perspective, cautiously eye the defenders, and then shoot. Given his angle, he must meet the puck with his speed and in one swing aim and shoot for the goal. His only chance at the upper right is to meet the puck square on at its pace, with his skating speed, in the midst of the aggressive defenders, and slap it in the net with the assessed amount of friction required to hit the mark.

In this case, the puck is far from static. It is kinetic and loaded with momentum. He has to therefore calculate his swing differently and adjust his necessary perceived power in the swing with the power already in the puck from another player. Then with precision and calculation, he has to connect his stick and swing, while in dramatic motion, to the moving puck and aim for the upper right. Like Pascale's example, the motion of the moving puck toward Gretzky is the disturbance to his previous, still position – e.g. radical, fast change. His assessment has to be dynamic because of the variables coming his way at a furious pace.

The disturbance of the puck's momentum causes his senses and talents to "froth" to the top, hone in on the solution, and nimbly apply the right amount of friction. Previously when he simply stood on the ice and shot, there was no disturbance to the system of his swing, he simply hit the puck. However, today's pace of change proposes that disturbances, like the speed of the passing puck, the movement of the other players, and the speed of his own skating serve to only interrupt traditional management. Instead, we need to insert dynamic alternatives. In this case, Gretzky has to process all the information and make a decision "on the fly." His ability to quickly adapt and apply new and quickly flowing information will invariable determine his success or failure. His agility is defined in the willingness to merge all of his resources (talents and knowledge) and open the system to the interconnectivity of his resources and talents to the system of the game.

Be Nimble

We need to learn how to be nimble within this speed of change and connect to the evolutionary advantage. Because a living system is interconnectedness between agents, we need to allow ourselves and organizations to intermingle, interact, and create conversations and relationships. With this newer structure, we need to likewise be able to sustain a system of rapid learning under a climate of drastic flux. We need to release the stronghold of a controlling structure and not fear the ocean and its undulating, connecting power. Instead, we need to paddle to the wave, spin around to its peak, paddle into its force, drop down the face of the wave, and surf.

Top down strategies don't win ball games today. Experimentation, rapid learning, seizing the momentum of success works better...the top can't possibly have all the answers. The leaders provide the vision and are the context setters. But the actual solution about how best to meet the challenges of the moment – those thousands of strategic challenges encountered every day – have to be made by the people closest to the action – the people at the coal face. Everything and everyone is affected.

Change your approach to strategy and you change the way a company runs. The leader becomes the context setter, the designer of a learning experience – not an authority figure with solutions. Once the folks at the grassroots realize they own the problem, they also discover that they can help create and own the answer – and they get after it very quickly, very aggressively, and very creatively, with a lot more ideas than the old-style strategic direction could ever have prescribed from headquarters...Once you give [the coworker] the context, they can do a better job of spotting opportunities and stepping up to decisions (Pascale, p. 191).

With real situations being pressed under the weight of varying forces of friction, like Gretzky's palpable but quick need to assess how to score, businesses, churches, and organizations need a system that is nimble enough to adapt and innovate in this rapid climate of change. How difficult is it to shoot a puck straight at a net without disturbances? Sure there are a few things like ice, a hockey stick, and balance, but they are "controllables" that the individual can easily influence. However, current trends of change demand greater agility.

Under a living systems approach, disturbances push an organism towards an edge. The organism, like Gretzky has to react openly as a whole system, evaluating and taking in all of the variables while "on the go" so they can score a goal by adaptable, flexible, nimble behavior.

However, the Newtonian mindset, like the first scenario of static controllables, diminishes nimble innovation because its emphasis is discipline, control, and precision while under a top down hierarchy, "...all those dense connections fuse like chemical bonds rather than flexing like a permeable network" (Pascale, p. 25). Until the people are prompted to engage with the issues, with each other, and with authority to collectively provide wise solutions, we will be ruled by a linear mindset incapable of Googles evolutionary advantage.

Finally, like whole systems mentality preaches, there is interconnectedness between the puck, the friction, and the outcome that will vary every time because of random disturbance to the system. It therefore requires the availability of the whole system to respond to the onslaught of change. Likewise, an organism that embraces a living system acknowledges that without the consideration of conversations from bottom up, adaptable behavior, and evolving solutions, we will likely only reach a lukewarm mediocrity.

Chris Langton, one of the pioneers of complexity science, has deepened our insight into the way equilibrium comes about. He programmed a series of simulations analogous to a beehive in which individual virtual "bees" were given simple rules to follow. When the rules became too rigid or too numerous, the beehive froze into inactivity. A little elasticity in the rules generated a repeating pattern in the hive; a few changes would ripple through the system, but the hive then reverted to its original state and the same pattern emerged again and again. In both instances, the rules evoked order and equilibrium.

With no rules, the opposite phenomenon occurred. The hive dispersed. But there was yet another set of rules described by arcane, hard-to-pigeonhole algorithms that proved most interesting. Along with some regularity, there was a flow of nonrepeating patterns. The algorithm was defined in such a way that it generated disturbances in its own regularity. Patterns would propagate in the honeycomb, disaggregate, and then recombine in perpetually novel ways. The "hive" always had enough internal variety to keep it from being locked into itself (Pascale, p. 25).

A Butterfly?

Similarly, Stuart Kauffman talks about the interconnectedness of the famed Lorenz butterfly effect. It states that the flapping of a butterfly's wing in London for example, could cause a tornado in Chicago. The flapping of the wings, or small disturbances, can have an immense effect on behavior within things highly connected, *and because of these interdependencies, or this sensitive dependence on initial conditions*, it is impossible to know the long range outcome. The variables intermingling with each other in a system cause so many contingencies that determinism has no power of prediction. This highlights several outcomes: 1) An intimately connected system could be greatly affected by a disturbance or com-

213

pletely unaffected, 2) a disturbance does not determine something good or bad will happen, 3) the "fitness" of a system will be determined by its adaptability to the disturbance, 4) a disturbance will likely evolve an organism forward if it is highly interconnected.

He describes disturbances or perturbations to the system as *essential* and how even the smallest of vibrations - i.e. butterfly flapping and floating - in an intimately interconnected system, like the weather or even an organization, can have tremendous effects on the overall outcome, or conversely none at all. Imagine the delicate, tissue paper-like wings of a butterfly adorned in amazing patterns of vibrant and unassuming colors having such an influence that it can alter weather patterns and change behavior of tremendous systems. It seems odd that such an intricate, small creature with wings that silently flutter and float on the back of the air can move things of such size. However, the key that we are looking at here is not necessarily the butterfly and its faint size, but the power of disturbance within an intimately connected system.

In a living system, it's not necessarily the size of the disturbance that is of concern but the nimble and adaptive capacity of the total system as it responds and moves with the disturbance, aka. its fitness level. It is first about the intercon- nectivity of the system and second about its adaptability from a disturbance. When a system is highly interconnected and filled with diverse relationships, the greater its "fitness" when it encounters a "non-linear" jolt or disturbance. In other words, the response of the system is ultimately a measure of its ability to innovate and adapt.

Conversely, because of probable behavior and indeterminate patterns, it also can distribute very little to no change. It's virtually impossible to tell what might happen or what might not happen. The disturbances can potentially jolt an entire system or conversely just send minor reverberations. It could form a tsunami or it might trickle a simple ripple. In the case of the butterfly, small disturbances can have random, unpredictable effects on the weather system. It might cause a hurricane, perhaps a few cumulous clouds, maybe just a little breeze or even nothing at all. The key however is that without these perturbations or these disturbances to a living system, nothing will change. Unless equilibrium is pushed to an edge or disturbed in a chaotic system, you will always have what you have.

What's important to comprehend and grasp here is that these threats, or these disturbances challenge the system and how well it works and or responds to hurdles outside the system. At the rate change is happening today, a system needs to be able to self organize and find solutions that best fit the immediate need and the long term nature of its adaptability. If it cannot mobilize and meet the opportunity, it will fall prey to change, be it good or bad, and be forced to wait out its fate. A system disconnected and run from the top for example will not be able to converge and circle their resources to adapt to the complexities tumbling down or hurdling themselves at the organism.

If the executives control the boardroom and the company, the rest of the workforce is at the whim of the few and the powerful and unable to move as a system when a perturbation hits. If it cannot immediately and collectively respond, it might be forced to perish or even worse, linger in the world of mediocrity. Also, the company and the entire workforce, the greatest asset of any organization, is forced to wait in anticipation of what and how they are told to respond.

Take this example: This scenario is like a crew of firefighters waiting for orders while they are smelling the embers of a forest fire, seeing the ash snow down on their camp, choking on the smoke, and anxiously watching the tips of the flames prick their heads over the ridge. They have to wait in the queue until some commanders in a far off, air conditioned office with maps and diagrams decide how to fight the fire through calculations and aerial photographs that are hours old. In other words, if firefighters are set as "self-knowing, intelligent entities" they can circle their own resources, study the fires movements, view the maps, and use their perspectives and experience to fight the fire as primary responders, they likely will have a fresh, true, and immediate understanding of what is needed versus the "suits" in the office far away from the heat.

Companies and organizations need to do more than mobilize the workforce. They need to let the workforce *mobilize itself* into innovative agents that can adapt and then redefine their interactions over and over. In so many cases, change becomes the only constant and this ability to collectively and immediately mobilize is essential.

Conscious learning and intention define a watershed in our exploration of what the science of complexity means for business – a line of divergence between humans and the rest of nature. Nature disturbs equilibrium through the threat of death and the promise of sex; it nudges species into an arena where chance mutations can thrive. Clear parallels exist between human system in general and business in particular. But humans have an important advantage. As self-knowing and intelligent entities, companies, at least in theory, are capable of recognizing danger (or opportunity) in advance and mobilizing to take appropriate action. They can wield the power of human intention (Pascale, p. 33).

The state of interconnectivity will produce outcomes, although unpredictable, that *can ultimately* surmount and circumvent the impending crisis. The key is to allow and continually encourage the lively and active interaction with disturbances. The ability to sustain constant behavioral change and dynamic outcomes will be the only thing capable of fighting change in a typically mechanistic driven bureaucracy.

Kauffman continues to explain the significance of small disturbances with sensitive systems, and although the outcomes will be unpredictable, what is important is how it responds.

Whatever winged creature is responsible, the point is that any small change in a chaotic system can, and typically does, have large and amplifying effects. Thus this sensitivity implies that the detailed initial condition – how fast, at what angle, and precisely how the starling flapped its wings – would have to be known to infinite precision to predict the result...Thus the familiar conclusion: for chaotic systems, we cannot predict long term behavior. Note again that failure to predict does not mean failure to understand or to explain (Kauffman, 1995, p.17).

The purpose then of these disturbances, whether purposeful from internal structure or unintentional from external influences, then is to create a place and environment where unlikely relationships can engage and flex through conversation and adaptability. It isn't simply to create more chaos on top of chaos to test stability and adaptability, or monitor the buoyancy of the system (although still a critical function of behavior), but it's primary purpose is to innovate and to create new opportunity that will lead to new heights of performance. The trick is that there is no way to find out exactly what it is because it is an evolving and emergent arena, except to put your hands to the plow and till the soil . Allowing a living system to prevail in its full form will open up the possibilities.

It Appears Like an Ocean of Colliding, Turbulent Waves

Yes a living system might feel like an uncontrollable ocean, but this sense of chaos is actually visible, living energy from entities interconnecting. Sitting in the ocean on my surfboard in a choppy, turbulent swell looks like and feels like bundles of energies hitting and colliding in a messy fashion: White caps rise up from the wind, meet, and slap together. Currents ripple on the waters surface while brewing like a witch's cauldron underneath. Foam from the white wash of a crashing wave bubble up and leave a white blanket of slop and froth trailing behind. Waves mound up, crash down, and cascade like a waterfall down their face. Winds whips up the chop and blow the lips of the waves around like spray from a misting rain. All of this teeming activity is a result of things colliding and then connecting, and this is the vitality of a living, breathing system.

When I am surfing, if I stare off into the horizon, feel the breeze on my face, and undulate with the current and the waves, I sense a power of convergence where properties emerge and collide to co-create and co-discover. I am engulfed in the immediacy of what is before me: the breeze, the lapping water, bouncing waves, swells, the shoreline, rip tides, currents, my undulating surfboard, and the waves I want to catch. It's this visual disorder that produce the wave that I surf.

Systems, like the sea for example, can be aligned to an image of what could happen. If this colliding power is allowed to create this seeming messiness of energy in the sea, imagine what similar structures could do if loosed through interconnectedness and collective intelligence. The possibilities are confined only by our own willingness to change and engage with emergence and rid ourselves of a traditional sense of control.

216

The Wave Heard Round the World

Have you ever seen the wave heard round the world ridden by surfing legend Laird Hamilton in Teahupoo, Tahiti? In a YouTube video Laird is said to have commented on the fact that this particular wave is an absolute freak encounter with hydrodynamics. It sucks so much water from the reef that it produces one of the most unique and most powerful waves on earth. It is not the highest wave but perhaps one of the most extraordinary because of its explosive power that erupts laterally onto a razor sharp, extremely shallow reef. It's possible that it is the most tenacious wave in its sheer mass and ferocity, and the wave heard round the world that he rode might be recorded as the single, heaviest wave ever surfed.

Because of the interconnectedness of the sea, the outlying swells and storms form energy, rush up to the reef with explosive might, and form the powerful mass of a wave. This is symbolically similar to the might that interconnectivity will bring to an organism. Like Laird surfing this mass of water, so to can we mingle with unfound might if enter into the scary and exciting cauldron of "letting go" and transforming a top down world into a bottom up mentality.

Buttons and Chemical Reactions

If a living system is a convergence of power and "chemical" reactions, a string connecting hundreds of buttons on a string, although interconnecting and corresponding to the movements of others, is not a non-linear activity (Kauffman, p.116).

If you take a single piece of string, tie it to a needle and begin threading the string through one button and then another and then another and then another until you have amassed a huge connection of buttons on one piece of string, you still only have a bunch of buttons connected on a string. There is nothing special but the amount of buttons you can connect. Even if you take this static connection and by one lift of the last button can hoist up the entire chain of buttons, you still only have a string of interconnected buttons that move together because of their new and unique relationship on the string. However, it is not dynamic connectivity.

A living system instead is dynamic and laced with evolving, almost explosive interconnections, that perform wild indeterminable behavior and randomly emerge. They are not like a slew of buttons connected together by a flimsy string. Although technically, they are interconnected, the buttons are not random, chemical relationships but rather staged connections that exist by the determinate planning of one movement. Ultimately, the buttons on that string belie only one relationship over and over again. Instead, Kauffman defines a living system under this light with a more explosive image of different relationships happening all over, all the time, and in no apparent pattern or regularity:

> Buttons and threads cannot do such odd things, but chemicals and chemical reactions can. Chemicals can be catalysts that act on other chemical

substrates to create still further chemical products. Those novel chemical products can catalyze still further reactions involving themselves and all the original molecules to create still further molecules. These additional new molecules afford still further new reactions with themselves and all the older molecules as substrates, and all the molecules around may serve as a catalyst for any of these newly available reactions. Buttons and threads cannot, but chemicals and their reactions can spill out the window, flood the neighborhood, create life, and fill the biosphere (Kauffman, p. 116).

I have a friend in the financial service business that works for a large and renowned firm and experienced this type of chemical reaction in the now historic financial crisis at Wall Street. One morning he was flying out to a major metro city to meet some stout clients that have invested a respectable size of income with his firm, and both he and his partner manage the portfolio. The main purpose of his trips was to fly out there and quell the storm of fear ransacking the minds of some of the clients of what currently is happening in the financial world both domestically and globally. I was talking to him the evening of the A.I.G. bail out, the Merrill Lynch purchase by Bank of America, and the debacle of Lehman Brothers. Within those last two nights – Monday and Tuesday – he logged about 3 hours of sleep so he was bit groggy, but the image he provided from his perspective was a very fascinating view of interconnectivity.

He explained it like this: Wall Street is an open system acting "religiously" under the principles of dynamic and indeterminate explosions and reactions. It is powered through its interconnectedness and probable not predictable behavioral patterns. He shared an image of the financial system that helped speed the crisis, and chemically it acted just as chaos alleges – indeterminate and unpredictable patterns emerged under disturbances to the system. Although the image is not entirely the shape and character of a living system, it does serve to explain a particular aspect of connectivity.

He explained to me how the financial world is like a pile of sand. If you take your hands, grab a scoop of sand and pour it out to a mound on the beach shore, it will pile up and hold some type of form. Although the shape that it takes is always different, the sand will some way and in some form always "pile' up. Literally, it will hold as a lump of connecting grains of sand, but what is important is that all of the grains that make up the pile or mound of sand are interconnected dynamically. They all have an interdependent "lien" on the grains of sand above, below, on the side of, next to, or near the other grains of sand. They all make up the mound and they are all interconnected and form "the pile" together. Where it gets radical is when you gently remove one grain of sand from that pile. It creates a disturbance to the system that could turn "violent" or do nothing at all. In a truly chaotic system, there is no way to know the way the pile will fall, if the pile will fall, if the pile will be stirred to a small or large degree, or if the pile will be completely undone by one small disturbance. The grains of sand are all interconnected and the theory states that in such a system, disturbance to the system, even as gentle as the butterfly's whisper or the undulation from a grain of gently textured sand, will have probable outcomes that are unpredictable.

The difference though in a sand pile and Wall Street is that one is static and becomes dynamic only when disturbed – the sand pile – while one acts alive and evolves – the financial market. Although the pile of sand contains interconnected agents, as does the string of buttons, it still is a system of pieces unless it is disturbed. In a truly complex adaptive system, like the ocean or an organization, combinations of entities are constantly bubbling, moving and creating new and unlikely relationships as it moves closer to the edge.

A system – Wall Street, an organization, a church, a school - that recognizes the power of living systems and applies it to leadership comes alive through its people, while the sand pile is only alive through disturbance and therefore becomes active only when prodded. Still, similar to the pile of sand, the financial market is intimately interconnected and the grain of sand that was removed caused great crisis in the market to the point that the pile seemed to tilt and almost completely crumble. Although I could by no means give a lecture on the technical meanderings of the fascinating complexity of the financial system, I do understand that it is most assuredly dynamically connected. The myriads of connections and relationships stretch out like patterns of a black widow's web or like the ocean's waves. They are erratic, seemingly disorganized, and even hard to see, but under the cloak of perceived confusion is the paramount stamp of something with a natural, deep order. The connections are like tentacles from thousand's of octopi overlapping and alive with touch and sense.

In this case, a living system was involved with adverse, negative effects in the financial sector, but the spiral was not *because* of it's principle interconnectedness. Financial leaders carelessly and unwisely gambled with too high a risk ratio and leveraged their firms beyond their ability to recover, and ultimately they were held accountable by the market. Their greed adversely affected outcomes while economic reality tipped the markets backward and sideways. The severe conditions of the risk were minimized and the probable returns were inflated; it made for a very bad equation. The economic facts of the market virtually spun an institution upside down while the *reality of a living system merely sped the process.* "Self organization is the tendency of certain (but not all) systems operating far from equilibrium to shift to a new state when their constituent elements generate unlikely combinations" (Pascale, p. 113).

However, a living system is tremendously powerful when the dynamic inputs flow through emergent, interconnected channels, and when harnessed under accountability it can move industries or it can transform behavior. "When systems become sufficiently populated and properly interconnected [through accountability], the interactions assemble themselves into a new order" (Pascale, p. 113). its behavioral characteristics and allowing a living system to flourish will enable dramatic unpredictable and indeterminate behavior.

Although it may at first glance look and feel like one big mess, it has an unfolding order that is naturally organized in its center. Our task as leaders is to learn to recognize it, harness its potential, then use it as an engine to maximize outcomes, and unfurl the hindrances Newtonian controls places on a system. The interconnectedness needs to be explosive and not static like the buttons and the sand pile. Although Wall Street is facing extremely adverse effects from its current circumstances, it still stands that Wall Street is a kinetic mechanism that is constantly developing new relationships and emerging patterns that are, as we are seeing, unpredictable. However, that is its strength, and if it not held accountable, its unmitigated and unsupervised autonomy will be its demise.

At the quantum level of reality, the paradoxes grow even larger. At the subatomic level change happens in jumps, beyond any power of precise prediction. Quantum physics speaks in terms of probabilities, not predictions. They can calculate the probable moment and location of a quantum leap, but not exactly (Wheatley, 1999, p. 22).

Traditional Solutions for New Problems

We still reach back to the archives of the science of management and look for older familiar answers in an era of unprecedented change. We can't do this anymore. Our world blends and blurs the lines into complicated networks that evolve. Today, when our equilibrium is disturbed, we right away want to restore stability with familiarity. We fall to things tried and true. We merely try to replicate the past.

When we do this, we intellectually and spiritually disengage from the process of discovery and fall back to sameness, or worse we rely on equilibrium. We remove ourselves from the issue and wait for it to fix itself while we are removed. We sit and wait for a "memo" from someone else to fix it so we can move on. We rarely think that the disturbance is actually the stimulus, the impetus that breaks us from equilibrium. Our Newtonian mindset prefers predictability and sameness, so we level out and throw "efficiencies" at it instead of effectiveness. We throw mechanistic thinking at an emergent phenomenons.

A Concrete Theory

Like the ocean may one day look chaotic and the next day calm and peaceful, so is the natural system's randomness and unpredictability. It is impossible to know the shape, size, or frequency of the outcome by studying the patterns of one event and then using that to predict its next pattern. Lewin says that the same butterfly in London that changed the weather in Chicago may again flap its wings causing small perturbations to the system and nothing will happen. "This is the second feature of non-linear systems: very slight differences in initial conditions produce very different outcomes. That's the basis of their unpredictability" (Lewin, 1999, p. 11).

220

In a conversation between complexity scientists Chris Langton and Roger Lewin, Langton described a living system by drawing too big, broad strokes on a chalkboard, "Totally ordered over here...Totally random over here. Complexity happens somewhere in between. It's a question of structure, of organization. The gas in this room is a chaotic system, very random, very little order. The science of Complexity has to do with structure and order" (Lewin, p. 10). For example, he goes on to explain how Newton's mathematics revolved around a world of clock- work precision and that this was a mandatory prerequisite of preparing for space travel. When scientists calculated travel patterns to the moon, Newton's law of motion was critical. If the numbers were off slightly, you'd be hard pressed to find any astronaut willing to get into the spacecraft without the stability of predictable results based on exactness. They relied on the precision of the calculations, on the predictability of the travel, and on the assurance they would reach their destina- tion safely. They could not blast off and hope that randomly they might hit the moon at an unknown trajectory at unknown speed.

And yet, our mindsets tend to linger only in this linear paradigm by default and training. We think we need to be precise and predictable like the flight pattern of the spacecraft all the time. However, not everything needs to be this linear, and more importantly, nor does linearity offer the best results and pro- cesses for everything seeking results, especially in this new global landscape. As evidenced by organizations like NASA, Newtonianism is their gospel and exactness is their mantra where exact calculations and defined processes are needed. Conversely, natural organisms instead repel it because they function more effectively under natural organisms –companies, churches, schools, organizations, and small busi- ness units –flourish under nonlinear mentalities through autonomy and account- ability if the model of a living system is driving the structure.

Chris [Langton] is at the board again, rapidly sketching a cluster of small circles, joined by double-headed arrows. "These are the components of your system, interacting locally." Above them appears what looks like a child's version of a cloud, and a volley of large arrows shoots up from the cluster below. He then added two arrows, one emerging from each side of the cloud, sweeping down toward the cluster. "From the interaction of the individual components *down here* emerges some kind of global property *up here*, some- thing you couldn't have predicted from what you know of the components. And the global property, this emergent behavior, feeds back to influence the behavior of the individuals *down here* that produced it." Order arising out of a complex dynamical system, global properties flowing from aggregate behavior of individuals (Lewin, p.13).

221

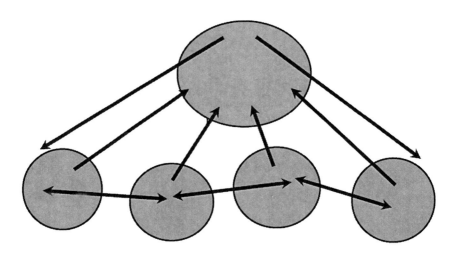

A cement company uses this randomness and unpredictability to increase its margins and ultimately their bottom line. They have tapped the vein of innovation through realizing it is better to move with chaos of one day and the calm of another by operating under a system that allows them to be prepared for either one to happen and still respond nimbly.

Cemex specializes in delivering concrete in developing areas of the world, places where anything can, and usually does go wrong. Even in Monterrey, Mexico, Cemex copes with unpredictable weather and traffic conditions, spontaneous labor disruptions, building permit snafus, and arbitrary government inspections of construction site. In addition, more than half the orders are cancelled by customers, usually at the last minute. Considering that a load of concrete is never more than 90 minutes from spoiling, those chaotic conditions mean high cost, complex scheduling, and frustration for employees, managers, and customers.

To help compete in this environment, manager looked for both technological and organizational innovations. Leaders call their new approach "living with chaos." Rather than trying to change the customers, Cemex resolved to do business on the customers own terms and design a system in which last-minute changes and unexpected problems are routine (Taft, p. 34).

Imagine wet cement being hauled around in cement trucks with no where to go specifically and with only probabilities on their call sheet and navigation systems for construction appointments. Imagine the fleet loaded down with cement leaving every morning with no exact street names and instead just general vicinities. They operate under the paradigm that they could maximize their production and therefore ultimately boost their profits by evolving with emerging demands with no clear predictable patterns. They realized that the "butterfly" could cause big market shifts or next to little or no market shifts, either way their nimble operating system prepared them for change. The company believed that because of the random nature of construction with its unpredictable time table and irregular performing contractors, it would be better to be free of set appointments and instead roam the streets like an ambulance and wait for a call. Their specific target was to launch the trucks with no ultimate destination and no exact route, instead they wanted to infuse them with the intent of producing dynamic results and innovating methods through random selections. They went where they were needed when they were needed in less than 2 hours through a complex technology package that communicated change on the fly from their headquarters.

This sounds crazy right? It's crazy that a company would send out trucks loaded with product, no place to go, and driving on hope and perceptions? Isn't it crazy? Or is this innovative and evolutionary learning? Although their system sounds chaotic in the bad sense of the word, a concrete company in Mexico called Cemex runs its organization based on the principles of a living organism. They disperse deliveries under the emergent and often erratic behavior patterns of construction (when have you seen a construction project be timely) and evolving needs of the customers. They are one of the world's largest and perhaps only global cement companies, and yet they thrive in the complex of world of unpredictable deadlines with a product that expires in a prescribed time – wet cement. Their promise is to deliver in a narrow window of time the amount of cement needed where it's needed. The problem is that when the trucks leave the shop, they don't know where they are going or exactly when it needs to be there. They send them out like bees *waiting* for pollen instead of bees *looking* for pollen. They dispatch "its fleet of cement mixers based on the same simple rules that govern how ants scavenge a colony's territory with ruthless efficiency" (Pascale, p. 8).

Cemex loads its fleets of cement trucks each morning and dispatches them with no preordained destination. The trick lies in how they make their rounds. Like ants scavenging a territory, they are guided to their destination by simple rules. Ants use chemical messages to convey these instructions; Cemex uses an algorithm based on greed (deliver as much cement as rapidly possible to as many customers as possible) and repulsion (avoid duplication of effort by staying as far away from other cement trucks as possible). It's scary to have a fleet loaded with, of all products, wet cement, which could harden before it is delivered. Yet the ant model works with remarkable efficiency. Cemex has obliterated competition in the eight nations where it operates. Cemex's decision to emulate a living system delivers an incremental return of $388 million per year to the bottom line (Pascale, p. 8-9).

A Collection of Collisions

A living system, as Lewin says in his preface, is "one whose properties are not fully explained by an understanding of its component parts" (Lewin, 1999,

p. x). Traditional thinking operates in the parameters of functions and responsibilities within prescribed boxes and then acts to the boundary of that description. We are taught to behave within our "role." Therefore, we usually perform or live within those designated boxes, but Lewin is describing a living system that maximizes its properties by randomly interconnecting and generally ignoring the prescriptive function and boundary. It's not that it seeks to rebel and therefore colors outside of the lines, rather it evolves through natural interconnections. It isn't anti-institutionalism. Rather, it's natural innovations through decentralization.

For a system to live or for a person to develop at potential, the parts cannot be the determining factor of its meaning. Like the butterfly that may or may not affect weather patterns, we must be nimble and able to adapt when an external force "bumps" or disturbs us or "our system." It isn't about controlling things.

This is about adaptability and flexibility. It's not that the butterfly is necessarily powerful, rather it is the system that is so intimately connected that a slight movement could potentially stir the whole thing or just little bits. We can learn to thrive under disturbance if we are nimble and adaptive. There is no way of knowing what effect the butterfly or a disturbance will have, but to prod results you have to let the butterfly float and flitter.

It is however in the randomness that there must be a balance of not too many rules but also not too few rules; it is a balance between freedom and discipline. If you tax a system with too much compliance, it will be restrictive, predictive, and flat. It will be unable to innovate because it cannot perform outside of what it is told it can do. If you let loose the system to do what it wills when it wants, you will have the utter anarchy and chaos within a system that will produce adverse results.

A living system is a delicate balance, a semblance of power and intimate connections nimble enough to move at whim.

- Complexity science concerns itself with non-linear effects where very small perturbations at the start may lead to avalanches.
- Complexity science is not built on the assumption that one can proactively control what will happen. Rather, it emphasizes nimble reactions: Expect the unexpected.
- [It] does not focus only on the path of an organism as it maneuvers across the competitive landscape. [It] also concerns itself with the way the landscape itself changes as the organism moves across it (Pascale, p. 105).

In other words, to think of it in parts and pieces and therefore to perceive that there is understanding at those individual points would be to miss a living system entirely. It is a gathering and intermingling of complex, unique, and specifically evolving relationships between agents that also then produce more evolving relationships. It's not about just "this" or just "that" or just "that person." It is about all of "that" and all of "them" and perhaps even sometimes it's none of them but someone or something else that is an offshoot of a previous relationships that ignited something dynamic. A living system is simply not about the parts but about encouraging systemic learning and creativity through conglomerate reactions from unique relations. It's about understanding the significance of something today by looking back at what happened perhaps yesterday, or perhaps 5 years ago, or even perhaps what may happen in the future. It's about what is probable instead of what one's "knows," because what one "knows" is not always the best thing to implement or use as a basis for final analysis.

For example, a factory with an assembly line, an airplane's landing gear, and a car's engine all have components that are for a specific function with a distinct ability that only serve to add meaning or function to the whole. Alone they cannot provide significance. Their existence is static and their components predictable. The factory, the plane, and the car all behave in a specific way because the parts are all understood by function and space and their activity is determinable.

Unlike parts with their distinct purposes, random relationships emerge and collectively collide and make it impossible to discern where the outcome came from exactly or in what form it originated simply by examining one of their "parts." The *total relationship* then includes any and all intersections from every angle that help to add meaning. It's the *journey of the emerging networks instead of a single relationship that determines the value*. It may just be one relationship of many that may lead to another and another relationship that may ultimately yield the change.

Computational Ability

A living system has these blurry, malleable lines with probable versus precise outcomes. Chaotic "organisms are complex dynamical systems, and what derives their evolution is increased computational ability" (Lewin, 1999, p. 137). This idea of *computational ability* is important. Traditionally, if something is left to itself it will always be capable of only what it is ultimately capable of by itself. Its computational ability in the traditional form is dependent on *its sole* strengths. It's possible that the "thing" may develop and advance, or the person may even improve existing skills sets, or an engine could be tweaked to improve its horsepower or output efficiency, but alone they will reach a level of innovation that is only as deep as what *they are immediately* capable and what *they are alone*. However, if another agent was introduced or multiple and varied agents were allowed to commingle and cross pollinate with the first agent to redirect purposes, realign meaning, introduce brand new discovery, or perhaps completely redesign a business unit, their power of computational ability will dramatically increase.

There is great power, not just in numbers, but in interconnecting, autonomous relationships that evolve randomly.

For example, to take a *snap shot* of something and seek a resolve or to tackle an organizational problem with a *CEOs perspective alone* decreases a unique and "crazy" solution. In this world of change, to rely on something so independent and limited, only spins sticky organizational webs and stirs sludge in already murky ponds. Such things of isolation and seclusion like snap shots, event mentality, or isolated executive committees, and lone individualism provide antiquated information and snuff out the flame of real change. A Newtonian pyramid, hierarchical structure only provide bits of the story, and it leaves out the other characters of the story and probable "chemical explosions."

Instead of linear predictions and understanding processes from direct cause and effect relationships, a living system can create computational ability. If we try and understand just with the parts, it's akin to looking at a *collage of images* and define meaning from a *single image*.

A Hillside

Every so often I take this drive to see my relatives on my mom's side and it takes me through a rather long and lengthy mountain pass called the Grapevine. It's beautiful in the spring, cold and windy in the winter and just plain brown and hot in the summer. In the winter months, when the roads aren't closed from storms, the mountain tops are blanketed with their winter white and the shaded valleys are strewn with frozen swaths of snow. My favorite time though is when spring starts to show its colors and the blooms begin to peak out of their wintry shells. Specifically, there is this one hillside that looks like an exquisite pastel painting. Every time I see it as I round the valley's edge, I experience the canvas that sheds its winter layers and blooms a warm, lush portrait of color. This particular hillside gets direct sunlight and therefore usually peels the snowy blanket early in the spring, and consequently it usually is the one place in the pass that first buds its smooth, easy mountain grass and blooms its brilliant orange wild flowers.

On this particular hillside, the greens and oranges adorn it like it was gently dusted by the smooth strokes of a masterful painter. The sway of the tiny flowers and slender grass under a gentle breeze and the sheer intricacy of the seeming portrait are brilliant. The entire hillside is dappled in sprits of orange and interwoven with slender, sleek blades of fine, delicate mint green grass. The whole hillside works in tandem to display this amazing image, from the crags in the boulders and rock clefts to the emerging blades of glass and the gentle petals of the flowers, the entire image is exquisite.

Looking through the lenses of a Newtonian mentality at this varied and complex landscape of flowers would be to take a single wild flower dappled against a mountain side laced with 1000's of wild flowers, various bushes, textured grass, roughly hewn rocks, and slipping patches of earth, remove it from the hillside and examine it in your car against the plastic, sun beaten dashboard, and then try to extrapolate the immense beauty of the entire hillside and all of its diverse relationships *from the one flower against the plastic*. This is an example of event mentality or a Newtonian mindset that measures a situation by its parts and applies interpretive meaning from an incident instead of compounding relationships. Sure, the single flower is beautiful, layered, frail and contributes to the total picture, but the power of the image is only realized when you step back and absorb the totality of the quilted hillside alive with color and vivid beauty. To understand the power of the colorful hillside is to put that single flower back into the myriad of other textures that form the total portrai. One flower does not make the hillside.

A living system, instead, takes the whole gamete and looks deeply and openly into the relationships, combinations, and uniqueness of its totality and assumes its amazing probabilities along side its unknown. Sure, the flower individually by itself held up against the sun bleached, plastic dashboard is still beautiful, but disconnected from the hillside it is isolated to just a flower with delicate petals. It's nice. However, when placed together with the thousands of natures dynamic brush strokes, it becomes intimately interconnected and forms a total painting ripe with details and amazing bursts that it cannot muster on its own.

These limiting, Newtonian mindsets tend to pluck one wilted, dilapidated flower from a hillside and tries to extrapolate the same beauty from that one flower that can only be found in the random relationships of nature's details from the *entire hillside*. In other words, if we engage the rules of a living system, it is very likely that odd, invigorating randomness becomes the new expected outcomes. If it is unfurled and nurtured through effective leadership, one flower can become, for example a mixture of intricate brush strokes weaving themselves together to form an amazing portrait that only the power of natures deep undulations can put together.

Surfers Understand Interconnectedness is the One Thing:

- Linear equations account for cause and effect answers, but because they emphasize isolated events and single loop learning cannot account for interconnectedness.
- A static puck is simple - aim and shoot- but a moving puck involves much more probabilities and careful evaluation of many different variables with many potential answers.
- The flapping of a butterfly's wings can have an immense effect on behavior within things highly connected, and because of these interdependencies, or this sensitive dependence on initial conditions, it is impossible to know the long range outcome.
- Sitting in the ocean on my surfboard in a choppy, turbulent swell looks like and feels like bundles of energies hitting and colliding in a messy fashion.
- If living systems is a convergence of power and "chemical" reactions, a string connecting hundreds of buttons, although interconnecting and corresponding to the movements of others, is not non-linear activities. Their relationship is still one to one.
- If a problem with irregularity and unconventional form is thrown into a hierarchical organization, the Newtonian mindsets will still throw mechanistic thinking at it.
- A cement company uses this randomness and unpredictability to increase its margins and ultimately their bottom line.
- A living systems as Lewin says in his preface, is "one whose properties are not fully explained by an understanding of its component parts."
- The whole hillside works in tandem to display its amazing image, from the crags in the boulders and rock clefts to the green blades of glass cutting up through the ground and the flimsy, colored tissue paper petals of the flowers, the entire image is exquisite.

Chapter 8

Constantly Create the Crazy and the Unusual

"There may, in fact, be a very thin slice of creators who arrive on the planet more able to go and even seek out that uncertainty- washed place that destroys so many others. But, for a far greater number of high-level creators, across all fields, the ability to be okay and even invite uncertainty in the name of creating bigger, better, cooler things is trained. Sometimes with great intention, other times without even realizing it" (http://the99percent.com/articles/7085/ Uncertainty-Innovation-and-the-Alchemy-of-Fear).

One of the fundamental properties of a living system is its power to create. A living system can do crazy things in crazy times, and it can do crazy things for you and me by prompting us to think with a new and "crazy" paradigm. I say "crazy" not because it is like the "crazy" of a junior high school classroom that is out of control when there is a substitute teacher with spit wads and unruly kids running amuck (I used to be a substitute teacher and full time teacher). I mean "crazy" for the Newtonian mentalities because they are used to precision and order and this mindset will likely will feel at least shaken as indeterminate things erupt.

You might be thinking that a living system rejects things like metrics and measurements and instead functions on "whim," and you might even feel like the patients are running the asylum. However, when the agents (people) of a living system form diverse relationships under shared values and interact with its laws through disturbances, new things emerge – "crazy and creative" things emerge. But in order for this to happen, the people have to be freed up.

For most of us chaos means random [crazy]. In the realm of nonlinear dynamical systems research, this is not the case. And for most of us, too, complex can mean almost the same as chaotic…[T]he molecules [in a] room are maximally chaotic, and to describe them would require the documentation of the position and activity of every one of them. No simpler description is possible. By some measure that would make the room full of molecules very complex. That kind of complexity did not interest [anyone]. [We] are interested in complex systems that produce order…[In other words, this craziness is] surface complexity arising out of deep simplicity (Lewin, p. 14).

Freeways and Trails

Our brains carve both freeways and trails depending on our inherent strengths and our developing skills. Our design is complex and detailed, filled with layers of unbelievable creative abilities. If we are given a catalytic environment that prods and nurtures our strengths, amazing things emerge. It's important to differentiate however, between developed skills and innate strengths. First, let's take a look at strengths.

Marcus Buckingham (and Curt Coffman) talk about this in a book, "First, Break all the Rules." His overarching emphasis is to focus on the strengths of people instead of always trying to develop what is naturally not there by design. In other words, leaders need to work more on developing the key, pre-existing strengths of people instead of always trying to develop weaknesses or establish new "skills." There is a newer management mantra that goes like this, "People don't change that much. Don't waste time trying to put in what was left out. Try to draw on what was left in. That is hard enough" (Buckingham, p.78).

Buckingham describes how studies in neuroscience have made it possible to document the strengths of a person by studying the brain and the patterns or frequencies of what is called synaptic firing. Namely, someone's primary strengths or dominating traits, can be traced to their communication network of neurons in their brains.

Discoveries in neuroscience in the recent past have concluded that a person's strengths are actually innate (genetic) and manifest as intuitive abilities early in their youth that develop throughout their life. These strengths can seen by observing what is called synaptic firing or the synapse between neurons in the brain. An actual synapse is the communication in the brain between neurons.

There are billions of neurons or brain cells in the brain from birth that will grow and will die on a regular basis. What he says is the colossal wonder is the amount of times these neurons or cells shoot off signals in the brain trying to communicate with other cells. When they connect or communicate, they form a synapse, or a synaptic firing. Neuroscientists have assessed that this intersection of connectivity is where the brain really exists. Its not in the cells or neurons but in the successful communication of the cells to each other. It is this synaptic firing, the synaptic connections, that shape and gradually chisel into definition the intrinsic strengths of every individual. "By the time the child reaches her third birthday...[there are] up to fifteen thousand [successful] synaptic connections for each one of its hundred billion neurons" (Buckingham, p. 81). He continues and says for the next 10 years the brain works at refining and focusing in on the synaptic connections that make the most sense and work the best for that individual, kind of the Darwinian effect. By the time they are a more mature younger person, their dominating strengths will have taken root and become established in the person's behavior. They will be like well traveled, highly efficient freeways.

It becomes especially intriguing how this neurological science illuminates the amazing detail of every individual and brings to light the benefit of understanding the talents and strengths of their people. If we figure out how to utilize those strengths to contribute to the throughput of the company, or church, or school, or business unit, the results will be unparalleled as well as surprising. If we learn how to recognize that we are all unique with distinction capable of unusual discoveries, and then build the system around that more natural structure, we can positively evolve people and each other forward. If we free things up, those "freeways" become even more traveled and kinetic.

Conversely, to force-fit people like widgets into a functional category, is to literally underutilize and misuse the potential of how we tick. This in turn decreases dynamic probabilities. If the person's strength are overshadowed by the perceived need of the position and the organization or leader instead try to develop anemic skills from neurons that never formed a true synapse, we miss out and the person miss out. Their real strength will be ignored, and instead of the well traveled and defined freeways you will be accessing remote, inefficient trails.

The more the synaptic firing that happens the more effectively that particular neurological freeway is carved into a wide thoroughfare. This thoroughfare or freeway is what we as leaders and people must learn to access. "Roads with the most traffic get widened. The ones that are rarely used fall into disrepair" (Buckingham, p. 81).

Let's take for example, someone who's strength (freeway) is to teach, train, and develop people. We could conclude that then every time he/she taught and/or developed someone's understanding, communicated a strategy, or enhance someone's very ability to learn and perform, the synaptic firing was responsible for carving that strength into their system. The neurons communicated and connected and carved a freeway. In that medium of teaching, developing, training, etc., that person will likely be very successful and effective because it comes naturally. Like an electrical current, the energy flows and produce a transference of that power.

Therefore, in this example where the person's ability to grow and develop people was easy and rewarding, it was the natural strength of that person to do so. However, if that same person was asked to be a controller of a financial company setting up the parameters for accounting practices system wide (trail) the person still might survive and do well, but the task would likely would be arduous and cumbersome. Every step might be a struggle, and the ceiling of success would be very low. They would be traveling a skinny mountain trail and not their natural freeway.

These genetic, "electronic" shots can be neurologically traced to their development and pervasive use. Like continual trips to the gym that build muscle, the frequent "firing" then builds a more definable, specific strength. Conversely, the infrequency of the firing reveals the neurons disassociations to other neurons. Nothing truly deeply develops. Symbolically, for our discussion a strength might look like the finale at the end of Fourth of July fireworks display where the night sky is charged with enormous activity. Conversely, an infrequent synaptic firing like a loosely developed skill might be more akin to the involuntary flickering of a dull light bulb at the end of a hallway on its last leg.

Unhappy at Work?

Statistics show that 6-8 out of 10 people in corporate America are unhappy with their job. Do you wonder if the 2-4 people that actually like their job are performing in a role that makes use of their strengths? In other words, the 60-80% that are unhappy in their jobs are probably the ones shelving their strengths and their "freeways" and opting to try and travel on a skinny "trail" that they are trying to newly define. Strengths assert that certain things come easier and a bit more natural like fishing with a huge net in a shallow pond stocked thick with rainbow trout. Your undeveloped skills on the other hand, takes more of concentrated effort to exert like walking on a tightrope with no training and no experience. Sure you might get lucky and make it to the other side, but keep on trying it and you will eventually fall. We lean towards our strengths because they are our dominant subset, feel incredibly natural and fulfilling, and come without having to dig deep. "On watchmaker, Nixon, USA's job availability web page, the company lists a simple, but universal motto that the industry [Action-Sports] lives by: 'Work because you want to, not because you have to'" (Striler, P. 31). I'm pretty sure it wouldn't be hard for most anyone to provide a quick and short list of their perceived strengths. Likewise, when we use them, there is a sense of fulfillment, almost a sense of joy. The argument could be made that it's probable "you were born to do" just such a thing. These strengths can further their contributions by helping define and validate the person by underscoring what they are naturally capable of doing, and it helps define a meaningful purpose.

What are you strengths? Do you like working with numbers? Do you like working theories? Do you like working with people? Do you like to analyze, teach, coach, engineer, construct, create, design, sell, etc. In other words, we all have a short list of critical strengths that coincide with our identity, the things that come natural to us that we have been using most of our lives. Like a river or a roadway, the wider the pathway the easier the travel patterns, and after years of use these strengths etch a wide swath of travel.

Conversely, skill sets that are developed through a new job title, a newly defined role, or a new challenge in life will have a slimmer pathway of travel and success because they are not necessarily innate or deeply developed. As opposed to a natural progression through neurological conditions - synaptic firing - they are forced to surface through survival techniques. They are more like a trail that has been lightly traveled but visibly evident. These skill sets define themselves or emerge in the person from circumstance, trial, and/or necessity. They arise from the fire. They will potentially become an established, reactive *skill* over time, but they will not be intuitive like their counterparts (strengths) because it takes a deeper, uncomfortable pull to bring forth the skill.

A new discipline (or skill) then is one that forges itself by way of the chisel of experience, obligation, and demands. Granted, one may develop the weakness of their skill, but it will never match the might of their natural strength. What happens though in this world is that people are pushed to better their skill that is defined by their role while underutilizing or ignoring their strength because we as leaders have made it our mantra to develop the skill and leave the strength alone.

To bring this around full circle, a living system would develop someone's skills if the contribution was effective for the whole system, but conversely and more importantly it would encourage their strength to flourish through random and natural connections because it quickly made the whole stronger. Because a living system doesn't promote linearity and a "parts and pieces" mindset, its more natural means encourages people to contribute in the place that makes the best use of their strength.

If a system or organization really is determined to grapple with the unpredictable landscape of global connectivity, then it would do its best to find a way to bring forth the talents and strengths of its people through things like open and transparent conversations, non-linearity, creative cropping, bottom up thinking, populating random relationships, and facilitating learning as a foundational paradigm. However, if they are instead determined to build and then fortify skill sets, as defined by function, they will be carving only a thin trail.

A Fire Road vs. A Hiker's Trail

I am not saying we shouldn't develop skills or to learn areas outside of our strengths, but the target should be to *uncover and develop* the strength that the skill set has shelved. Two images from the local mountains here in California might help define the difference between the wide path of someone's strength versus the slender, skinny trail of a developing skill: a fire road and a hikers trail.

Out here in California, we have mountains spreading out and winding themselves all up and down our coast, and they are layered with a labyrinth of jaded peaks and sharp valleys. In these mountains, you can see two types of trails: 1) huge, wide firebreak roads (because of our fire season) that stretch out long as though God took the palm of His mighty hand and effortlessly carved huge roadways all over the mountains and 2) a slew of skinny, winding trails that meander, dip, and roll as though God took his fingernail and scrapped skinny lines in the dirt.

The strengths or "synaptic pathways" might look like the huge and wide fire roads that split and decorate the looming mountains like freeways. Because of the extreme fire danger we have every fall, local fire crews bulldoze these massive fire "breaks" and carve these wide fire roads. They are very wide, very long, etched deeply in the dirt, and they stretch for miles and miles across great stretches of land. They resemble the width of about a 4-5 lane highway and are designed to break a wildfire's speed and potentially halt its path of travel.

Conversely, the trails are treaded into existence by hiker's boots, runner's sneakers, and an occasional mountain biker. These trails are random and their patterns are decided by the frequency or infrequency of hikers and where they decide to put their boots. Unlike the connecting firebreaks, these trails are etched by random selection, and their purpose is only found in the whim of the hiker. That is why they pop up and spatter themselves all over the mountainsides. They are in random places all over the hills, but unlike the fire road they are skinny and allow perhaps 1-2 hikers wide versus 4-5 freeway lanes. The brain will have both the wide synaptic pathway (un-congested and developed) along side the trails of the skill set (congested and narrow).

These mental pathways are [the] filter. They produce the recurring pattern of behaviors that makes her unique. They tell her which stimuli to respond to and which to ignore. They define where she will excel and where she will struggle. They create all of her enthusiasms and all of her indifferences.

The carving of these pathways is the carving of her character. Neuroscience is telling us that beyond her mid-teens there is a limit to how much of her character she can recarve.

This does not mean that she cannot change...she can learn new skills and hew knowledge. She can alter her values. She can develop a greater sense of self-awareness and a greater capacity for self-regulation. And if she does indeed have a wasteland for confrontation, then with enough training, coaching, and encouragement, she can probably be helped to build a thin path so that she is at least able to cope with confrontation. But it does mean that in terms of these mental pathways, no amount of training, coaching, encourage-ment will enable her to turn her barren wastelands into frictionless four-land highways.

Neuroscience confirms what great managers know. Her filter, and the recurring patterns of behavior that it creates, is enduring. In the most impor-tant ways she is permanently, wonderfully, unique. (Buckingham, p. 82)

Skill Set Mentality

This skill set mentality is often the focus of the Newtonian mind because they conform to a defined parameter and generally take little consideration of the persons strengths. In other words, the question often asked by the executive and the organization is not whether the strengths (natural gifting) of the person will enhance or amend the role but will the person be able to conform to the required skill set that defines the role.

As a business man and a leader in a company where people answer to me, I clearly understand the importance of a job description that helps create direction and purpose for the initial landing, but to then only stay there and never let the role, person, or organization improvise from there is a danger. I have seen first hand how a job description or performance review creates silos and inherent boundaries. It quells innovation and weakens nimble reactions. The role's parameters should guide and not control. Instead, a skill set mentality generally isolates strengths into dark corners and puts all of the emphasis on a scripted skill.

What if the role description is wrong, the position itself is poorly defined, or perhaps it needs more illumination or a wider scope? Do you see how this disconnects the potential of the strengths interconnecting, commingling, and creating diverse relationships because the parameters are too tight or too defined? This skill set mentality prohibits interconnectivity, and it cripples the learning community in an age where emergent, unpredictable patterns are the norm.

Simply put, such restrictive parameters limit us. If we are defined to a singular role that is all and only about a skill set for a job description, we are serving the purpose of a lifeless, predetermined directive which dates back to an era of deterministic behavior and control. If we stay in this mindset, the current erratic behavior of change will pillage and ransack our lives because we are stuck in nonconforming boxes that are incapable of responding. It's like trying to run from a grizzly bear while your hands are tied behind your back, barefoot, and at night in the woods.

Our mental fortitude in this new era is dependent on our ability to use the power of diversity that willingly form new relationships over and over, but if we stay stuck in a skill set mentality we become inflexible. We are controlled and predetermined. This wild state of change will not permit organizations much less teams or individuals to succeed if they are not readily pliable and easily elastic and willing to break free from the incessant need to develop within a defined parameter.

Strengths Alongside Skill Sets

Instead, we need to ignite our strengths *alongside* developing skill sets in order to produce a full range of lasting, sustainable value. We must be willing to throw out the predetermined role if it doesn't work and replace it with a newly emerging structure. This will organically deepen our ability to be nimble and innovative. In other words, we are very skilled and determined at finding ways to better someone's weakness - tuning a skill set - while neglecting the opportunities to develop and utilize someone's strengths (Marcus Buckingham).

A way to materialize this transformation is to interconnect the community. Break down the walls and borders of function and precision and allow skill sets of predetermined roles to intermingle with the strengths of others to find a new meaning and purpose through relationships that "combine and combust." If *conversations* like this are encouraged, it is probable that the community will learn to intermingle with each other's strengths and skill sets. Here, discoveries will emerge and behavior will evolve. But in order for this to happen, we must unhinge our need to control and let the autonomy of emergence manifest nontraditional solutions.

People can do amazing things through these combined synergies because they can feed off each other. They perceive strength and see the "light" of discovery in another, and then draw out a new response from their own reservoir. Good ideas beget better ideas when creativity and stimulus are introduced, promoted, and valued. Others are inspired to risk, believe and act. When we are encouraged to tap into our ideas, voice them, and let those ideas percolate up, there is a buy in.

Be an Evangelist of Your People

If the individual and community add value added content to the "conversation," meaning infuses itself into the organization. Even though not every idea will work and not every idea will materialize, we learn to reach outside our "lines" and experiment with unorthodox, intellectual capital. We become citizens of creativity that collaborate with emergent trends.

I remember in my classroom when I taught English Literature, the occasional rogue students that were rejected by a colleague were solid performers for me. Granted they were not straight "A" students, but they did perform way above the label they were branded with. Four things happened that contributed to the results:

1) I was an evangelist of the student which prompted an organic strength in their creativity to emerge by validating unfound talent (strength), 2) I charged the environment with the belief that they could produce dynamic results by utilizing their strength and developing new skill sets, 3) I allowed myself to be amazed by better ideas from my students that exceeded mine and not be threatened by insight that was beyond what I introduced, and finally 4) I encouraged unlikely relationships to form through discussions that were more interactive and less "canned and traditional."

The Target: Self-Organize

It is this catalytic function, or the ability to ignite, where these interrelationships mutate and create channels of innovation. If the system is interconnected, having a slightly unpredictable run is not necessarily a bad thing. If the system is thinking in a living system approach, it produces nimble responses capable at moving with evolution. We can improvise through varying conversations across unorthodox lines that uncover strengths and converge on potential. In order to achieve this improvisation however, we must become "hierarchically flat" and decentralize our thinking.

In this arena, when we learn to break it down, we are poised to breach a *point of transition, or a point of incredible change.* When this happens, the interactions peak and form catalytic functions, "order for free" emerges and *self-organization* arises naturally (Kauffman, 1995, p. 71).

This "order for free" is a vital state because this is where it happens, this is where self organization buds like a rose and blooms brilliant colors like the hillside I drive the pass in the spring. It is a delicate balance between a tumultuous (unpredictable) and a static (controllable) environment that nurtures the connectivity to this place of "bloom," or point of transition. When the static and the malleable combine and compromise, new shapes and forms take place.

> A living system must first be able to strike an internal compromise between malleability and stability. To survive in a variable environment, it must be stable, to be sure, but not to stable that it remains forever static. Nor can it be so unstable that the slightest internal chemical fluctuation causes the whole teetering structure to collapse (Kauffman, p. 73).

This point of transition is like the crest of a wave where the energy that has traveled its distance across the depths of the ocean, converges on the rising ocean floor, peaks, pitches, and throws itself into form. When the rise of the shoreline meets the evolving and emerging swell, the collision forms and shapes the beauty of the wave. It's this colliding of the diverse relationship that gives way to the power of the wave. By themselves – the shoreline and the traveling power of the swell – are simply what they are and they would stay singularly in their form, but together they converge on each other and create the wave so that I can surf. The wave requires both if it is to rise up and explode. The wave is a result of relationship. The wave by existence is a relationship.

Similarly, it is this "order for free" that Kauffman talks about that powers self organization and is thought to undergird entire systems. This happens because living organisms are made up of complex, diverse agents that converge on each other in autocatalytic bursts of emergent co-evolving and co-creating non-linearity's (random new relationships).

In other words, to break down the science of it all, as individuals, pastors, leaders, community members, we need to peel back the layers of control and allow ourselves and those around us to find their strengths and manifest them to their fullest by combining them with the resources of other peoples strength. By using change as an influencer and motivator and then connecting our systems, we become better because our systems are trained to perpetually learn. We need to disrupt our own system of stayed patterns so that change can be tweaked and trimmed into unsuspecting, productive turns. For example, every carve a surfer puts into a wave is a catalytic function of friction and interactive momentum. When our strengths become products of our bottom up thinking, we will infuse our lives with adaptability through an environment that encourages perpetual behavior that lives on an innovative edge.

While autocatalytic networks arise spontaneously and naturally because of the laws of complexity, perhaps selection then tunes their parameters, tweaking the dials, until they are in the ordered regime near this edge – the transitional region between order and chaos where complex behavior thrives. Systems capable of complex behavior have decided survival advantage, and thus natural selection finds its role as the molder and shaper of the spontaneous order for free. (Kauffman, 1995, p.90).

When I surf and the wave is ever changing before me, I am forced to constantly improvise. Because the wave is kinetic and not static, it is always changing and throwing disturbances at me- size, direction, angle, speed, ripple, form, shape, etc. I have to improvise and create on the quick with the wave beneath my feet. If for example while I surf a wave, I decide I only want to travel one trajectory and hold that line no matter the shape or directions the wave decides to fall, it will at some point throw me.

Likewise, Gleick similarly noted that Lorenz (butterfly effect) also saw these perturbations (disturbances) as dynamic inserts to the system ultimately disrupting predictability. "Yes, you could change the weather. You could make it do something from what it would otherwise have done. But if you did, you would never know what it would otherwise have done" (Gleick, 1987, p. 21). There are wave pools and wave parks where the wave is controlled by machines and pool borders, but the options to innovate on the ride are severely limited and become static.

Likewise, we can continue to control and manipulate the micro and the macro of our company, our church, our school, our organization, our people, or our life, etc., and at that, even those predictions and forecasts may come up short. I'm not asking or suggesting that you play "Vegas" and simply inject disturbances into your system to then see what happens and how nimbly it moves. That would be unwise and sloppy. What I am suggesting is that when the system is set up to interconnect within shared values like a living system and comfortably move within random patterns and uneven undulations, we will be able to innovate and use the power of disturbance. "...[Y]ou would never know what it otherwise would have done" (Gleick, 1987).

A Starfish and a Spider

If you cut off the legs of a spider, it eventually dies, but if you cut off the legs of a starfish they grow back. In a great book called "The Starfish and the Spider," we learn that most organizations closely resemble the spider. If you cut off a leg or cut it in half it will die because all of its "pieces" connect back to a center, a head. With a spider, the head is running the body. Although a starfish looks like a spider with many legs, if you cut off one of its legs, another will grow back. In fact, some of the species, if you cut it in half, are capable of replicating itself from a single piece of an arm. "They can achieve this magical regeneration because in reality, a starfish is a neural network - basically a network of cells. Instead of having a head, like a spider, the starfish functions as a decentralized network. Get this: for the starfish to move, one of the arms must convince the other arms that it's a good idea to do so" (Brafman and Beckstrom, p. 34-35). These are the 10 rules from their book that apply to us here:

1. Diseconomies of Scale: Small size combined with a large network of users gives the companies both flexibility and power.
2. The Network Effect: The network effect is the increase in the overall value of the network with the addition of each new member.
3. The Power of Chaos: Institute order and rigid structure, and while you may achieve standardization, you'll also squelch creativity. Where creativity is valuable, learning to accept chaos is a must.
4. Knowledge at the Edge: The best knowledge is often at the fringe of the organization.
5. Everyone Wants to Contribute: Not only do people have knowledge, but they have a fundamental desire to share and contribute.
6. Beware of the Hydra Response: Attack a decentralized organization and you'll soon be reminded of Hydra, the many headed beast of Greek mythology. If you cut off one head, two or more will follow.
7. Catalysts Rule: Catalysts in organizations are crucial because they inspire people to action.
8. The Values Are the Organization: Ideology is the fuel that drive the decentralized organization...Take away the ideology, and the organization will crumble.
9. Measure, Monitor, and Manage: Just because these organization tend to be ambiguous and chaotic doesn't mean that we can't measure their results.
10. Flatten or Be Flattened: Yes, decentralized organization look messy and chaotic. But when we really look at their full potential, what initially looks to be entropy turns out to be one of the most powerful forces the organizational world has seen (Brafman and Beckstrom, P. 201-207).

Surfers Constantly Create the Crazy and the Unusual:

- When the people of a living system like an organization form diverse relationships and interact with its laws through disturbances, new things emerge – "crazy" things emerge.
- Leaders need to work more on developing the key, pre-existing strengths of people instead of always trying to develop weaknesses or establish new "skills."
- The skill set mentality pushes aside natural strengths of the individual and focuses instead on the task and function of the role while ignoring the probabilities of a system dynamically interconnected.
- Organizations are very determined at exploiting someone's weakness in order to build a self-serving skill set, while they neglect the opportunity to develop and utilize someone's innate strength (Marcus Buckingham)
- If you cut off the legs of a spider, it eventually dies, but if you cut off the legs of a starfish they grow back.

Chapter 9

See a Relationship not Limited to Meaning in Itself

"The connectivity and force that emerge from the enterprise's governing principles and enterprise intent are strengthened by an increase in interdependence and turbulence and a decrease in hierarchical control" (Twomey, 2006, p. 13).

"As to methods there may be a million and then some, but principles are few. The man who grasps principles can successfully select his own methods. The man who tries methods, ignoring principles, is sure to have trouble." - Ralph Waldo Emerson

Command and Control Deny Interconnectedness

Newtonian, mechanistic thinking is chunky, metallic and bulbous. "The pyramid, the chief organizational principal of the modern corporation, turns a business into a traffic jam" (Semler, 1993, p. 185). This more linear thinking says that people and organizations are broken down into pieces usually by function and title, and then held to a value only of its place in the machine. Outside of its function and outside of its intended purpose, it possesses little or no value. Like science, organizational structures generally operate under this Newtonian view.

Pioneered by Fredrick Winslow Taylor, scientific management emphasizes scientifically determined jobs and management practices as a way to improve efficiency and labor productivity. Taylor proposed that workers "could be retooled like machines, their physical and mental gears recalibrated for better productivity..." To use this approach, managers develop precise, standard procedures for doing each job, select workers with appropriate abilities, train workers in standard procedures, carefully plan work, and provide wage incentives to increase output (Taft, p. 23).

This practice of efficiency or the science of management isn't "The Dark Lord of Mordor" (Lord of the Rings) nor is the notion that we can become quantifiably and qualitatively better at outcomes by becoming more efficient. What is accurate and true is that times have changed and consequently draw out the design of the human element and our natural order instead of just "retooling the human." A flatter grid mentality and an interactive, interconnected system is therefore required to positively manipulate the flow of real information so the whole system has interactive capacities. If we are to be transformed through collective interaction, we must open the system wide. For example, the practitioner Semler felt that for this learning to flow, he needed to flatten typical hierarchical structures, "After taking a good look at ourselves, we whittled the bureaucracy from twelve layers of management to three and devised a new structure based on concentric circles to replace the traditional, and confining, corporate pyramid" (Semler, 1990, p. 6).

As I previously stated, I used to run a company that was steeped in Newtonian mindsets both locally in my location and industry wide. I was the minority partner and operating manager that took on a business model and management philosophy reaching back decades with three distinct and separate business units, three distinct profit centers, and three distinct operational mentalities subscribing to and trained in the "Newtonian Way."

I'm not saying that a living system will instantly eradicate all of our human frailties and faults. We are flawed and tend to look out for ourselves through the lenses of our egocentric perspectives, and we generally stick to whatever makes us look better and more astute. However, a living system does by its very nature and design operate on a much more transparent pulpit through collaborative community building, and its core practice is set up to decrease much of the distrust and fear that generates this isolation and "turf Dom."

For example, Whole Foods strategy was about innovation but with accountability. A critical function within a living system is accountability that carefully measures and monitors contributions both internally and externally. Like a wave harshly and immediately corrects a surfer, so to the system will critically hold accountable its participants.

We need to consider the *whole* conversation, the entire relationship and all of its various implications before we rush to judgement on an event or person. We need to acquire an ability to communicate alongside a willingness to interconnect random relationships that contain unpredictable outcomes. The ripples of connectivity will stretch further and further out the more conversations and interactions a system is encouraged to have.

The Iceberg

Our current volatile climate is change incarnate, and falling back on the past could be our demise. The reality however is that to redirect this older mentality is daunting. And yet, the alternative – to stay the course – is like seeing a massive iceberg in the path of your ship and not changing course.

Many people today have the sense that as change accelerates, the world's problems are multiplying faster than solutions. Slums are growing daily; affordable and sustainable energy is elusive; we are failing to provide adequate health care for many citizens. Whatever the issue may be, we believe that the most powerful and profitable answer is often a new form of partnership [relationship] between business and the citizen sector, which is now composed of millions of competent and competitive organizations, often led by entrepreneurs. The more eye's we have on society's problems- and opportunities- the better our chances of coming up with variable solutions (Harvard Business Review, p. 64, September 2010).

A living system requires more "eyes." In other words, it permits more people to contribute more value. However, we are used to a structure where we are "fac- tory assembly liners" that make widgets and perform only in our function. In this structure, if we were given the opportunity to break free and orchestrate diverse solutions and rally new communications, we might at first get lost because we have been taught to work "heads down," reach back for the same piece we have been grabbing and connecting for years – Part A into part B into part C will produce product D. We are reduced to function and role void of purpose and relationship.

"This mechanistic outlook reduce[d] reality to a set of basic elements or elementary particles and forces. Each elementary particle embodied[d] an essence that determine[d] its nature and value; each is what it is apart from other particles...[This] mechanistic view suggests that these elements interact with each other mechanically but these interactions do not affect the inner natures of the particles" (Grenz, 1995, p. 50).

Under this, we excommunicated our "nature" from our existence. We missed the power of relationships intermingling and intersecting with vitality. Instead, we sought to control outcomes by controlling the community and by controlling the person we thought we could manage a future. We believed coordination and planning was our engine to an efficient existence. "The basic thrust of [our] thinking is captured in the idea that management is a process of planning, organization, command, coordination, and control" (Morgan, 1998, p. 24).

However, we now have learned that this creates a build up of residue, a shellacking of the arteries, like a person bound for a heart attack. For decades, older

243

systems have run void of the human element and the relationships. We have given way to traits that are more thick and mechanical. Outcomes are the measuring tool, profitability is the reward, and "more and more" is the mantra.

Over the years, the system has been allowed to only partially perform, and because of that today we are left stagnant and stranded. Under this machine like mentality, we morphed into chunky, bulbous, jaded pieces of cold metal, like the computer of the 1980's that filled up an entire office room – big and unnecessary.

The First Cell Phone versus the iPhone

Consider the organizations under Newtonian structures like the first chunky cell phones and a living system more like the iPhone. The first cell phones used to be as big and heavy as two bricks tied together and just about as useful. They were hideous with little functionality compared to the new iPhone from Apple that is sleek, gently slides into your pant pocket, and fits in the palm of your hand. It surfs the internet with amazing speed, sends text messages, takes digital photos and video, checks the weather, follows stock market and checks your email in real time, shows full length movies, can update your Facebook page, holds up to 16 gigabytes, and can download amazing 3rd party applications that will make your head spin. They are slim, innovative, intuitive, creative, collaborative, and unique. In contrast, the first cell phones were *just* bulky and used only as mobile phones like the older management systems was just for precision and control. Comparatively, the iPhone is an invention of the new age with near complete functionality in its breakthrough performance based entirely on a platform of innovation and unique collaboration - mini computer, digital phone, personal planner, and gaming tool.

The First Computer and the Mac Air

Similarly, those old, clunky computers that used to fill up an entire room produced far less functionality and were as inferior compared to the MacAir that is sized to a legal pad of note paper and nearly as thin. The new organizations are symbolically akin to the MacAir because they are strategically and intellectually innovative and nimble and filled with unintentional, random relationships that promote upward thinking from the "bottom." Consider the newer behavior of organizations called discovery driven planning versus the more traditional conventional planning.

Discovery driven planning is a practical tool that acknowledges the difference between planning for a new venture and for a more conventional line of business. It recognizes that at the start of a venture, little is known and much is assumed. When new data are uncovered, they are incorporated in to the evolving plan. The real potential of the venture is discovered as it develops. With conventional planning, managers can extrapolate future

244

results from a platform of past experience. Deviations from plan are considered a bad thing. By contrast, new ventures call for entrepreneurs to envision what is uncertain and not yet obvious to the competition. They must make do with assumptions; and because these assumptions generally turn out to be wrong, new ventures inevitably experience (often huge) deviations from original targets. Entrepreneurs must establish checkpoints at which they convert assumptions into firmer knowledge before making major investments (Harvard Business Review, p. 70, September 2010).

The logic for the older thinking, the conventional approach according to Stumpf is laid out very deterministic, "We see the problem. We isolate the problem. We solve them." However, where he says the *real problem* occurs is the disconnection between the events and their connectivity to other events, other implications, and ultimately other people. We have ignored the bounty of fresh perspective that relationships bring. If you take out the human element and with it the natural order to replace it instead with mechanical precision, we will be unprepared to truly innovate.

A Place for Precision and Perfection

There is a place for precision and perfection and obviously some organizations require this model of determinate outcomes like NASA and space travel or Northrup Grumen Newport News which builds nuclear powered aircraft carriers like the Nimitz. "Putting together an aircraft carrier is an incredibly complex job involving 47,000 tons of precision-welded steel, more than 1 million distinct parts, 900 miles of wire and cable, and more than 7 years of hard work by 17,800 employees" (Taft, p. 13). Clearly, there is an obvious place for determinate outcomes and results that use precision. I am not saying there is little room for coordination, processes, and strategic planning, but to have that does not also mean we get to alienate the power of emergent community, interconnectivity, and evolving relationships.

Excluding connectedness with a machine mentality is to miss real solutions because we miss the real problems. Becoming living system thinkers, pushes us to deeper levels of understanding because we are permitted to look beyond the obvious. We are encouraged to examine implications and possibilities. "Where our solutions fail to take into account the interconnectedness of events [and relationships], we may make matters worse. If this occurs, we tend to define the situation as a new problem, ignoring or not seeing the links between the initial problem, our solution, and the new problem" (Stumpf, 1995, p. 40), – are not encouraged, other harmful but adaptive conduct gradually takes over" (Nielson, 2005, p. 1).

When our natural impulse is sidelined, we are weakened. We are bound and gagged. We are set to perform at minimal levels. This is noted in second part of Nielson's comment; something else will take over the "healthy impulses" and be replaced by adaptive, maligned behaviors that will usurp the natural system.

245

When I taught, a common misnomer that education alleged was to not let the student's thinking venture to far "out of the box." The unspoken mantra seemed to be to help them learn but contain them within certain parameters. The perception was that if you do that you never know what you might open and from that angle you cannot discipline the intellect appropriately, or control the learning. It was like the system was afraid of a Pandora backlash – too much freedom will loose pandemonium and quell true learning.

However, what I loved about teaching was the *learning I encountered* because of my students. They opened my mind up to things I either forgot about over time that age sidelined or they pointed me to an angle I never considered. As I taught, they helped me learn. The corporation, the church, the classroom, the organization, and the board room, all need to adapt this idea of cooperative learning and collaborative contribution.

It was the best part of the classroom experience because I'd have a classroom of 40 plus students talking about one character, one theme, one perspective, or one viewpoint that I assigned, and from that one lecture through class conversation I might all of a sudden have 40 new angles to consider with 40 more discussion points and 40 more micro themes that I never explored. All of this only happened through conversation as I opened the platform to exploration and discovery *with* my students and through a *willingness* to see beyond my own ideas. At once in this moment of discovery, we'd have this kinetic energy. Symbolically, the collaboration is as scintillating and as gentle as the migration of butterflies every year from Mexico to the central coast where the they vibrantly blanket the skies for days in delicate flight and textured colors.

We are intrinsically designed to drive toward betterment and the manifestation of our purpose, and we are charged to lead this frontier on our own behalf. We are the drivers of an energetic, creatively driven community that potentially could forge an entirely new landscape of discovery. However, if we merely dictate what we want them to "find" and "how they are to find it," we will always only live on a linear plateau barricaded by canyon walls.

In Harvard Business Review, October 2010, they ran a brief quip on applying open-sourcing to an organizations processes to increase creativity, like Wikipedia for example. They commented on how it applies to human behavior:

Impingements on physical freedom can trigger reactance. Confine people in tight spaces and they'll respond with independence-asserting behavior, say Jonathan Levav of Columbia and Rui (Julie) Zhu of the University of British Columbia.

In a lab experiment, the researchers found that subjects who were asked to select a candy bar from an assortment made more-varied choices after being placed in a narrower, more cramped space.

The researchers replicated the findings in grocery stores: When crowding impinged on personal space, shoppers increased their purchase variety in more than 70% of product categories (HBR, October 2010, P. 32).

Our minds work on stimulation, our souls thrive off of purpose, and our productivity is maximized or minimized through their utilization; it's where we find hope and meaning. When we learn through these healthy stimuli, there is a mechanism that comes alive in the human element, and if we can make the workplace, where 60-80% of the workforce is unhappy, a place where people can add meaning to their role then productivity, innovation, and the bottom line will multiply beyond the traditional results of arid, mechanical precision. "This machinery imagery leads to the belief that studying the parts is the key to understanding the whole" (Wheatley, 1999, p. 10).

Gary Hamel wrote an article I quoted earlier (which bears repeating) in the Wall Street Journal called *"Management a la Google"* (April 26th, 2006, Opinion) that talked about this ability of companies to evolve ahead of and beyond its originally intended business model and business targets, "The capacity to evolve is the greatest advantage." He continues, where many businesses may have the engine to hit their original forecast numbers and fulfill the projections of its business model through sheer determination and force, few have the capacity to then innovate past their original projections. They get stuck at their goal. That is the problem with engines, they are destined for a single purpose and designed to only perform in their functionality. They cannot innovate.

Companies, organizations, churches, institutions, governments may get to their desired targets, but then what? Is their goal now merely to sustain that place, maybe make an adjustment, a tweak in a process, get more, or perhaps advance with more market share? They get what they planned for and then maybe hope to get a *little bit more of the same*? The question should not only be how much more of the same but how do we continue to innovate? What does it look like and are we flexible enough? As I previously stated, "The ultimate test of any [leadership] management team is not how fast it can grow its company in the short-term, but how consistently it can grow it over the long-term."

> Google has invested heavily in building a highly transparent organization that makes it easy to share ideas, poll peers, recruit volunteers, and build natural constituencies for change. Every project team, and there are hundreds, maintains a Web site that is continuously monitored for peer feedback. In this way, unorthodox ideas have the chance to accumulate peer support – or not – before they get pummeled by the higher-ups. It also helps that Google is organized like the Internet itself: tightly connected, flat and meritocratic. (Wall Street Journal, Wed, April 26, 2006, Opinion, Hamel).

A Living System Promotes Discoveries

"Companies and organizations must be redesigned to let tribes be. They must develop systems based on coexistence and not some unattainable idea of harmony. Fixed working hours, organizational charts, and policy manuals are all so negative. They strip away freedom and give nothing in return but a false feeling of discipline and belonging" (Semler, 1993, p. 287).

New discoveries and emergent conditions are forcing change. A newer study of quantum mechanics specifically linked itself to systems thinking; *a relationship in itself is not isolated to its meaning in itself. It is connected to other previous relationships that therefore help define its probable meaning.*

A Quick Lesson in Quantum Physics?

Quantum physics says *probability not predictability* is the rule. Things are not what they seem. In other words, classic physics is limited because it can only account for principles of movement that are measurable in particles that exist on a human scale, like traditional management. However, quantum physics defies the classic rules of measurements because the particles they discovered are so very, very tiny, and on these smaller scales, or massive scales, or varied velocities, the particles didn't behave with *typical Newtonian characteristics like* traditional management. For example, classic physics says if you apply forward pressure to a sitting ball, it rolls forward. In quantum physics, movements and measurements can't be predicted. In quantum physics, you applied forward pressure to a ball and it might roll forward, it might push backwards, it might roll sideways, or perhaps nothing at all.

In fact, if you try to engage and get close to a quantum particle (very, very tiny) to define its location or size, the more the results will skew. *It became impossible to measure or predict anything because meaning was discovered in the relationship of the particle to its surrounding particles and not its individual location.* This concept stretches over to a living system. The closer you get to a person, an organization and just look at its singularity to determine its "state," the more inaccurate your observation becomes.

The lesson we take from quantum physics and its application to a living system is our ability to, 1) integrate the multiple and random interactions as opposed to isolating and controlling pieces, 2) dig into the interrelationships and provide feedback to deepen learning, and finally 3) examine our context, proximity, and environment and weigh our effect on those interrelationships. Such openness will instigate us to create and sustain learning as we become engaged through *interactive instead of static feedback.* It is not enough to know about something or someone – place, definition, description, function. Instead it is essential to also know about connections, reverberations, and random relationships.

For example, in quantum physics, the more precise the scientists got with an object's location in the atomic world, the more erroneous the predictions became. In other words, if you got too close you would automatically adjust its position and any and all future interactions would be contaminated.

The Whole Picture

We must view and study the "whole picture" and move into a living systems thinking and away from event mentality, because like quantum physics predictions are inaccurate. The more you examine an event (like a particle in the quantum world) and isolate the interaction to a single point, the location becomes tainted. We must look at the relationships that surrounded and preceded the event and even the relationships that may come from it.

I know this quantum world of varied meanderings and unpredictability versus the familiar world of precisions, measurements, and controls raises eyebrows. I also realize that the dominant mindset is that effective and proper organizations are not operated and organized on probabilities and maybes, but they are generally founded on careful analysis, discipline, and a solid, executable plan.

However, even though this all looks messy, it is not to be mistaken with the idea that leaders simply set out on the wild, wild west with a relative idea, throw it on the wing of a prayer and hope that it might happen. Or just because you examine something closely or in immediate proximity doesn't mean it is always wrong. I say again, this is not abdicating frivolous and audacious ventures under the impression that "chance" and luck will cohesively bring it all together through weird relationships. The critical difference between the older principles and the newer ones is not how they get there, how it looks, and did they meet their goal, but rather how do we create systems that can grapple with malleability, random burst of innovation, shapeless formations, and blurry, emergent relationships.

An article in The Wall Street Journal article titled "The Ingredients Of His Success" about Texas Billionaire and entrepreneur Sam Wyly who built companies like University Computing, Bonanza Steakhouse, and the Michael's chain of craft stores, talks about how Wyly gives a respectable level of autonomy and "blur" to his managers to achieve set goals. He knows that if he gets too close or controls too much, that he could skew and/or diminish the results.

> The principal idea is to set goals and then give managers the freedom to meet them – but only after a brutal process of review. A division manager at Wyly Company does not have to seek headquarters approval for daily decision on hiring or marketing; in fact, he enjoys a remarkable amount of autonomy. But he had better be ready to defend himself at quarterly strategy sessions. "We dragged all the business unit managers kicking and screaming into a room to present their performance against their plan...Anyone who had a smooth story with no substance never tried that twice" (Wall Street Journal, Monday, December 11, 2008, A11, Opinion, Mr. Freeman).

Even though this observation is a brief snippet, it serves to emphasize certain aspects of the nature and potential of "random particles intersecting." Namely, Wyly emphasized the critical components of autonomy *and* accountability and used to it to explode productivity through creativity and relationships. A living system helps to govern this trajectory because it is designed in a flatter structure. It specifically helps to navigate through these radically undulating landscapes. Instead of just violent tides pushing forward and pulling backward unusual conditions and unlikely markets, leadership can find order within the chaos if they can let go of control and create autonomous, accountable behavior.

Probable

Predictability has been replaced by probability. The world is now dynamic and emergent and difficult to measure and predict. The closer we get to individual things or the more we try to manipulate outcomes, the greater the likelihood that we will miss great moments and new discoveries. The randomness of probabilities now percolate up and challenge the stayed theories of Newtonian principles.

When we can learn to handle this living systems thinking, its unique thrust will pull us out of the pond sludge of control.

How can we be sure the Newtonian model is giving way to the natural one? Two reasons: for one, the marketplace leaves companies no choice. In an era when change arrives without warning and threatens to eradicate entire companies and industries overnight, organizations can survive only by engaging the eyes, ears, minds, and emotions of all individuals and by encouraging them to act on their knowledge and beliefs. Second, and far more importantly, the new living systems model will thrive and persist because it bears more closely to what we as humans are (Pascale, 2000, p. 14).

As markets realign and the global landscape brings change and diversity upon life as we know it, the older mindset is becoming invariably ineffective and systems are in need of things more human and real. The information is coming too fast and it is far too random to then put through an older system of control and precision. Information must become widely dispersed and real transparent collaboration must become common in order to become efficient within uncertainty.

Pliable Like Clay

Leaders, employees, and organizations need to be *participants* and work with the clay of change together as opposed to a few leaders issuing top-down initiatives. We must learn to facilitate an environment where the "elements within the system [can] interact and create new forms of reality...[We need] to release the potential of those within the [system]" (Keene, 2000, p. 17). This paradigm shift emphasizes a "focus of holism rather than its parts. Systems are understood as whole systems and attention is given to *relationships within those networks*" (Wheatley, 1999, p. 10).

In table one I describe a competitive posture adopted from Daniel Twomey's article called "Designed emergence as a path to enterprise sustainability." Here

I showed the difference between an conventional enterprise and a sustainable enterprise.

Conventional Enterprise	Sustainable Enterprise
Control and Win	Create and Preserve
Defeat and Dominate	Align/create synergies with others
Short Term Goal	Principles, competency, relationships
Reward top talent only	Develop talent at all levels
Impact Society to exploit outcome	Align capability with society needs
Beat the Opposition	Raise the level of play
Outperform/Diminish opposition	Leverage/develop long-term synergy
Increase firm value	Increase total industry value
Stretch rules, control/limit information	Change rules, generate/share information

Within a living system, information flowing throughout the system is central to its openness and rapid exchanges. The Newtonian bureaucratic structure is like a river that gets congested upstream with debris from the shore's edge – boulders, branches, trash, sediment, etc. - that clogs up the water's momentum and diminishes its surge of power versus the river that is flowing freely.

The more interconnected the system and transparent the information the greater the flow of information. A river that is constantly flowing is always alive and full of energy. There is a sound and sense that something is healthy and robust like when the information is disseminated rapidly and easily throughout the interconnecting links of the system. Under this canopy of fluidity, bureaucratic policy can be gutted and re-contented with more intuitive and natural processes. "The key is that the volume of information keeps the organization in a perturbed [energetic] state, allowing independent agents to work in parallel as they refine models and innovate" (Clarke, 2002, p. 5).

Leap of Faith

Very often it is difficult if not impossible to believe and then act on things that appear to circumvent the practical or proven, but sometimes even though crazy ideas might just seem crazy, perhaps it is the "crazy" that pushes us out and up to the next frontier. Perhaps the crazy is the innovative and the intuitive that has been suppressed by stayed mentalities stuck in familiarity. It is very easy, even in the face of radical challenge, to stay in entrenched in old behaviors. It does require a little faith.

251

Allow me to share a story of faith. Put aside any religious prejudices and listen to a story. The patriarch Abraham from the Old Testament in the Bible was credited as one of God's most faithful and deeply believing servants. He *believed* in the unseen hand of God and *acted* on an incredible mystery. His faith garnished him the title a man of righteousness because of his unswerving, deep belief and faithful obedience. He had to believe and move in spite of some seemingly dooming circumstances, unconventional proposals, and very dynamic, new relationships. First, for a crazy example, at 75 years old he was told to "Leave your country, your relatives, and your father's house and go to the land I will show you" (Genesis 12 vs. 1, NLT). If you notice in the text, God doesn't say where he is to go, how he is to go, or precisely what "land" God had in mind. The command was simply go, leave all that you know, all you have, and have faith that it will be shown to you. Abraham was faithful and obeyed and left everything to go somewhere with no map of destination. Second, an even crazier example, while Abraham was nearly 100 years old *and childless* (his wife 90 years old) God told him he would become father of a multitude of nations, "I am going to give you so many descendants that, like dust, they cannot be counted" (Genesis 13 vs. 16, NLT). Childless and at 100 years old God makes a promise of a seemingly ludicrous nature, and yet, after a brief chuckle of bewilderment, Abraham believed. Finally, the most outlandish leap of faith and absolutely craziest example, after Abraham and his wife had their miracle son, God asked Abraham to kill his son as a sacrifice, the very one that might fulfill the "father of nations" promise. This was pure craziness, and yet Abraham believed. As he brought his son to the altar of sacrifice, hand raised with knife in grip, God stopped him and said, "Lay down your knife…You have not withheld even your beloved son from me" (Genesis 22 vs.12, NLT).

This might sound improbable and perhaps "religious" to you, but the example highlights the need to act with an intelligent faith when encountering the unparalleled combinations of acting agents. This is not a proposition to go blindly into the night, but it is a challenge to venture into challenging the model of the machine and dawn the evolution of our living system.

One clear fear that sprinkles itself all over this model is the seeming call to abandon authority and "just surf dude." That is not the case. The call instead is to abandon the "false security" that control brings. The call is to structure the system so that innovation can happen through creative and constant connections rich in meaning. It denies traditional control but encourages accountability and innovation. Like a wave, if a surfer is in the wrong position, it will administer relentless consequences. The wave will push him over the falls, suck him up the tube, crush him beneath its falling face, or pull him under its curling form. A living system does not seek control, rather it seeks innovation through fusing a new life into our system. Peter Senge believes that organizations and people work certain ways "because of how we think and how we interact. Only by changing how we think can we change deeply embedded policies and practices" (Senge, 1990, p. xiv).

By faith I mean we need to let go of perceptions and practices that always and only made sense - the "tried and true." We need to explore a new "religion" and search its foundations. It's the tangibility of the familiarity that keeps us focused on short term trends instead of managing future vision. "Organizations [and people] lack this kind of faith, faith that they can accomplish their purposes in varied ways and that they do best when they focus on intent and vision, letting forms emerge and disappear" (Wheatley, 1999, p. 18).

This "faith" component is critical to the success of a living system because it is dynamic, unique, and unpredictable. Our conditional response to things is generally a microwave mentality where everything has to happen immediately and the results have to be "hot" and immediately apparent. Faith has an element of this uncertainty but it has a slowness, an evolving nature. In order for it to work, it must be allowed to mix and mingle unencumbered with possibilities (developing relationships) and produce results that are not always instantly successful but potentially fruitful.

I know that this might sound "fluffy," but the secret is to let relationships of all kinds flourish under proper stimulation and effective leadership models of accountability; it is in these very random relationships that happen through a faithful (committed) perseverance which allows a system of continual learning.

An End Point?

Learning should never reach an end point because human potential if unfettered will always inspire, dazzle, and surprise. The problem is that we constantly fence it in. "A complex adaptive system consists of a large number of agents, each of which behaves according to some set of rules. These rules require the agents to adjust their behavior to that of other agents...[and then these] agents interact with, and adapt to, each other" (Webb, 2006, p.34). And if these agents are therefore interacting and adapting to the behavior of the other, they are learning through and with each other as they move forward.

A living system "provides a holistic understanding of our underlying dynamics; that is, organizations are self-organizing, non-linear systems whose elements are interdependent and mutually causal" (Twomey, 2006, p. 13). The difficult thing to intellectually mitigate is its alleged randomness because organizational life is used to planned outcomes.

Typically, companies hand down these plans like God handed Moses the Commandments. The owners decide who gets what, when. At Semco, profit sharing is democratic. We negotiated with our workers over the basic percentage to be distributed – about a quarter of our corporate profits, as it turned out – and they hold assemblies to decide how to split it. It's up to them. labor contract, a union leader argued that too big a raise would overextend the company (Semler, p. 4)

And to build on this and promote perceived and real value we "must … redesign the internal structures of our 'mental models' [and our entire organizational life]" (Senge, 1990, p. xv).

> Some people have likened the Semco philosophy to socialism, in the old, Eastern European sense. *Nonsenseskaya.* I think we're proving that worker involvement doesn't mean that bosses lose power. What we do strip away is the blind, irrational authoritarianism that diminishes productivity. We're thrilled our workers are self-governing and self-managing. It means they care about their jobs and about their company, and thats good for all of us (Semler, p. 5).

Ricardo Semler practiced and practiced and practiced redesigns through internal structures in order to break free from his mental constructs. He embraced new models so the system at Semco could learn to be flexible and respond naturally. "Self-organizing means that agents interact with each other on the basis of their own local organizing principles, and it is in such local interaction that widespread coherence emerges without any program, plan or blueprint for that widespread pattern itself" (Stacey, 2005, p. 11).

Here are some unique practices Semler implemented in his company. For example, his company changed the way departments buy from one another by allowing them, if they are unhappy, to buy outside the company. This kept competition thriving and the departments critically alert. On occasion, they even sponsored employees to go out and start their own businesses, and then Semco would lease them company equipment and provide resources to help them get going. If these companies then established a market presence Semler would buy from them if they were competitive, and yet these same companies could then sell to the competition. In doing this, he fronted their entrepreneurial venture and the spirit of innovation and helped create a new series of relationship that were dynamically interconnected. "This program has made us leaner and more agile, and given them the ultimate control of their work lives. It makes entrepreneurs out of employees" (Semler, 1990, p. 6). A living system seeks "to address: uncertainty…For the past 50 years, organizations science has focused on controlling uncertainty. For the past 10 years complexity has focused on how to understand it so as to better 'go with the flow' and perhaps channel that flow" (Clarke, 2002, p. 4).

Surfers See Relationships as not Limited to Meaning in Itself:

- Traditional models constrict the natural flow of information and prohibit transparent conversations only to focus on events and a disconnectedness.
- The alternative – to stay the course – is like seeing a massive iceberg in the path of your ship and not changing direction.
- A relationship in itself is not isolated to its meaning in itself. It is connected to other previous relationships that therefore help define its probable outcome and significance.
- The world is now dynamic and emergent and less and less precise and controllable while predictability has become archaic and "squishy."
- The new leaders need to facilitate an environment where the "elements within the system interact and create new forms of reality to release the potential of those within the organization."
- A living system challenges traditional and conventional means used to explore solutions by producing randomness, unique relationships, and seemingly crazy ideas.
- A living system requires some faith.

Chapter 10

See Dynamic Interconnectivity

"The secret to high performance and satisfaction - at work, at school, and at home - is the deeply human need to direct our own lives, to learn and create new things, and to do better by ourselves and our world" (Pink, Book Cover)

"Effectiveness is doing the things that get you closer to your goals. Efficiency is performing a given task in the most economical manner possible. Being efficient without regard to effectiveness is the default mode of the universe" (Ferris, p. 68).

An Interconnected System

We need to create companies, schools, churches, and teams that are self organizing entities with naturally emergent properties, and to do this well we need to redesign the way we think and not just the way we structure our systems. An interconnected system over time and through careful attention becomes emergent and self-organizing that develops into "co-managed networks where the goal is to create synergies between... the [people, the organization, and the end user]" (Twomey, 2006, p. 18).

Today's youth has the ability to share passions and opinions in ways that prior generations never imagined. Technological innovations are connecting an increasing number of people across the globe. The seven degrees of separation that once linked us to others have materialized and now unite us through growing social networks and online communities. Our privacy is limited only by the ability and cooperation of others. Our education is limited only by our willingness to discover. In a world where every citizen has a cell phone, and every cell phone has a camera, our personal lives are becoming public as mobile uploads and viral distribution share our actions with virtually anyone any time.

This transition of the way we interact has profound implications for business and celebrities, who themselves are brands. Where information flows freely, we have the ability to learn from others and use their experience to improve on our own. As like-minded groups of individuals congregate in communities and share knowledge, good intentions have the ability to grow into great movements and small brands can grow into large organizations. Personal brands and business brands are connecting with others like never before" (Striller, P. 5)

Peaks, Valleys and Triathlons

Have you ever been running on a back mountain trail or logging miles on a treadmill and your heart rate nears its threshold at about 80-90% of capacity, your breathing becomes arduous and heavy, your legs feel like lifeless tree stumps, and your brain seems to runs out of the juice to push your body? These are signs that your body is measuring and manifesting your fitness level and telling you either to push forward or press the brakes; these gauges are telling you this is either your wall or you need to tap your reserve. Therefore, the frequency, discipline, and intensity of your workout routine, will determine your "fitness landscape" or your fitness level, and ultimately determine whether to stop at the wall or tap the reserve. It will determine whether you are a toad or a wild stallion or whether you have grit and grind to push through it, over it, and beyond it. Obviously, how fit you are determines how capable your body can adjust to these physical changes and challenges. In this example, your cardio condition therefore is the manifestation of your body's fitness conditioning, similar to an idea of a fitness landscape for an organization.

Another one of my hobbies besides surfing is competing in and training for triathlons. I try to stick to what is called the Olympic distance or international distance – 1 mile ocean or lake swim, 25-40 mile bike, and 6-10 mile run. I have yet to do the full Ironman, but it is on my bucket list. Obviously, the key to these races is the discipline of training, the willingness to press and press your body beyond typical thresholds, and a little bit of craziness. Ultimately, it is about intersecting the capacities of the physical body and the discipline of the mind and the will power of the spirit.

There are many days where training is the last thing you want to do, but you have to press through the mental hurdle and then press beyond the whims of the physical chants from your body urging you to find a sofa and a cool drink. The key for a triathlete, any athlete really, is the ability to create new *peaks* in your fitness level and then press through those to again create higher peaks within your fitness level the next time. The goal is to have a "rugged fitness landscape" of higher peaks and valleys so that your soul, body, and mind are familiar with and capable of pressing past where it's been and draw on the reservoir your training created .

For a visual effect, if a line is drawn out on a piece of paper from corner to corner representing a stout or impressive fitness level, it is marked with multiple valleys and punctuated with numerous peaks. And as the line progresses further on the page, the peaks ascend to higher and higher elevations representing the ability to respond to difficulty and challenge. A solid performing triathlete's "landscape" or "line" would be marked with a vivid ruggedness - many peaks ascending higher and higher across the page with many valleys in between marking recovery. This run of multiple peaks illustrates increasing "highs" or broken thresholds that give way to new benchmarks or new thresholds because they've challenged where your fitness levels were and create new peaks to over- come. The more "rugged," or the more ups and downs in the landscape, the greater the athletes fitness level, and the deeper his/her ability to peak, recover, and then ascend to a higher peak.

An organization, a church, a person, a business with a rugged fitness land-scape is therefore probably advancing and innovating at stellar and dynamic levels where an organization with a relatively mediocre fitness landscape is bumping along in status quo. In other words, a chart or graph that depicts the amount of peaks and valleys of an organization's fitness landscape, tells the health level of the system and its ability to "peak" the challenge, recover, respond and inno-vate again by climbing the next peak. Therefore the fitness landscape pertains to the level of dynamic outcomes: the higher the "peak" than the one before it and the more of them, the greater the level of innovation from the agents. If there are fewer peaks with minimal "elevation" spikes then it means the system has plateaued. The greater its "fitness" equates to the greater its ability to perform, recover, evolve and emerge and push up and over more peaks.

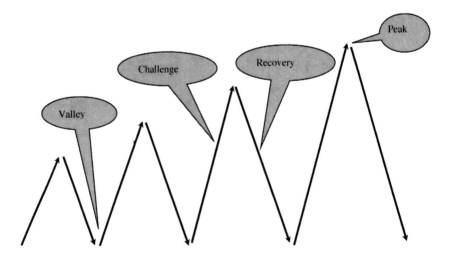

It's a positive thing if an organization has rugged fitness, but this ruggedness requires two key components: 1) the system must be intimately connected in order to enable a collective and immediate response to change or "peak" and 2) leadership must but catalytic and flat so the players can constantly intersect, interconnect, evolve and learn. If a system is interconnected and woven together in such a way that the whole thing can alter its behavior to meet an emerging challenge or evolving parameter, it can increase its "ruggedness" of its own landscape. It can do this because of its rapid ability to respond to a problem; it's similar to the ants we discussed in an earlier chapter being able to move around an obstacle quickly and alerting the other ants to change patterns accordingly and immediately.

For example, if the agent population of a system reaches a "peak" and is then challenged through an issue, it needs to be able to climb off of its last peak, recover in the "valley" so that it can quickly scale the next, usually more complex challenge. Therefore, the more disconnected a system, during a challenge or problem the greater its probability of an anemic response, like an undisciplined, unconditioned athlete. If it is not interconnected, it cannot rise above its level of competence. "By altering the fitness landscape of which individual agents are trying to adapt, [leaders] can change both the trajectory of emergent behavior and the diversity of behaviors in an organization's repertoire" (Anderson, 1999, p. 229).

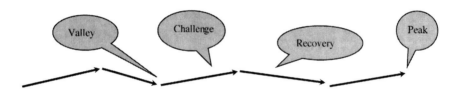

These connections within an organizational system and its ability to build on the learning of its working relationships produce innovation at greater speeds with greater efficiency. Like the interdependencies of a living system, "organizations [are] widespread patterns of interactions between people, [with] widespread narrative and propositional themes, which emerge in the myriad [of] interactions between people, both those between members of an organization and between them and other people" (Stacey, 2005, p. 11).

What the older way seems to miss is the power of these myriad of narratives (unfolding personal stories) interacting and commingling to produce their landscapes. If leadership ignores this electricity through narratives, it will miss the power of connectivity and how it betters the processes of problem solving while adding both value and diversified content.

Interacting Narratives

We are a people with individual stories or narratives that interact all day with each other intersecting and crisscrossing like the Los Angeles freeway system swarming with energy. Instead of trying to subdue this energy through a contrived, disconnected structure, we must unleash the power of the narratives and let the stories intersect. People's stories bring value and unique perspectives, and to ignore how they interact with the system misses the power of individual collectiveness. As leaders, I am not suggesting that we sit down and tell each other's stories, but I am saying let the individual exhibit their strengths and passions so that natural value will exist.

The Alps

I remember while attending a year of graduate school in Oxford, England I took a ski vacation to Switzerland. I stayed in this little village quaintly nestled on the valley floor that was surrounded by the towering Swiss Alps. The image vividly set in my mind. As I peered out of the window of the charming chalet, the perimeter of the valley was lined by the daunting canyon walls jutting straight into the sky. I felt like I was in the middle of the J.R.R. Tolkien book *The Lord of the Rings* with Frodo set to saunter around the corner and offer me some crumpets and tea. Thin streams creased the canyon floor like wrinkles in a shirt and gingerly carried the water down to the valley below. Swiss houses, perfectly manicured with firewood stacked in precise rows, delicately dotted the landscape. It all looked surreal against the "pikey" peaks of Switzerland.

As I stood on the valley floor and peered up, the mountains loomed large like Greek gods guarding the heavens. The train that I took up the mountain to the slopes every day climbed higher and higher, passing through the storybook towns, and gave a closer view of the Alps that towered still higher. I remember their peaks that sharply etched undulating lines up and down across the sky as though carved by the finger of God. The ruggedness of their jaded peaks beautifully marred the skyline's canvas. They made me feel small and totally lost in the mighty hands of Creation, like I was engulfed in the palms of giants.

Obviously, this picture carries a slightly romantic notion, but the symbolism I am emphasizing is the sharpness, the up and down from one peak to the next. It provides a picture of an organization's vivid diversity within its fitness landscape. The image of the Alps is a symbol of the rampant potential within an organization of any kind that gives it the ability to rally, assemble resources, and climb the peak of the next challenge through dynamic connectivity. Let's take a look how the Alps and endurance training might explain a living system.

A living system has an ability to take on a challenge, interact with that disturbance, and then flexibly respond through connectivity and transparency. In an open systems, every agent is charged to act under the drive of the mission and not the directive of the hierarchy. When we come against a change, a challenge, a barrier, or an unlikely influence, historically we typically freeze and wait for the hierarchy to evaluate, analyze and then react with a linear stance. Instead, we need to be able to respond on our own within the autonomy of the system guided by endemic priorities. For a system or person to really be able to continue on its own agility, it is specifically dependent on its ability to scale and conquer a peak and then corporately and autonomously move on to the next one. What is called our *fitness level* is determinant not just on our ability to climb a peak but our ability to recover from that peak systemically and then be able to conquer the next one that is higher than the last.

Strategy development has traditionally been the domain of the C-Suite, employing structured tools for analysis and tightly managed decision making. The Wikipedia Foundation (the nonprofit that operates Wikipedia) took a different approach by open-sourcing it strategy formulation, drawing on the community of Wikipedians around the world. The process took place in public, on a strategy wiki that anyone could contribute to.

The yearlong experiment, which wrapped un in July 2010, yielded a cohesive strategy for Wikimedia that will steer its priorities for the next five years. Clearly, the extreme openness of Wikimedia's strategy formulation process may not be suitable for every organization...some elements of traditional strategy creation remain - for instance, senior executives set priorities and synthesized the final initiatives into a business plan....

In particular, this approach can help firms more closely align their activities with the interests of their communities, be they customers, suppliers, or even colleagues.

Open sourcing strategy brings the customer inside to shape and support strategy from conception to execution. To be sure, Wikipedia traded away control, but in return it fostered a sense of ownership of strategic problems among contributors, who are the lifeblood of the organization. Wikimedia expects that will translate into a desire to stick around and execute on the solutions (Harvad Business Review, P. 32, October 2010).

As a leader, you want your team to climb a "peak" and descend it rapidly to then be fit enough to do it all over again on a higher, more complex peak. You see, it's not just about being able to climb and conquer. Many of us can force ourselves to do that. We can shout a command and push ourselves or the team up that one peak, but to only lead like this will ultimately prove ineffective. The leader alone cannot continually and effectively push the entire organization through and out and up time and time again to the point that the system is self organizing. If we are simply pushing to the top, what are we learning? More importantly, what are we teaching?

Our target is to build a community that acts like the ants or open-sourcing that encounter an obstacle and instantly assess, decide, and communicate to the system in real time what they are gonna do. Then they do it. We must be empow- ered to react in tandem through our diverse contributions and connections. That way we act as a complex, adaptive system overcoming the moment together and communicating rapidly with flexibility so that we can do it even better the next time.

A Living System Understands

Living systems understands the importance of getting off that peak and on to the next one. It recognizes that equilibrium and status quo is death. It's an image of perpetual forward motion advancing higher with the intent of getting better. I don't mean to say "hurry up and get fit" forgetting wisdom and caution. There does need to be a slowness.

However, an organization that is rich in random relationships and intimately interconnected centered in common foundational values and clear mission will have this sense of extreme peaks and valleys like the Swiss Alps because it is adaptable and flexible. It's constantly co-creating within itself.

These difficult climbs bring increased challenges like steep ravines, wide crevasses, loose shale, sheer rock faces, insurmountable boulders, incumbent weather, and even a billy goat or two, and an organization, a person, a business, a church determines its fitness level through their collective ability to immediately overcome and use these challenges to learn.

Change is the Rule

Like the constantly developing strengths of an organization, continual change with ingenuity is the rule of a living system. Sameness is status quo. It's fundamental that the system is organically responsive and proactive and even unusual so that it can be nimble. For an organization to rest at a point of excellence, freeze new relationships, or remain in a particular pinnacle of achievement (a fitness peak), the organism will loose its ability to be mobile and fluid. It will not climb again. The system stops learning, the people stop learning. And like a listless student in the classroom, there needs to be a stimulus infused into the employee, or the church member, that inspires the individual to be invigorated and disturbed upward.

A Storm of Interconnections

We tend to miss the entire enterprise when we only look at the storm. To look at all that it touches is to see the enterprise of interconnections. The storm is the event but how its external and unlikely variables interact with other external variables tell a more complete story.

Ultimately Connected

Even though events caused by that storm occur at different times with different results, they are not separated. The water run off filling up the ground water, the clouds swirling above, the invigorated health of plants, the rain spattering on the forehead of an onlooker, and the emerging sunshine are all connected in the system. One cannot happen without some connection to the other.

Structures of a complex adaptive system, like the human body with its structures of systems, control the behavior of the simple interrelationships. "In human systems, people often have potential leverage that they do not exercise because they focus only on their own decisions and ignore how their decisions affect others" (Senge, 1990, p. 29). Systems thinking dialogue doesn't discuss local iterations as isolated effects because what is happening in that the iteration is directly connected to iterations before and after. It is tied to the diversity of the network, just like the storm.

"Systems thinking show us that there is no outside; [rather, it says] that you and the cause of your problems are part of a single system" (Senge, 1990, p. 66). This isn't just a simple thought that redirects blame. It communicates a radical principle of connectedness where solutions are found within a process of learning where blame is an afterthought and replaced with feedback, learning and growth.

Meaning is not located in any individual but emerges, and is continually iterated, in interaction between individuals. This is a very different model of communication to the sender-receiver model of mainstream thinking. Instead of regarding communication as an engineering problem, the perspective of complex responsive processes regards communication as human relating where power, ideology, ethics and morality are central" (Stacey, 2005, p. 14).

Seeing Wholes

Nothing emerges from just one direction or one cause and effect. Everything is cause and everything is effect. Feedback loops use reinforcing behaviors through "subtle interconnectedness. Systems thinking is a discipline for seeing wholes. It is a framework for seeing interrelationships rather than things, for seeing patterns of change rather than static snapshots" (Senge, 1990, p. 68, 69).

It is in this traditional mindset, where the possibility of learning is diffused and diluted because the leaders are unwilling to be changed by the people they lead. They want to be the ones issuing the change as opposed to the humility of admitting their own limitations. "The changing characteristics of individual agents impact the evolution of the system, while the characteristics of the system impact the evolution of the agents" (Hazy, 2006, p.61). In this exchange within a living system, internal change happens – the system and agents mutually change each other.

In feedback loops, an endless supply of interactions percolate up, out and sideways while non-linear occurrences become common though disturbances and new relationships. Therefore, this way of thinking is dynamic complexity and not detailed complexity (Senge, 1990, p. 72). From a linear perspective, these feedback loops can help us see the problem and recognize the characteristics, but there is no impact to our learning by simply recognizing it like a blurry image in a photograph. Until we are able to develop an understanding of the interdependencies influencing one another and looping back to create unique outcomes, we are stuck in sameness. Living systems call us to change our thinking and delve into the blurry lines where there is no such thing as a one way street. "Actions not only proceed along feedback loops, they can also change these loops. Traditional causal models [are fixed], but in complex adaptive systems models, the evolution of the network that links agents is an important object" (Anderson, 1999, p. 225).

No Destination – A Lifelong Journey

These fluid, random interactions promote a constant state of learning under a constant changing state of development.

All companies have a culture, some companies have a discipline, but few companies have culture of discipline. When you have disciplined people, you don't need hierarchy. When you have disciplined thought you don't need bureaucracy. When you have disciplined action, you don't need excessive controls (Collins, 2001 p. 13).

Personal mastery is an ever-present discipline of learning and growth. It is a state of creative tension where fears pull backward from reality while the visions and dreams of the future pull forward to the possibility. Picture a rubber band being stretched by two fingers. Their outer ends are being stretched out while the center (reality) stays static. This is a dynamic place where people are literally and figuratively stretched. They press away from their fears and forward to their visions. Although there is a possibility that they will snap back in both their fear and vision, the structure of the system beckons them out and up yet again and again. "People with high levels of personal mastery are continually expanding their ability to create the life they truly seek. From their quest for continual learning comes the spirit of the learning organization....Traditional, hierarchical organizations aren't designed for people's higher order needs" (Senge, 1990, p. 140-141).

Ricardo Semler - A Catalyst

Imagine a young, autonomous college graduate, brimming with revolutionary ideas, college theory, and no real experience with business or people, put in place to run an ailing, million dollar paternalistic, vertical family business filled with hundreds of people, tradition, policies and processes. Ricardo Semler was that graduate, son to the founder and owner. He was put in place to run a successful, patriarchal, hierarchical company severely struggling during a rough economy. What he did was just short of amazing. He took a company set in traditional controls of a top-down mentality and exploited the system under an emergent, self-organizing structure of a living system. He transformed a good company into a great company through people and profits by letting the employees decide what was best and allowing them some "skin" in the game to make it tangible. For example, he flattened management and let communities of 6-12 run the company. Tyranny was dethroned and democracy set in place. What was once regimented and controlled through reams of processes, policies, and reports became a thriving enterprise of emergent behavior and non-linear solutions. "Theories departing from a Cartesian – Newtonian model of physical systems are becoming increasingly popular…when theorizing social and natural systems as differing from the mechanical models…" (Styhre, 2002, p. 344).

Ricardo Semler of Semler and Company (Semco), a Brazilian company of shipbuilding products, reorganized his company to a magnitude that virtually all traditional, command and control aspects were purged and eradicated.

He has made it known as the world's most unusual workplace. Instead of the militaristic regime where things were ruled under a sense of control, cog mentality, and mechanistic thinking, he wanted a truly democratic workplace: individual freedom, individual responsibility, limited but energetic leadership, economic opportunity, with free market enterprise and economic growth. He wanted to positively contaminate the system in order to undo the traditional structure that damaged the workers and stifled creativity.

For example, to ensure that creativity wasn't snuffed out by hierarchical management, subordinates interviewed potential managers for employment. If those subordinates decided to hire those managers, they also performed peer reviews every six months on the manager's performance. They could at that point decide to keep them or terminate them. Semco asked their current workers and their incoming potentials what they think they should be paid according to their role and how they arrived at that figure. If they were hired, their pay ultimately was measured by their input and put up against internal, external, and affordable measures to decide what was best. Managers were hired by subordinates and pay was determined by community.

Today at Semco: receptionist arrange their own schedules, work teams don't stay in the same station more than two days in a row, leadership isn't concerned when employees come or go because ultimately its unimportant, and they are passionate about an even exchange between employee and company – what you do for the company and what the company can do for you.

His theories brought drastic, positive results while his style created a huge chasm between traditional management and his style of new leadership. His philosophy was controversial to say the least because it challenged decades of a working machine, but the premise of the challenge was that the older way didn't work. "The desire for rules and the need for innovation are, I believe, incompatible. Rules freeze companies inside a glacier; innovation lets them ride sleighs over it" (Semler, 1993, p. 97). Truth at Semco to him was subjective and there was no need to make sameness the platform for process. According to the rules of a living system, "Thus, leadership that catalyzes an exploration and experimentation process to increase the variety of possibilities available to the system also creates the conditions that enable transformation from one attractor to another" (Hazy, 2006, p. 59).

When he took the company as a majority share holder with reigning authority, he instituted the principles of self organization and emergence, by taking out the levees retaining and corralling creativity and spontaneity in his people by creating a non-linear, free thinking organization. "My role is that of a catalyst. I try to create an environment in which others make decisions. Success means not making them myself" (Semler, 1993, p. 3).

He abandoned the notion of control that ruled for centuries. He didn't want to be in charge and sit high above on his throne and rule with a golden scepter. Instead, he was a self proclaimed catalyst propelling innovation into action. He starts the chemical reaction by mixing the solutions and then lets the relationship of the elements shape itself and define its own outcome. He wanted unconventional thinking, spontaneous reactions, and probable solutions. His push and determined drive away from hierarchy ushered in this fluidity of randomness and allowed these crazy swings. His company became flexible and nimble. Instead of bracing for change like a seawall taking the brunt of a wave, Semco was able to roll with the impact of change and shift its weight and its response no matter the direction or angle of the wave. He turned his company into a dissipative structure; "a semi stable configuration that does not correspond to external pressures and manipulations in a linear manner" (Styhre, 2002, p. 344)

Ricardo Semler became what Dee Hock formerly of VISA coined as a chaordic leader – a blending balance of chaos and order. Hock described this type of leader as one "who symbolize, legitimize and strengthen behavior in accordance with the sense of the community – who enable its shared purpose, values and beliefs to emerge and be transmitted. A true leader's behavior is induced by the behavior of every individual choosing."

Semler became an evangelist for cutting edge capitalism with a socialistic bend. Instead of a calcified system under the older mentality where employees are "dumbed" down, merely learn how to survive, and where most of the work day is filled with waste, he allows crazy manifestations of individual and communal influences that defy traditional set ups: hammocks in the lounge to rest and regroup your thoughts, individual business units choose their own furniture based on their vision of the unit, expenses are managed by these units according to their own end, and then ultimately share in its profits, and even factories are painted according to the whim of the working community,

He believes in the natural and sometimes ruthless underpinnings of democracy in the workplace and an aspect of socialistic thinking where communities participate together and then share together. He thinks the mentality that *we alone* (senior leaders) can be trained to know the answer is a very dangerous notion. This very idea takes away power and influence from the human element congregated together for a common purpose and autocratically places it in the power of one or an elect few. To enforce his philosophy that decidedly breaks away from this anachronistic, pyramid structure, he created ownership and belonging for the workers.

He instituted "employee stock" or profit sharing with Semco. By sharing in its profits through their direct input and contributions they were able to feel their effort, target advances and see the real value of their involvement . They became apart of an "otherness." They became part of something bigger than themselves because their contributions mattered not only to themselves but for their own community. Immediately, meaning was exchanged for meaning, and the people belonged to something other than themselves and were held accountable by real and reachable targets and visions.

Although the model may sound duplicitous, the goal of Semler was really to let go of control and let the people be held accountable to the truth of innovation alongside of peer evaluation and profitability. There came an incredible freedom with an incredible pressure to perform. If you didn't perform for the work group or business unit, you could be voted out of a job whether you were manager or subordinate. Semler used a catalytic structure of self regulating freedom- managing without managers - but governed it through the unforgiving, accountable hand of capitalism.

He has seen that companies cannot sustain themselves very long. Historically, they fall down from their own doing; they crumble because their strength is obligatory and defined within the parameters of a job description. It's generally incumbent upon the leaders to be militaristic in their leadership where teams are built with a chisel and a hammer. Instead, his notions are radical and he believes that employees should do what you need to do and what you think you want to do to contribute to the shared vision of the end. For example, he says meetings are optional. "Attend the meting if you find it interesting and if you want to contribute value. If you don't, then don't show up."

He multiplied possibilities and created probabilities through opening up the system to true participatory practices. He distributed authority, let employees communally provide solutions, and allowed the interconnectivity to establish endless emergent reactions.

To speak in the scientific language of the complexity science, "If the number of kinds of molecules is N, the number of kinds of reactions is N squared. N squared increases rapidly as N increases. If there were 10,000 kinds of molecules, there would be about 100 million kinds of two-substrate, two-product reactions among them" (Kauffman, 1995, p. 120). By increasing probabilities (as mentioned above) through the spontaneous relationships with his workers, Semler believed firmly that the expanding potential would unfold beyond unbelievable. Who are we to calculate the limits of probabilities while we sit among a sea of budding human potential, ingenious design, and natural talents? *The concept is that within the incalculable number of seen and expected relationships sitting dormant in organizations or within the very souls of people, there is at least that much unfound potential merely sitting in isolation.* If you unfurl those relationships to unlikely combinations, or unseen and unexpected relationships, the numbers of probabilities is exponentially greater.

This point is the travesty that has for decades hindered our life. By herding people into departments and job descriptions, we are telling them how, where, and to what extent to perform. It's like a teacher telling a young child to simply, always and only connect the dots to see the shape the institution wants them to draw. We excommunicate the innate design of the human from the workforce instead of trying to find a way to unravel its ability. There is no generative learning because creativity isn't allowed to drive and push human innovation. Instead we serve a machine. We are designed with an incredible caliber and yet the mechanistic character of leadership has fenced us in like cattle. Instead of having people merely connect the dots, leadership must teach them to create the dots that then define the shape they designed with their diverse and emergent team.

Semler hoped his action would change an autocratic environment to a democratic semblance of non-linear conversations in a complex system. He wanted the agents or workers to learn together through interconnections within the whole system. Let the people rule, but hold them strictly accountable to results steered by core, foundational values. He opened organizational mobility, "After taking a good look at ourselves, we whittled the bureaucracy from twelve layers of management to three and devised a new structure based on concentric circles to replace the traditional, and confining, corporate pyramid" (Semler, 1993, p. 6). Semler instituted three key principles that describes leadership's ability to leverage change:

1. Leadership operates to catalyze convergence of the system to a more deeply formed structural attractor basis.
2. Leadership operates to catalyze an increase in the variety of alternatives to the system, experimenting with new internal configurations of capabilities and exploring the environment for new sources of resources.
3. Leadership operates to balance the system's convergence to peak performance, assuming known and relatively predictable conditions in the environment, as well as the system's variety of alternatives should conditions in the environment change in unpredictable ways (Hazy, 2006, p. 67).

"Rather than assuming that reality is well-ordered, structured and predictable as in the Cartesian-Newtonian conception, it may be seen as consisting of flows of energy and information" (Styhre, 2002, p. 348). Semler believed that in order to revitalize his ailing family company, he had to break from the controlling and report driven community. The atmosphere beckoned unproductive but dutiful workers to perform arid responsibilities.

Ricardo was eventually loosed to apply his theory of open systems and interconnectivity to real applications in Semco. His message was diversification. He said that Semco didn't "have time for slow, herbal medicine. It needed emergency surgery" (Semler, 1993, p. 22).

Contrary to his father's mechanistic view, he believed a living system "puts into question the linearity and single direction of such organizational change models. Complexity theory [or a living system] suggests that changes are produced on the basis of a multiplicity of interconnected causes and effects whose interrelationships are complicated to conceive from with analytical framework assuming linearity" (Styhre, 2002, p. 349). In other words, things intimately connected drive dynamic change, and things that are linear cause the same thing again and again.

This inept interconnectedness of the company stalled change. As Ricardo tried to introduce a more participative environment, the employees became more skeptical. "There was a deep split [in the company] between those who believed in law, order and organization above all those who felt that people, motivated by a sense of involvement, could overcome any obstacle" (Semler, 1993, p. 55). Ricardo had to get more involved in the implementation. Similarly, leaders need to do the same and engage the change:

1. Realize it's futile to approach leadership development in a deterministic manner by assuming that if the leader does X then Y will occur.
2. Leaders cannot be separated from efforts to behave as a leader. One must be an active observer and player in active partnership with the organization and its environment.
3. Defining reality in an open system is a challenge. Perception is reality for each individual and there is no perception in isolation (Stumpf, 1995, p. 41)

He realized he had to change a traditional, paternalistic environment to a self-sustaining, non-entropic, open system. "Entropy, a process of continual disintegration to a state of randomness, is a predictable outcome of any system in the absence of inputs. Open systems overcome entropy by interacting with the environment- taking in needed resources" (Stumpf, 1995, p. 42). He too found himself imprisoned to controls and reports. "The receipt of cold numbers, even when they are current and correct, is not enough. In addition to comparing the numbers that arrives every month with the budget, it is essential that they be compared with the expectations of the person who is going to use them." (Semler, 1993. p. 65).

Older Models

Older leadership models exclude these dynamic probabilities of emerging relationships that Semler promoted. Most leaders know the numbers but are separated them from their people. Instead, they think in categories. They put their people in one column and the organizational numbers into another. Instead of drawing a connecting line developing a relationship and then creating an umbrella of structure that fosters a deeper development, they separate and categorize them. They do not show a natural relationship. They accentuate a divide, a disconnect, a factory assembly line. They measure the numbers and weigh them against benchmarks, but they miss the power of evolution when they don't converge on relationships, open landscapes, and probabilities.

Like Semler, I want information to be valuable and not just visible. "The nature of [leadership] expertise became the creation of control of constants, uniformity, and efficiency, while our needs have now become the understanding and coordination of variability, complexity, and effectiveness" (Hock, 1996, p. 4). Wheatley talks about organizations as living systems with "adaptive, flexible, self-renewing, resilient, learning, intelligent attributes" (Wheatly, 1996, p. 1).

Semler was building "communities of practice [as] webs of connections woven by people to get their work done. People organize together based on their perception of needs and their desires to accomplish [those needs] " (Wheatley, 1996, p. 1). He realized that the behavior would be without a blueprint but that emergence and new patterns of behavior would disrupt the system to something better. The system would be bumped or moved to a new and higher peak. His total renovation of the company was closely aligned to what Dee Hock described as five critical attributes of a complex, emergent organization:

1. It must be equitably owned by all participants.
2. Power and function must be distributive to the maximum degree.
3. Governance must be distributive.
4. It must be infinitely malleable yet extremely durable.
5. It must embrace diversity and change (Hock, 1996, p. 5-6).

We must learn to see that "emergence arises both from the complexity of internal interactions in systems with their external environment [through] the open character of complex systems" (Byrne, 1999, p.2). I borrowed and adapted Table two (below) from Jim Collins in an article called "Turning goals into results: The Power of Catalytic Mechanisms." He was using it to compare the benefit of using catalytic mechanisms, (like Semler) in an organization as opposed to what he called "big hairy audacious goals" (Collins, 1999, p.4) where the end seems unattainable. I showed the difference between the characteristics of a someone in a living system using catalytic mechanisms (like Semler) and the more traditional, hierarchical controls (his father).

Traditional Management Devices	Catalytic Mechanisms
Reduced variations with democracy	Results in unpredictable ways
Hierarchical, top-down, centralized control	Distributed power to benefit the system
Executives provide mere intentions	Metrics have sharp teeth
Right behavior with wrong people	Right people, bad resource expelled
Short term impact in isolated event	Ongoing, long term effect

Ricardo wanted to flatten management, diffuse the bureaucracy, and open Semler & Company to true democracy while his father wanted to keep it paternalistic and rigid. Ricardo using a living system cared about the significance of events in their relationship to meaning. He valued not only what happened but also what it implied to other actions, relationships, and events. He saw the problem with his father's mentality and its abrasive rub against his open system thinking. It was like trying to mix oil and water. "...The epistemological problem of non-linear modeling can be crudely summarized as the dichotomy between engineering and science. As long as a representation is effective for a task, an engineer does not care what it implies about underlying mechanisms; to the scientist though, the implication makes all the difference in the world" (Byrne, 1999, p. 3)

As a teacher, I felt this unique burst happen between the student and their learning when they connected with the content intrinsically. They connected meaning to their development and I connected to them and their growth when learning happened. What we traditionally miss is this connection. We minimize the effect that value added learning can have on the organization and its ensuing outcome.

Ricardo firmly believed that small perturbations to the system can have big effects (butterfly effect). Ricardo realized that, like Gladwell points out in his book *The Tipping Point*, we have a "rough approximation between cause and effect." We think the effect will equal our estimation of the whole. Because of our deterministic thinking and alleged power of predicting, we think we can produce accurate outcomes when we are given the data. But Gladwell talks about geometric progression in epidemics, for example where results double and then double again.

> As humans beings we have a hard time with this kind of progression, because the end result – the effect – seems far out of proportion to the cause...We have to abandon this expectation about proportionality. We need to prepare ourselves for the possibility that sometimes big changes follow small events, and that sometimes these changes can happen very quickly (Gladwell, 2002, pp. 10-11).

Semler administered these applications of a living system as a catalyst hoping to expand the previous mentalities of cause and effect, "Applying complex adaptive systems models to strategic management leads to an emphasis on building systems that can rapidly evolve effective adaptive solutions" (Anderson, 1999, p. 216).

Real Results – A Living System Works

Semco's revenue jumped from millions to billions, and the firm grew from several hundred employees to 5,000+/-, with employee turnover of about 1 percent. The firm has eight businesses, or so says Semler, 'nine, depending on the week,' having expanded into outsourcing management (for four of Brazil's biggest banks), to environmental site remediation and engineering risk management" (CIO Insight, 2004, p. 2). Semler asked, "What if we could run the business in a simpler way, a more natural way. A natural business, that's what I want" (Semler, 1993, p. 67). A living system proposes just this type of accommodation- a natural influx of energy that ignites under a diversified platform of dynamic connections and emerging relationships. He believed that deep down in the nature of humanity people want to contribute, innovate, create, and develop meaning through communities of connections.

He believed that there was something inherently wrong with constant emulation. There is no stimulus for us to want to be a part of something he (or she) knows cannot be changed. Organizational life continues doing what it has always been doing instead of integrating and encouraging intuition. For example, why are we forecasting 5 year business plans? He says that as long as organizations design and forecast these "five year" business plans, it is ok if they are wrong they just have to be "precisely wrong." In other words, know why and exactly by how much you are going to be wrong so that it will at least look like you are emulating tradition and the mechanism. Who knows even what tomorrow looks like so why worry about tomorrow or tomorrow five years from now. Change is inevitable and unpredictable. Integrate, instead momentum with your people by freeing them up to perform through intuition and innovation because they are inspired and passionate about what they do.

Instead of five year business plans, Semco plans and forecasts in an educated six month stint through communal wisdom and pragmatic observations of the market trends, Semco's productivity, and the perspective of the workers. They have realistic goals and strategic targets but are willing to move within them or even stray from them.

He says that we spend 60% of our time doing "silly" things at work. These things are nonsensical and play into the arms of control and manipulation instead of autonomy and innovation. We do these things because the machine demands that we do them simply because that is how it's always been done. The model cannot stray from its path because the path is all it knows. Instead of admitting fear that a participatory structure through systems thinking is anti-Newtonian and is set to dismantle an anachronistic model, they feign a dire need to hold the organization in close grips to minimize chaos and anarchy. Semler astutely and pointedly responds to that claim. He says we send our sons and daughters to defend and ultimately potentially die for our democratic society while we enforce an entrenched philosophy of an autocratic and tyrannical workplace.

He built a living system into the framework of the company and slowly pushed out controlling systems that undermined collaborative efforts. Because he created a network of connections, he facilitated disturbances to routine and encouraged deviations from sameness by letting employees solve a range of issues through their interconnected networks.

Semco became a complex adaptive organization and then operated as a "system made up of a large number of parts that [had] many interactions [and a] set of interdependent parts, which together make up a whole that is interdependent with some larger environment" (Anderson, 1999, p. 216).

What Semler didn't want is for the system to only operate in and of itself to only interconnect within its own relationships. That would set up barricades and stunt growth. This way it would become ultimately isolated and locked within its own universe to eventually implode. The goal was to enable the system to become dynamic with itself and then to multiply its effect out to other systems to multiply again and then again and then again.

If the complexity stays within itself, there is no ultimate power in its manifestations and therefore no multiplication in its internal relationships. The network is concealed within its own meandering as opposed to unrealizable ventures in unfound lands. However, if it swirls from within to form a power structure that can influence and change other systems that are outside its domain, it can then spin out from its own center and intermingle with other organisms and fully innovate beyond imagination. This is where the power is found: total systems interconnecting and unfolding true dynamic discovery.

Star Wars?

I know you may think this sounds like I am promoting a new episode of Star Wars or that I am traveling with Captain Kirk through unknown galaxies darting to and fro narrowly missing asteroid storms. However, even though this may sound a bit romantic and idealistic and you may be wondering if I am plotting for a Sci Fi thriller, there is a tremendous connection to our intrinsic design within a living system that is often and continually overshadowed by harsh realities of life and work. This shadow doesn't let the light in on what we as humans were "built" for and it snuffs out the creativity flickering in all of our souls. And specifically, the hands of control through older leadership models won't allow the reality of our potential to come forth and extend beyond. True, reality is the hand of manipulation and it potentially distorts the mind's eye of what is conceivable, but we have to let the human spirit reveal its secrets beyond what the shadow of real life circumstances have covered. A living system promotes this potential through relationships and autonomous, democratic cultures.

Semler decentralized all authority. He institutionalized a collaborative effort every time for every decision by drawing on the power of a co-evolving system and altered the stayed mentalities through whole systems thinking.

> The edge of chaos images arises in coevolution [like Semco] as well, for as we evolve, so do our competitors; to remain fit, we must adapt to their adaptions. In co-evolving systems, each partner clambers up its fitness landscape toward fitness peaks, even as that landscape is constantly deformed by the adaptive moves of its coevolutionary partners (Kauffman, 1995, p. 27).

The People Made the Decisions

From establishing salaries to hiring and firing bosses, the people made the decisions. He removed strict dress codes, parking space regulations, time clocks, and established worker lead teams that innovated according to community engagement and enlistment of specific issues. For example, they picked the color of the uniforms, the color of the factories, and the order of the locker rooms.

They even picked the physical layout of the factory floors in regards to machinery placement and the work teams. He implemented true participative management instead of a consultative management (Semler, 1993, p. 83). It wasn't that he was lazy and wanted to go and sit under the cabana and sip latte's. His desire to have it run on its own accord through the people was a desire for true effectiveness and increased and diverse productivity. He realized that he couldn't always provide the answers that the market, culture, or economy demanded armed only with a few executives and his own insight. His organization needed to be able to flex and move with emergent needs and unpredictable patterns.

In a living system, small disruptions to the system can lead to dramatic alterations for the whole if the system is intimately connected. He cites an example of a marketing manager whose team put a particular problem back in her lap to solve. She was concerned whether it would be a successful implementation and if the group would approve. Ricardo said, "One of two things [will happen]. If sales go up, they will learn to trust your judgment. If they go down, they won't...This group puts together the budget, and they'll only include you in it if they think you're a good investment" (Semler, 1993, p. 83).

"Complex adaptive system models typically show how complex outcomes flow from simple schemata and depend on the way in which agents are interconnected...they show how such outcomes evolve from efforts of agents to achieve higher fitness" (Anderson, 1999, p. 220).

Self Guided Teams

It became such that self guided teams "took it upon themselves to hire and fire co-workers and bosses by democratic vote [based upon productivity and efficiency for the team] ... Flexibility guided by common sense became the rule, rather than the exception" (Thunderbird, 1993, p. 4). Instead of org charts and rigid structures that generate distrust and squander dynamism, he wanted to bring out the natural energy and ingenuity in people because the conventional model wasn't working. He encouraged his "employees to suggest what they should get paid, to evaluate their bosses, to learn each other's jobs and to tolerate dissent – even when divisive (CIO Insight, 2004, p. 1).

Separate, self-organized groups randomly spun off of work teams that weren't established by Semco to deal with issues and concerns central to their specific factory. "They formed spontaneously, as the bracing winds of democracy swept through the food service equipment unit" (Semler, 1993, p. 86). These self appointed groups helped lower wage earners afford meals in the factories cafeteria by spinning a descending scale of food pricing based upon income. The less money one made the less of a percentage they had to pay for the food and vice versa. Managers, for example had to pay say ninety-five percent where the grounds crew had to pay ten percent. He wanted the different factories to be run by the wisdom unique to each factory and to each worker (Semler, 1993).

In typical linear organizations, outcomes at one level are directly connected to relationships and causal factors in that same level. Like Semler's applications, "They ask how can changes in agents decision rules, the interconnections among agents, or the fitness function that agents employ produce aggregate outcomes" (Anderson, 1999, p. 220). Like the rocks dropped into a lake, ripples from that disturbance eventually stretch out to the whole system.

He built rapport with the highly unionized community of the Brazilian business structure through ongoing negotiations. For example, strikes were allowed, but not appreciated at Semco. It provided "exciting, new opportunities for analyzing complex systems with out abstracting their interdependencies and nonlinear interactions" (Anderson. 1999, p. 220). If there was a strike, perhaps the company had something to learn:

> The strikes taught both sides large lessons. We realized that being participative was not enough. We would have to learn to communicate better, because as much as anything people's perceptions generate strikes (Semler, 1993, p. 105).

When big decisions were evaluated by management council, total information was shared and employees were sought to help find solutions. For example, employees were gathered and petitioned where to move a struggling factory, decide on appropriate pay increases, what diversified business ventures to pursue, what businesses to buy, and what new machines to purchase in ailing factories.

Self-organization and emergence can only happen in open systems because they are capable of bringing in energy from the outside through interconnectivity. They import the energy where closed systems are entropic. "A dissipative structure is an organized state that arises when a system is maintained far from thermodynamic equilibrium because energy is constantly injected into it" (Anderson, 1999, p. 222).

An entropic system would be one run top down under an autocratic format. All of its energy is drawn from a single source – senior leadership, board of directors, CEO, pastor, teacher, Administrator, etc. – instead of energy being infused into it from without and through internal dynamic connections. Eventually this source will lose its own source of power. Simply put, a system isolated within itself under the power structure of a few will become an atrophied like a muscle after injury or surgery. These times demand that we run open systems that are exposed to external power sources and unique influencers so that we have more options and greater chances to advance our influence within our system and out into adjoining systems.

Semco provided a unique form of profit sharing with the employees that were different than the traditional model. Usually, executives provided at whim their own discretionary and random formula for allocation of profits or bonuses, if any at all. In Semco, they were provided with discretionary percentages according to title, responsibility, business unit, and specific contributions from the bottom line of company profits. The company accountants got together with leading management and worked out a percentage that would work and still keep them in line with profitability and growth; this information and how they arrived at the conclusion then was all shared openly and totally to everyone that wanted to learn about company financials and allocations. The more the people wanted to learn, the more the company would teach them about the details, and the more they learned the more they wanted to participate and affect real change.

Semco sought to share all corporate information by teaching them how to understand the business through fully comprehensible information. He wanted to recruit mentalities that are willing to reach out to other systems and draft in new energy sources to feed its core. He wanted, "Those with influence and/ or authority turn the heat up or down on an organization by recruiting new sources of energy [with] new sets of challenges that cannot be mastered by hewing to existing procedures" (Anderson, 1999, p. 222). By interjecting this outside energy into the system, it disturbs unconventional relationships and new and different realities to emerge.

> "No one can expect the spirit of involvement and partnership to flourish without an abundance of information available even to the most humble employee. And a company that doesn't share information when times are good loses the right to request solidarity and concessions when they aren't" (Semler, 1993, p. 136).

He enabled the system to begin thinking up and out and transformed the top-down mentality to a bottom-up mentality. For example a small group of engineers, cognizant and versed in Semco's new leadership culture, challenged Ricardo to let them loose and take their relationships, under company backing, to find, form, and create new relationships of innovation and product as entrepreneurs on a business venture. He let them go out and take with them the mentality of "order for free" (Kauffman, 1995).

> Chemicals can be catalysts that act on other chemical substrates to create still further chemical products. Those novel chemical products can catalyze still further reactions involving themselves and all the original molecules to create still further molecules. These additional new molecules afford still further new reactions with themselves and all the older molecules as substrates, and all the molecules around may serve as catalysts for any of these newly available reactions" (Kauffman, 1995, p. 116).

The trio of engineers that Ricardo let loose became prolific through inventions and ingenuity. They established an autonomous new business unit under Semco that added profitability and authenticity to Semco and leadership of KT. "A defining feature of complexity is that self organization is a natural consequence of interactions between simple agents...When there are too few components or not enough interactions among them, patterns tend to die" (Anderson, 1999, p. 222).

The living system at Semco was put to the test. For example, in one of the factories that were slated to close because of hard times, all of the workers convened in a meeting and instead of agreeing to laying off a percentage of the workforce and perhaps closing their doors, they all agreed to the following conditions: A thirty percent wage reduction, forego the ten percent raise that was due, managerial wage reduction of forty percent, and cut subsidized meal plans, transportation allowance, and other benefits. However, the caveat that was no doubt spawned by the newly cemented democratic collaborative culture, was that the workers would take over "all of the services at the plant provided by the outside contractors and third parties and perform them themselves, slashing the company's costs" and manage all activities of the plant (Semler, 1993, p. 245). After the first month, the workers had saved so much money that the profit sharing program kicked in from the Semco contracts and made up for the wage reductions.

> "Local adaptations lead to the formation of continually evolving niches, so complex adaptive systems operate far from equilibrium of globally optimal system performance. [This] apparent disequilibrium facing co-evolving adaptive agents is actually a dynamic equilibrium" (Anderson, 1999, p. 223).

Semco developed satellite programs that instead of terminating the employee, funded ventures and satellite movements that kept people employed, paid them based on performance, and formed new units of business with Semco as a customer. They built a paradigm around the ideology of democracy, trust, and transparency and sustained autonomy and profitability. The living system at Semco kept working through disturbances to the system. "In his or her role as an organizational architect. The strategist influences the extent of improvisation, the nature of collaboration, the characteristic rhythm of innovation, and the number of experimental probes by changing structures and demography" (Anderson, 1999, p. 229).

Implications for Leadership and the Newtonian Mindset

Semco's applications drew on natural elements in human nature. By drawing on these natural elements like a desire for a meaningful exchange, a mutually engaging relationship, value added contributions, creative outlets, relationships, and an influential presence in an organization that actually means something, people can propel the output of their organization and compete in markets that they could have never touched. Such systems "evolve to the edge of chaos, the point where small and large avalanches of co-evolutionary change cascade ... because this state gives them a selective advantage. Systems that are driven to (but not past) the edge of chaos out-compete systems that do not" (Anderson, 1999, p. 223-234).

Semco suffered set back with plant closures and employee loses, however they did this without incurring more debt. They broke even in the worst years and made good money in the middle years following. On average Semco grew an impressive 27% over 25 years of the company. Their employees produced goods at four times the national average from 1980 and their productivity rose six and a half times. Even though their sales per year dropped from their peak at $35 million in 1987 as did their number of employees, Semco rose from $4 million a year to approximately $20 million [in that year] (Semler, 1993, p. 261).

"Life, in this view, is an emergent phenomenon arising as the molecular diversity of a prebiotic chemical system increases beyond a threshold of complexity. If true, then life is not located in the property of any single molecule- in the details – but is a collective property of systems of interacting, molecules. Life, in this view, emerged whole and has always remained whole. Life, in this view is not to be located in its parts, but in the collective emergent properties of the whole they create" (Kauffman, 1995, p. 24).

He removed himself as CEO, and broke down the primary stage of autocracy and displaced his own authority. He flattened management but did not do away with leadership. The proposal through the implementation of a living system is not to rid any organization of all leadership and simply let the people run the system. Leaders are essential and leadership is fundamental. Someone has to lead and steer with vision, compassion, and discipline, but the significant difference is that power is displaced and distributed while control is democratic and shared. Leadership does not have to imply, like it typically does, that power and control automatically accompany its title. Leadership is actually a role of humility that teaches creative ingenuity, taps the human spirit, and supplies direction to the community and catalyzes. There is a willful dissemination of wisdom and an exchange between meaning being exchanged for meaning.

What Semler did was set up a committee of counselors, each owning one percent of the company, and let them run the organization, while employees shared in the profits of their business units. He built the structure with his leaders around circles and not a pyramid. Every six months, to further alleviate the lure of power, they took turns and rotated as chief counselor. He joined the counselors in shared leadership.

This commitment to democracy, trust, and transparency led the organization through economic turbulence all the while allowing the very nature of turbulence - chaos and complexity - to disrupt and birth new and successful evolving connections. Instead of "punctuated equilibrium" where inertia builds up through time and eventually pops and creates a crisis, a living system "suggests that a pattern over time of large and small changes is what one would expect from a system of co-evolving agents subjected to selection pressures" (Anderson, 1999, p. 224). As a system is geared to continually and constantly deal with disruptions and then handle these disruptions effectively, the tension is spread through out the system and dispersed to end up in *effective and creative tension as opposed to stress.* The system then through this creative tension or dissipative momentum moves itself to new and higher peaks instead of building to a point of catastrophic collision.

Leadership freed up collaboration to run naturally and creatively through the employees. Through a living system's power to self organize, Ricardo Semler became the chief catalyst of a new leadership style at Semco. The Newtonian solutions became antiquated and the natural organism of Semco self-organized into an evolving system.

> I propose that much of the order in organisms may not be the result of selection at all, but of the spontaneous order of self-organized systems. Order, vast and generative, not fought for against the entropic tides but freely available, undergirds all subsequent biological evolution. The order of organisms is natural, not merely the unexpected triumph of natural selection (Kauffman, 1995, p. 25).

Non-linear reality is the new paradigm, and the living organism became hyper- competitive because of its interconnectivity,

> "Their non-linearity leads to unpredictable behavior and a rapid rate of change, because changes in one's agent's behavior reverberate to influence others in a chain reaction. Unlike systems with fixed point or cyclical equilibrium, there is more dynamic equilibrium in which actions can lead to small, medium or large cascades of adjustment" (Anderson, 1999, p. 228).

He promoted movement and momentum from causal feedback loops and networks of multiplicity. His philosophy was to find answers from diversity and seeming chaos. He found new solutions from these disturbances with his employees, communicated openly and honestly with the community, and never accepted equilibrium. Semler is a revolutionary and defied leadership paradigm because he let the people define the company and not the company define the people. Margaret Wheatley encapsulated his philosophy,

> "As we let go of the machine model of organizations, and workers as replaceable cogs in the machinery of production, we begin to see ourselves in much richer dimensions, to appreciate our wholeness, and, hopefully, to design organizations that honor and make use of the great gift of who we humans are" (Wheatley, 1999, p. 14).

The Anxiety of Learning

Semler believed philosophically that the "application of complexity theory to strategic management [would allow] single business units to achieve rapid evolutionary progress through improvisational moves based upon a few rules, responsibilities, goals, and measures" (Anderson, 1999, p. 228). Semler built mangers as facilitators, self-guided and democratic work teams, profit sharing for all employees, hands off management styles, committee decision processes on all issues, a shared duty roster where all employees participated in general office duties – there was no central office – and finally a culture of people instead of a culture of a company. Company, volunteer committees created values, hired and fired new employees, started new companies, established their own working hours, and developed their own pay grades and salaries.

"In a dissipative structure, anything that disturbs the system plays a crucial role in helping it self-organize in a new form of order. Whenever the environment offers new and different information, the system chooses whether to accept that provocation and respond" (Wheatley, 1999, p. 21).

"There's an inherent paradox surrounding learning: Anxiety inhibits learning, but anxiety is also necessary if learning is going to happen at all" (Coutu, 2002, p. 6). In this anxiety is the reality that managers also have to motivate the employees to "unlearn what they know and learn something new" (Coutu, 2002, p. 6).

The risk and possible distraction is found in the very chaotic nature of a living system where things are constantly evolving and continually under disturbance. These challenges to traditionalism and routine command and control can threaten certain community members and those comfortable with the Newtonian mindset. It can create a disorderly chaos. If buy in from the top management is not complete and if commitment by leadership is not firm and disciplined, a living system could cause unproductive and damaging ripples that splinter and fracture the organization. "These running an organization, if they want maximum learning and growth, have a very fine line to tread to maintain this. If there is too much freedom, then the system can tip over into chaos, witness what often happens in a revolution" (Lewis, 1994, p. 16).

There is also a risk in giving up control and allowing a living system to self organize without the controls. Things go wrong and some decisions that emerge and relationships that bubble up damage progress and hurt community if no one is guiding and steering the ship.

There is a dark side to complexity as Dee Hock points out, " One of my deepest beliefs is that everything with capacity for good has equal capacity for evil. Chaordic, self-organization is no different" (Hock, 2005, p. 16). The traditional, reactive hand of management must be coerced to slow down and let a living system happen naturally under its own undulations. The system might allow collaboration to happen, but for how long can it sustain itself? "Chaos refers to the issue whether or not it is possible to make accurate long-term predictions about the behavior of a system in flux. [For Semler] it's future will unfold as the feedback from a growing community continues to cause disturbances with unpredictable outcomes" (Clarke, 2002, p. 13). Guidelines must be provided that encourage positive ripples to ring themselves throughout the organization that produce a mentality of thinking up from an invigorated bottom-up mentality.

A Need for Slowness

We must be willing to discipline this ability of reflection, or a mentality of "slowness" (Cilliers, 2006). The cult of speed and reactive management will cripple a complex system. Therefore, a living system demands that leadership be patient and thoughtful in approaching business dilemmas. Ricardo Semler experienced much resistance to his style and business confessions and consequently many of his ideas caused distress, and what at first seemed like negative results. However, he was *committed to the process* and permitted time and natural iterations, often uncomfortable, to continually and progressively seek out non linear solutions under these disturbances. Cilliers says this commitment to slowness "is not merely backward looking nor a glorification of what has been... the argument for slowness is forward looking; it is about an engagement with the future as much as with its past. The argument is against unreflective speed" (Cilliers, 2006, p. 106). He goes on to say,

> Complex systems unfold in time, they have a history that co-determines present behavior and they anticipate the future... The behavior of complex systems is not symmetrical in time. They have a past and a future that are not interchangeable" (Cilliers, 2006, p. 107).

Ricardo Semler wants a culture where "everyone should be willing to listen, and admit when they are wrong" (Semler, 1993, p. 171). He believed that leadership within a living system, would generate greater innovation by freeing up undulations and new relationships throughout the enterprise. Future, successful organizations will learn "to tap people's commitment and capacity to learn at all levels in an organization" (Senge, 1990, p. 4). The following is a chart contrasting a Traditional platform and a Living System:

Traditional	Living Systems
Linear	Non-Linear Thinking
Isolated Event	Causal, Learning Loops
Compartmentalized	Highly Connected
Parts	Interrelationships
Deterministic	Indeterminate
Centralized	Networking Connectivity
Confined	Blurry Boundaries
Job Description	Dynamic Complexity
Short Term Gains	Life Long Learning
Command and Control	Interdependent

Although the changes facing us today in the fast paced, relatively flat global landscape are circumstantially different, change is just as dynamic of a phenomenon as it was when electricity was discovered or the automobile was produced (Collins, 2001, p. 15). However, the way we need to address the change is unique. We need to be able to recognize the difference between the Newtonian mentality of parts and the interconnectivity of a living system. Recognizing this will bring non-linear, emergent solutions. To succeed today, we must get our teams out of the box and into the wave. We must learn the The Art of Surfing.

Surfers See Dynamic Interconnectivity:

- Leadership must promote innovation through a natural learning structure of interconnectivity with people and systems as a foundation for progress and innovation.
- Leadership must change the person in order to change the system, and to do this leadership must discipline itself and enter into a contract of life long learning.
- Instead of leaders issuing commands about what they want the employees to do and alone deciding the direction of things, they are now responsible for the learning of their people and not the controlling of their people.
- Steer away from the arid process of organizational restructuring as a tool to foster change because it's merely shifting the boxes.
- If a system is woven together in such a way that it can alter its behavior to meet an emerging challenge or evolving parameter, it can increase the "ruggedness" of its own landscape.
- The image of the Alps is a symbol of the rampant potential within an organization to rally, assemble resources, and climb the peak of the next challenge.
- If the structure is democratically set forth where the system monitors its own behavior, is accountable for its own performance, and is connected and compensated from its results; the system will judge itself and fix itself.
- Meaning is not located in any individual but emerges and is continually iterated in the interaction between individuals and their combined relationships to.
- Seeing beyond snapshots is about being willing to change the system through itself and then be personally changed from within by the system through these interrelationships.
- "Models of organizational life that build on complex adaptive systems... need not simply endow agents with schemata, connections, and adaptive behavior. They can also allow these elements to evolve."
- Semler transformed a good company into a great company through people and profits by letting the employees decide what was best and allowing them some "skin" in the game to make it tangible.
- Leadership must positively contaminate the system in order to undo the traditional structure that damage workers and stifle creativity.
- Much of leadership is in trouble because all their confidence is in one ailing product arena and in one aging, command and control philosophy.
- "There's an inherent paradox surrounding learning: Anxiety inhibits learning, but anxiety is also necessary if learning is going to happen at all."

References

Anderson, P. (1999) *"Complexity Theory Organization and Science."* Organization Science, Vol. 10 No. 3 (May – June 1999) pp. 216-232

Anderson, L., & Anderson, D. (2001) *"Awake at the Wheel: Moving beyond Change Management to Conscious Change Leadership."* Accessed 2/20/2006 from http://www.odnetwork.org/odonline/vol33n3/awake.html.

Anderson, P. (1999) *"Complexity Theory Organization and Science."* Organization Science, Vol. 10 No. 3 (May – June 1999) pp. 216-232

Babbie, E. (2005) *The Practice of Social Research (Third Edition).* Belmont, CA: Wadsworth Thomson Learning.

Brafman, Rod and Beckstrom, Rod A. (2007) *The Starfish and the Spider: The unstoppable Power of Leaderless Organizations.* Penguin Group, New York, NY.

Boje, D. (2000) *"Phenomenal Complexity Theory and Change at Disney."* Journal of Organizational Change Management, Vol. 13 No. 6 (2000) pp. 558-566.

Buckingham, Marcus., Coffman, Curt. (1999) *First, Break All the Rules; What the World's Greatest Managers Do Differently.* Simon and Schuster, New York.

Bunker, B., Alban, B. (1997) *Large Group Interventions: Engaging the Whole System for Rapid Change.* San Francisco: Jossey – Bass.

Byrne, D. (1999) *"Complexity and Postmodernism."* Accessed 2/2/2006 from http://jass.soc.surrey.ac.uk.2/2/review1.html.

Cilliers, P. (2006) *"On the importance of a certain slowness."* E:CO Vol. 8 No. 3 (2006) pp. 105-112).

Clarke, J. (2002) *"eBay: Symbiosis between enabling technology and the complex adaptive system."* Unpublished Master's Thesis, Santa Barbara, CA: The Fielding Institute, Master's Program in Organizational Design and Effectiveness.

Collins, J. (2001) *Good to Great: Why Some Companies Make theLeap and Others Don't.* New York: Harper Collins.

Collins, J. (1999) *"Turning Goals into Results: The Power of Catalytic Mechanisms."* Harvard Business Review (July – August 1999) pp. 1-13 [HBR reprint # 99401].

Collins, J., and Porras, J., "Built to Last." Harper Business, New York, NY. (1994).

Coutu, D. (2002) "The Anxiety of Learning." Harvard Business Review (March 2002) pp. 1-8 [HBR reprint #RO203H].

Donigan, A., Hughes, J. and Weiss, J. (2010) *"Extreme Negotiations. What U.S. Soldiers in Afghanistan have learned about the art of managing high- risk, high-stakes situations."* Harvard Business Review, Nov. 2010, pp. 66-75.

Drucker, Peter F., (1995) *Managing in a Time of Great Change.* Penguin Group, 375 Hudson Street, New York, NY.

Drucker, Peter F. (2001) *The Essential Drucker.* Harper Collins Publishing, 10 East St. New York, NY,

Ferris, Timothy. 2007, 2009. *The 4-Hour Work Week.* New York. Crown Publishers.

Freeman, Mr. (2008). *"The Ingredients of His Success."* Wall Street Journal, Monday, December 11, 2008, A11, Opinion.

Friedman, Thomas L. (2006) *The World is Flat: A Brief History of the Twenty-First Century.* Farrar, Straus and Giroux, Union Square West, New York.

Gates, Bill. (1999) *Business at the Speed of Thought; Succeeding in the Digital Age.* Business Plus. Hachette Book Group USA, New York.

Geitner, Jr., Louis V., (2002) *Who Says Elephants Can't Dance*. Harper Collins Publishers Inc., East 53rd Street, New York, NY.

Gibbons, Dave (2009) *The Monkey and the Fish: Liquid Leadership for a third-culture church*. Zondervan, Grand Rapids, Michigan.

Gladwell, M. (2002) *The Tipping Point: How Little Things Can Make a Big Difference*. New York: Time Warner.

Gleick, J. (1988) *Chaos: making a new science*. New York: Penguin Books

Godin, Seth. (2008). *Tribes, We Need You to Lead Us*. The Penguin Group. New York.

Grenz, S. (1996) *A Primer on Postmodernism*. Grand Rapids, MI: Wm. B Eerdmans.

Gyllenpalm, B. (2003) *"The Organizational Cone."* (This is a revised chapter to be published in the ninth edition of *Management of Organizational Behavior* by Hersey, Blanchard and Johnson). Pp. 1-14.

Hamel, Gary (2007) *The Future of Management*. Harvard Business School Publishing, 60 Harvard Way, Boston, Massachusetts.

Hamel, Gary (2006) *"Management a la Google,"* Wall Street Journal, Wednesday, April 26, 2006, Opinion.

Hazy, J. (2006) "Measuring Leadership effectiveness in complex socio-technical systems." E:CO Vol 8 No. 3 (2006) pp. 58-77.

Hirsch, Alan. (2006). *The Forgotten Ways*. Brazos Press. Grand Rapids, MI.

Hock, D, (1996) *"The Chaordic Organization: Out of Control and Into Order."* Accessed 5/18/2006 from http://www.newhorizons.org/future/hock.htm.

Hock, D. (2005) *"Out of control and Into Order."* Accessed 9/25/2006 from http://www.newhorizons.org/lifelong/higher_ed/hock.htm.

Katzenbach, Jon R, and Smit, Douglas, K. (2003) *The Wisdom of Teams*. Harper Collins Publishing, New York, NY.

Kauffman, S. (1995) *At Home in the Universe: The Search for the Laws of Self Organization and Complexity*. New York: Oxford.

Katel, P. (1997) "*Bordering on Chaos – The Cemex Story.*" Accessed 4/6/2006 from http://www.mexconnect.com/mex_/travel/pkatel/pkcemex.html

Keene, A. (2000). "*Complexity theory: the changing role of leadership.*" Industrial and Commercial Training Volume 32 Number 1 (2000) pp. 15-18.

Lencioni, Patrick (2007) *Three Signs of a Miserable.* Josey-Bass, San Francisco, CA.

Lillian, K. & Perez, Francisco, P. (1998) "*Ricardo Semler and Semco S.A.*" Thunderbird, the American Graduate School of International Management. A15-98-0024 pp. 1-12.

Lewin, R. (1999) *Complexity: Life at the Edge of Chaos (Second Edition).* Chicago: University of Chicago Press.

Lewis, R. (1994) "*From chaos to Complexity.*" Vol. 7 No. 4 (pp. 16-17).

MacMillan, Ian C., Thompson, James D., (2010) "*Making Social Ventures Work,*" Harvard Business Review, September 2010, pp. 67-73.

Morgan, G. (1986) *Images of Organizations.* Beverly Hills: Sage.

Murray. (2010) Wall Street Journal, Sat/Sun, Aug. 21-22, 2010, pp. W3.

Neilson, G., Pasternack, B., Van Nuys, K. (2005) "*The Passive Aggressive Organization.*" Harvard Business Review (October 2005) pp. 1-11. [HBR reprint #RO510E].

Newstead, Barry. (2010) "*Can you Open-Source Your Strategy?*" Harvard Business Review, October 2010, pp. 32.

Pascalle, T., Millemann, M., Gioja, L., (1997) "*Changing the Way We Change. How Leaders at Sears, Shell, and the U.S. Army Transformed Attitudes and Behavior–and Made the Changes Stick.*" Harvard Business Review 75:6 (Nov 97), 126-139. [HBR reprint #97609]

Pascalle, T., Millemann, M., Gioja, L., (2000) *Surfing the Edge of Chaos: The Laws of Nature and the New Laws of Business.* New York: Three Rivers Press.

Pink, Daniel, (2009) *Drive: The Surprising Truth About What Motivates Us. New York.* River Head Books.

Rosenhead, J. (1998) *"Complexity Theory and management Practice."* Accessed 2/13/2006 from http://human-nature.com/science-as-culture/rosenhead.html. (Pp. 1-27)

Rosenweig, P. (2010), *"Robert S. McNamara And the Evolution of Modern Management,"* Harvard Business Review, December 2010, pp. 87 - 93.

Schaffer, R. (2002) *High – Impact Consulting: How Clients and Consultants Can Work together to Achieve Extraordinary Results.* San Francisco: Jossey – Bass.

Semler, Ricardo (1993) *Maverick: The Success Story Behind the World's Most Unusual Workplace.* New York: Warner Books.

Semler, Ricardo (2004), *The Seven Day Weekend*, Penguin Group, Hudson Street, New York

Senge, P., (1990) *The Fifth Discipline.* Currency Doubleday, New York, NY.

Stacey, R. (2005) *Experience Emergence in Organizations: Local Interaction and the Emergence of Global Pattern.* New York: Routledge.

Striller, Alex. (2011) *X Play Nation of Action Sports Game Changers.* Copyright Alexander R. Striller.

Stumpf, S. (1995) *"Applying new science theories in leadership development activities."* Journal of Management Development Vol. 14 No. 5 (1995) pp. 39-49.

Styhre, A. (2002) *"Non-linear change in organizations: organization change management informed by complex theory."* Leadership & Organization Development Journal 23/6 (2002) pp. 343 –351.

Tickle, Phyllis (2008) *The Great Emergence: How Christianity is Changing and Why.* Baker Books, Grand Rapids, Michigan.

Twomey, D. (2006) *"Designed Emergence as a path to enterprise sustainability."* E:CO Vol 8 No. 3 (2006) pp. 12-23.

Webb, C. Lettice, F., Lemon, M. (2006) *"Facilitating learning and innovation in organizations using complexity science principles."* E:CO Vol. 8 No. 1 (2006) pp. 30-41.

Wheatley, M. (1999) *Leadership and the New Science: Discovering Order in a Chaotic World*. San Francisco: Berret – Koehler.

Wheatley, M. & Kellner – Rogers, M. (1996) *"The Irresistible Future of Organizing."* Accessed 7/6/2006 from http://www.margaretwheatley.com/articles/irresistiblefuture.html.

Wieners, B. (2006) "Ricardo Semler: Set Them Free." Accessed 3/11/2006 from http://www.cioinsight.com/print_article2/0,1217,a=124700,00.asp

http://www.theamericanscholar.org/solitude-and-leadership/
http://the99percent.com/articles/7085/Uncertainty-Innovation-and-the-Alchemy-of-Fear
http://the99percent.com/articles/6973/Francis-Ford-Coppola-On-Risk-Money-Craft-Collaboration
http://the99percent.com/articles/7074/Vision-Without-Obstruction-What-We-Learn-From-Steve-Jobs

(http://business.transworld.net/50009/features/upstarts-nemaki-industries/)
http://agile.dzone.com/videos/sue-mckinney-agile-2009
http://www.sqe.com/conferencearchive/agiledevpracticeswest2010/Summit.html
http://www.youtube.com/watch?v=hyZRS0BnpAI&feature=related
http://online.barrons.com/article/SB121763156934206007.html).
http://edition.cnn.com/2004/BUSINESS/05/19/go.semler.transcript/index.html).
http://www.youtube.com/watch?v=LUtxEsc10B&feature=related
http://www.strategy-business.com/press/16635507)

CPSIA information can be obtained
at www.ICGtesting.com
Printed in the USA
FSOW01n0737180817
37744FS